A
POCKET BOOK

Authors
Major (Retd) John Hobbis Harris
Elizabeth Rosalie Davison

ISBN 1-874528-04-7

THE CHARTER OF THE ARMY CADET FORCE

THE ARMY CADET FORCE IS A NATIONAL VOLUNTARY YOUTH ORGANISATION.

IT IS SPONSORED BY THE ARMY AND PROVIDES CHALLENGING MILITARY, ADVENTUROUS AND COMMUNITY ACTIVITIES.

ITS AIM IS TO INSPIRE YOUNG PEOPLE TO ACHIEVE SUCCESS IN LIFE WITH A SPIRIT OF SERVICE TO THE QUEEN, THEIR COUNTRY AND THEIR LOCAL COMMUNITY, AND TO DEVELOP IN THEM THE QUALITIES REQUIRED OF A GOOD CITIZEN.

THIS AIM IS ACHIEVED BY:

a. PROVIDING PROGRESSIVE CADET TRAINING, OFTEN OF A CHALLENGING AND EXCITING NATURE, TO FOSTER CONFIDENCE, SELF RELIANCE, INITIATIVE, LOYALTY, AND A SENSE OF SERVICE TO OTHER PEOPLE.

b. ENCOURAGING THE DEVELOPMENT OF PERSONAL POWERS OF PRACTICAL LEADERSHIP AND THE ABILITY TO WORK SUCCESSFULLY AS A MEMBER OF A TEAM.

c. STIMULATING AN INTEREST IN THE ARMY, ITS ACHIEVEMENTS SKILLS AND VALUES.

d. ADVISING AND PREPARING THOSE CONSIDERING A CAREER IN THE SERVICES OR WITH THE RESERVE FORCES.

THE MOTTO OF THE ARMY CADET FORCE IS:

"INSPIRE, TO ACHIEVE"

The Cadet Training Centre, Frimley Park, Camberley, Surrey

CONTENT

Chapter 1 General Information.
Banner of the Army Cadet Force, The Cadet Prayer, Enrollment
Ceremony, Personal Details, Being a 'full member', Cadet and the
Community, Welfare, Childrens Act, Safety, Annual Camp and
Preparation, Medical Certificate, Insurance cover, What to do & What
not to do at camp, Know who's who in your community, Kit check list,
Questions .... 1 - 14

Chapter 2 The Army Cadet Force Past & Present.
The Early Days, The Volunteers, Octavia Hill, First World War,
Second World War, Army Cadet Force Association, Amery Report,
Duke of Edinburgh's Award Scheme, Adventurous Training,
Hundredth Anniversary, New Rifles introduced, Direction of the ACF.
Reserve Forces & Cadet Association, The County Cadet Committee,
Your County Cadet HQ and Staff, Army Cadet Leagues,
Questions .... 1 - 24

Chapter 3 Personal Turnout and Drill
The Brassard, Care of Uniform, Care of Boots, Desirable Kit, Personal
Tunout, Compliments, The Queens Commission, ACF Banner, Badges
of Rank, Introduction to Drill, Introductory Words of Command,
Changing Direction, Marching and Dressing Off, Teaching Drill, Words
of Command, Questions .... 1 - 19

Chapter 4 Fieldcraft
Natures' Skills, Place of the Section in a Battalion, Individual Skills,
Judging Distance, Personal Camouflage and Concealment, Movement,
Target Recognition, Range Cards, Fire Control Orders, Night Vision,
Duties of a Sentry, Section Battle Drills, Section and Platoon Field
Signals, Section Formations, Choosing a Route, Pacing, Navigation, Aids
to keeping Direction, Selecting Lines of Advance, Observation,
Searching Ground, Scanning,
Patrols: Reconnaisance, Standing, Fighting Patrols, Sequence of
Action to Mount, Carry Out, De-Brief a Patrol. Brief the Patrol,
Ground, Situation, Mission, Execution, Service and Support, Command
& Signals, Reports, Ambushes: Types and Principles, Orders and
Preparation, Rehearsals, Patrol Harbours,
Safety with Blank Ammunition 1-55

CONTENT

Chapter 5 Map Reading
The Grid System, Map References, Setting a Map, The Silva Compass, Prismatic Compass, Bearings and Types of Bearings, Taking a Grid Bearing, Re-section, Relating Map to Ground, Relief, Contours, Vertical Interval, Scales and Measuring Distance, Pacing, Finding North, Route Cards, 24 hour Clock System, The Protractor Romer.
Orienteering. How organized, Check Points, Equipment & Clothing, Keeping Direction, Getting Lost, Navigating Techniques, Choosing a Route, Aiming Off, Info on Maps, Terms used in Map Reading, GPS, Questions 1-40

Chapter 6 Skill at Arms : Air Rifle, .22 Rifle & L98 GP Rifle
Safety Precautions for handling all weapons. Personal Declaration, Air Rifle explanation, standards and handling.
Introduction of L98 A1 CADET GP Rifle. General Description, Safety Precautions, Low Port Position, Component Parts, 90 Pattern Infantry Webbing, Questions 1-12

Chapter 7 The Duke of Edinburghs' Award Scheme.
Main Principles, The challenge, Advantages, Opportunities, Conditions of the Bronze, Silver & Gold Awards. Value to the Cadet, How the Award Scheme works with APC, Scoring for Sport and Physical Fitness Tests for APC, Descrition and Conditions for Tests, Questions ...1- 20

Chapter 8 Expedition Training.
The Country Code, Personal Health and Hygiene, Personal Kit List, Load Carrying, Choosing a Camp Site, Construction of Latrines, Preparing Food in the Field, Menu Planning and Preparation and use of Pouched Rations, Food Hygiene, Water Purification, Hill Walking skills, Improvised Shelters, Emergency Procedures, Insurance Cover, Safety, Planning and Preparation of Exercises, Prevention of Accidents, Communications, The Wind Chill Factor and Hypothermia Description of Rope,
Knowing the right Knot to use at the right time, Illustrations of Knots and how to tie them, Questions 1- 36

Chapter 9 First Aid & Health and Safety
Assessing D.R.A.B.C, Action in an Emergency, Severe Bleeding & Treatment, Burns & Scalds -Types of Fracture & Treatment, Shock - Causes Recognition & Treatment, Head Injury. Extremes of Temperature, Motor Cycle Helmets,

CONTENT

Substance Misuse; Tobacco, Alcohol, and the misuse of presecription drugs, Questions 1-26

Chapter 10 Signals
Security, Codes, Phonetic Alphabet, Voice procedure, Pro words, Disciplines, Organisation of a Radio net, Questions 1-14

Chapter 11 Bands in the ACF
Band Units, Drum and Bugle Bands, Finance and support, Recognition of Effort, Band Practice, Qualifications, Band- APC Qualifications, Drum and Pipe Bands, DofE Award, Skills required, Team Effort 1-4

Chapter 12 Method of Instruction
The Six P's, Qualities of an Instructor. Preparation & Planning, Questioning technique, The Lesson Plan, Stages and Key Points, Training Aids, Improvised Training Aids Questions 1-7

Chapter 13 Opportunities after 2 Star
Duties & Opportunities, Personal Development, Responsibilities, Chart showing courses and opportunities open to cadets, Details of MOD Technical Courses visits and attachments at home and abroad, Conditions Chart The Defence 6th Form College. The Army Foundation Colleges, Harrowgate, Arborfield, and Bassingbourne. Army Education Grants & 'Golden Hellos', Army Scholarship Scheme, The Undergraduate Bursary. 1-35

Chapter 14 Life After Cadets
Further Education,Facts of Life, Leaving Home, Our Country, Hobbies and Interests. Decision Making and The S.W.O.T. List, Do you see yourself as others see you, World of work, Applying for a Job, 'Selling Yourself', Writing a Letter, Personal History - your CV, Before going for an Interview, What are they like to work for?, The Interview, Your Image, Sample Questions to ask, Now at work, The right Attitudes, After your Interview, Your Job and the value of being a cadet, the Cadet NVQ 1-6

Abbreviations in common use... 1-2

Pictorial History of the Cadet Force.

Within some of the Chapters there are illustrations of Cadets in uniforms of the period, or scenes from the activities they were involved in.

These are samples taken from a set of 24 Post Cards that were commissioned to celebrate the125th anniversary of the Cadet Movement in1985.

The purpose of including them in the Cadets Pocket Book is to show you the Cadet of today, the history that is your heritage; how in spite of many problems the Cadet Force has survived and grown over the years.

The orignal post cards are printed in attractive full colour and make up an interesting pictorial history of uniforms and annual camp scenes of the day.

An album was also produced in which to keep the cards along with a short explanation of the illustration on each card.

The logo above was designed for the ACFA to celebrate the 125th Anniversary in 1985 and was used on many items for the Cadet.

What will the logo designed to celebrate the 150th Anniversary take the shape of?

PERSONAL DETAILS

Surname ....

Other Names ....

Home Address ....

.... Post Code ....

Date of Birth   /   /   Nat Insurance No ....

Blood Group .... Home Telephone No ....

Next of Kin Relationship .... Tel No ....

Address .... Post Code ....

Religious Denomination ....

Relevant Medical Information, Allergies, etc ....

School Attending/Employer ....

....

Date Joined .... Date Passed Basic Training ....

Enrolled on .... at ....
Sponsors:-

      1 ....

      2 ....

Signed .... Detachment ....
              Officer i/c

Unit .... Date ....

THE BANNER OF THE ARMY CADET FORCE

The Banner of the ACF was first presented on 9th Feb. 1960 at the Tower of London, by his Royal Highness the Duke of Edinburgh as Colonel in Chief, on the Occasion of the Centenary. A new banner was presented by His Royal Highness the Duke of Edinburgh at the Chapel of the Royal Hospital, Chelsea on 27th March 1982. The original Banner was laid up in St. Peter's Church, Frimley, Surrey in July 1982 where it may be seen to this day.

THE CADET PRAYER

O God our heavenly father, who hast brought
us together as members of the Army Cadet Force;
help us to do our duty at all times,
and be loyal to each other.
May all that is good and true prosper among us;
strengthen us to defend the right; and bless our work
that it may be acceptable to thee.

Chapter I

GENERAL INFORMATION

INTRODUCTION

The first Cadet Pocket Book was published over twenty years ago. It is designed to help you learn or revise correctly and safely. With its help, you will attain a high standard in the Army Proficiency Syllabus (APC) subjects. Some of the contents do not relate directly to APC training, but it does relate to you as a person and the way you will develop as a young adult. Cadet Instructors will find the Pocket Book an invaluable aid when planning lessons.

RESPONSIBILITIES

This chapter contains advice on what is expected of you by your Officers and Adult Instructors. Like you, they are volunteers; the Army Cadet Force is their hobby.

Your Detachment will only be as good as you and other Cadets make it. Your Detachment Commander and Adult Instructors are there to encourage and train you. Work as a team - even if you do not particularly like someone; let's face it, it could be useful to learn how to work with people you do not like! Being a member of the ACF gives you opportunities to grow in knowledge and experience.

THE ENROLMENT CEREMONY

The first few weeks you parade at your Detachment you will take part in your Basic Training. Providing you attend regularly, you will be ENROLLED in about six to eight weeks. You are then officially allowed to wear the Cap Badge of the Regiment or Corps to which your Detachment is affiliated.

The format of the Enrolment Ceremony varies, but usually your OC will have invited your parents or guardians, and possibly the Padre to help officiate in the ceremony. Normally, each Cadet being enrolled has two friends from the Detachment who are appointed as his/her 'sponsors'. They will help you through this milestone in your Cadet career. The Enrolment Ceremony serves as a reminder to the other Cadets of their commitments to their Detachment and the ACF.

GENERAL INFORMATION

The Enrolment Ceremony is personal to the Cadets taking part. Usually not more than two cadets are enrolled at a time. It is not a photo opportunity for the PRO or local press to be involved in a publicity stunt, it is very much a personal matter for all the Cadets. Many County ACF's allow Cadets to join after their 12th birthday this is a young age to measure up to becoming a member of your Detachment and therefore will need to be made welcome straight away. Their Sponsors have a special responsibility to se that this is carried out.

YOUR DETACHMENT COMMANDER WILL EXPECT YOU TO:

1. Be smartly turned out both in uniform and in your normal clothes.
2. Wear your uniform correctly - keep it clean and well pressed.
3. .Walk tall, don't slouch - you can look ten centimeters taller!
4. Read and comply with notices and orders put up on the notice board.
5. Obey orders - if they seem unfair, obey them and complain after.
6. Remember your good manners.
7. Look after new recruits; make them feel part of the Detachment.
8. When your Detachment is "Open to recruit" encourage those who you feel would make good Cadets to attend a Detachment Parade.
9. Be ALERT, be SAFETY and SECURITY CONSCIOUS AT ALL TIMES
10. Treat other peoplesproperty with respect ; prevent damage and vandalism.
11. Never be afraid of doing more than you have been asked to do.
12. Keep fit, play and work hard, take part in sports and games.
13. Work in the Detachment as you SHOULD DO at home - be prepared to help with the 'chores' without having to be asked. Be tidy; do not rely on others to clean up after you.
14. Never be afraid of doing more than you have been asked to do.
15. Be on time - five minutes before time!
16. Remember to let your Detachment Commander know in good time if you are unable to attend a weekend/camp etc. Just not turning up is not good enough, nor good manners

GENERAL INFORMATION

BE A "FULL MEMBER"

Whenever events, parades, sporting events, weekend training, Annual Camps are planned, your Detachment Staff and others at Company and County/Sector level will have spent many hours in planning a full and interesting programme. This is all organised for your benefit.

What does being a **"Full Member"** mean?

Like your Detachment Commander and Adult Instructors, you have other responsibilities outside the ACF, with the time you have available for Cadets, put maximum effort in to becoming a good Cadet.

A good Cadet is a full member, and is expected to:

1. Take an active part in the life of the Detachment and make the progress required not only in training but also as a person.
2. Help others who find it difficult to learn new skills.
3. Look after new recruits; make them feel part of the Detachment.
4. When your Detachment is "Open to recruit" encourage those who you feel would make good Cadets to attend a Detachment Parade.
5. Be ALERT, be SAFETY and SECURITY CONSCIOUS AT ALL TIMES

THE CADET AND THE COMMUNITY

A part of the Army Cadet Force Charter reads:

"To inspire young people to achieve success in life with a spirit o f service to the Queen, their country and their local community, and to develop in them the qualities required o f a good citizen".

As an individual, a Cadet, you are a CITIZEN. You live in this country, in your own town, city or village. You have family, friends and are part of the community you live in. Every community depends upon people who are prepared to work towards making it a better place to live. During your training, depending on how your Detachment staff plans it, you should be taking part in various projects and activities in your local community. This is an excellent opportunity to meet the local "Movers and Shakers", Civic dignitaries such as the Mayor, local Councillors and those who actively support the community in many ways, through business, profession or charitable work.

It also presents the opportunity for them to meet you and the other Cadets in your Detachment. The impression you make is reflected on you and your Detachment - let it be a good one! If you are taking part in the Duke of Edinburgh's Award Scheme, you may chose to undertake community project work as part of your award.

GENERAL INFORMATION

Getting involved in the community can often be difficult and demanding, but it can also be great fun and very rewarding.
You may find that you continue working in the community long after you have left the Cadet Force.

YOUR WELFARE AND SAFETY

The purpose of the following information is to make you aware of what laws there are for your protection and how they are put into action.

Welfare

The Children Act 1989

This Act is designed to ensure that children (up to the age of 16 years) and young persons (up to the age of 18 years) are treated properly. What does it mean within the ACF? Firstly, it means that Adults who express an interest in working with the Cadets are vetted to try and prevent people who might wish to harm young persons physically or mentally from joining the ACF. Secondly, it means that the adults in the ACF must think at all times of your welfare and safety. It is termed "Duty of care".
How does this work? There are systems and procedures in place on a County or Sector level that provide a 'listening ear' for any problems there may be. It is confidential, but you should be aware that serious problems will be passed on to trained personnel for further action.

What do you do?

If something has happened that makes you feel really bad, share it; talk to an Officer or Adult Instructor you get on well with, it is pretty certain that they will have experienced something similar.
• If you feel that you are not being treated properly, talk to a person you can trust. Be truthful, enlarging on the truth will not help you.
• In your cadet activities, there could be some training that you feel you just cannot cope with; you know you will fail. Give it your best, you've tried and that is not failing.

SAFETY

All Officers and Adult Instructors have to comply with official safety requirements. There are strict safety rules all cadet activities. If these rules are followed, the risk of someone being injured is reduced.

GENERAL INFORMATION

Failure to follow the safety rules can lead to disciplinary action and possibly court proceedings particularly if someone is injured.

How does this work?

Your APC syllabus contains safety training where required. When you are out on exercise, there are briefings to inform you of how, what, when and where. Before you receive your briefing, the Adult Instructors and Officers have carefully planned the activity and have had their briefings, including the safety aspects.

What do you do?

• Remember your safety rules ALWAYS follow them
• Watch the more junior Cadets, ensure they follow the safety rules
• Listen, (take notes if necessary), when you have your briefing
• Do not fool around at the wrong time
• Know the telephone numbers of.
  Your Detachment Commander and all other Adult Instructors in your Detachment
  Your Company/Area Commander and the Cadet County Headquarters.
• When out on exercise - the mobile number(s) to call in an emergency.

ANNUAL CAMP

For many years the Army Cadet Force and the Combined Cadet Force have enjoyed the training camps provided by the Ministry of Defence. Annual Camp has always been the highlight of the cadet year. You should always make a special effort to attend. It is a time when all the training you have received during the year is put into practice in 'the field', by taking part in exercises and expeditions. You will be a full time Cadet for the duration of camp and is an ideal opportunity to make new friends and learn new skills.

Another opportunity Annual Camp offers you is the chance to be in a very different part of the country, perhaps for the first time in your life. Try and find out as much as you can, what the area is famous for, what is made there, local customs and history.

Many counties, depending upon the location of the camp have "Open Days", when parents and friends visit the camp. The day is often planned as a Sports Day, with demonstrations and displays, many of which are organised by the Cadets. Some events are set up to involve visitors to make it an entertaining day.

GENERAL INFORMATION

ANNUAL CAMP "DO'S and DON'TS

The following information should make your camp enjoyable by helping
you get the most out of it and keeping you our of trouble.

Remember that while you are under the supervision of your Officers
and Adult Instructors they are responsible for your SAFETY and
WELFARE.

This applies to ANY Cadet activity no matter where it is. Annual Camp
like weekend training means you are away from home; your Officers
and Adult Instructors are responsible for you even whilst you
sleep! The rules, instructions and orders given by your Officers and
Adult Instructors are there to protect you. Make sure you follow the
rules, if you are an NCO, make sure that you set an example by
complying and seeing that they are properly carried out.

BEFORE CAMP - PREPARATION

1. Save up for camp - be ready to pay your camp fees when asked.
    (Note: if you have difficulty in this, see your Detachment
    Commander, help may be available).
2. Get to know when and where you are going as soon as possible.
3. Get to know the programme and what you are to be doing.
4. Practice some of the training that you will be carrying out at camp,
    particularly those you are not very good at.
5. Get your OC to provide a map of the camp and surrounding area,
    build up a picture in your mind of what it will be like.
6. Do a project on places of interest, special features of the
    countryside, the people, industries and other interesting
    information.
7. Do you have any friends or relatives in the area - if so you may be
    able to visit them?
8. Check that your uniform fits you properly, if not try and get it
    changed early enough to give the Quarter Master a chance to help
    you.
9. Check all your kit for camp. Make a list of all your needs, get it
    organised well before hand. Your OC will give you a checklist for
    camp; you may find the Annual Camp Check List at the end of this
    section useful.
10. Do your own packing. If you have never packed before, ask for a
    demonstration. Do not start packing the night before you are due
    to leave.

GENERAL INFORMATION

11. Have your MEDICAL CERTIFICATE (sometimes known as the FFI form - Free From Infection), make sure it is correctly completed and SIGNED by your parent or guardian. Put it into your coat pocket when leaving home for camp.

MEDICAL CERTIFICATE

You will be given a Medical Certificate for your parent/guardian to complete and sign before you go to annual camp. Procedures vary; you may have to hand it back to your Detachment Commander, or hand it to the Adult in charge of your coach. (see page 1-13 for Certificate) The reason for this form being a requirement is that the Ministry of Defence cannot entertain certain risks and these must be eliminated by regulations, for example:

1. Condition - Epilepsy. Not allowed to undertake such activities as Rock Climbing, Swimming, Shooting, Canoeing, Orienteering, and Expeditions in Wild Country etc.

2. Condition - Asthma. Whether or not they are receiving any form of therapy is not allowed to undertake activities involving strenuous activity.

3. Condition - Diabetes. Those dependent on Insulin treatment may not undertake activities involving irregular meals or long periods of exertion.

4. Condition - Heart problems. These are of such a variable nature that a cadets' medical practitioner must judge them individually. Should any doubts exist on a Cadets' ability to undertake all the activities listed below, a doctor should be consulted by the parent or guardian before the certificate is signed.

EXAMPLES OF PHYSICAL & SPORTING ACTIVITIES

Rock Climbing, Canoeing, Hang Gliding, Hill walking on Expeditions, Life Saving, Parachuting, Par ascending, Sailing, Rafting, Offshore and Windsurfing.
Skiing: Cross Country and Downhill, Water Skiing, Caving, Sub-Aqua Diving. Athletics, Boxing, Circuit Training, Cricket, Cross Country Running, Cycling, Mountain Biking, Football, Rugby, Hockey, judo, Orienteering, and Swimming.

IMPORTANT NOTICE - INSURANCE

The Ministry of Defence and the Army Cadet Force Association have insurance policies for Cadets who may have an accident.

GENERAL INFORMATION

THIS INSURANCE IS ONLY VALID IF YOU ARE TAKING PART IN AN ACTIVITY THAT IS PLANNED AND ORGANISED AS PART OF YOUR CADET TRAINING.

WARNING

Therefore if you decide to organise an expedition or exercise WITHOUT AUTHORITY and as a result someone is injured, they would NOT be covered by insurance.

ON YOUR WAY TO CAMP

When traveling by coach or public transport: **Do Not:**
Make unnecessary noise to the annoyance of other travellers
Leave your kit unattended, or in a place dangerous to others.
Cause problems for coach drivers or those responsible for you.
Do not deliberately spill drinks, leave litter or cause damage.
Go wandering off without permission.

WHEN AT CAMP - DO THE FOLLOWING:

1. Put most of your spending money in the camp bank or other means of safe keeping organised by your adult staff at camp.
2. Listen and make note of the camp Standing Orders for Security, Fire and Safety instructions. Observe 'Out of Bounds' notices.
3. Read daily routine orders and comply with them.
4. Write or phone home to let them know you have arrived safely. Remember to keep in touch.
5. Remember to wash yourself every day. Leave the ablutions as clean as you would wish to find them.
6. Clean your kit daily, wash out dirty socks and underclothes - remember to rinse them properly or you will get sore!
7. Carry out all duties and "chores" cheerfully and properly.
8. Help others - especially the junior cadets who are away from home AND at camp for the first time.
9. Be polite to people you meet in the area, particularly the civilian staff in the camp and those who run the NAAFI
10. Watch out for bullying or signs that another Cadet is really unhappy. If you see it, report it.
11. Be safety conscious, report any suspicious persons or events.
12. Pull your weight - work hard, play hard, keep your bed space clean and tidy. Most important of all, ENJOY CAMP

GENERAL INFORMATION

WHEN AT CAMP DO NOT:

1. Make work for yourself and others by dropping litter or leaving kit lying about.
2. Leave the toilets or washbasins in a dirty state; you will probably have to clean them.
3. Never wander off on your own, or in a group without telling anyone where you are going.
4. Be a nuisance to local residents by being noisy or 'fooling about' in the streets or other public places.
5. Hitchhike in uniform - it is not approved of.
6. Stay out of camp later than permitted, without first having asked for special permission.
7. Leave valuable items of personal kit lying about, lock them away safely.
8. Do not touch or pick up strange objects in the training area, (remember Camp Standing Orders).
9. Get involved with 'trouble makers' - unless you do not want promotion.
10. Be tempted to 'do drugs' in any form.
11. Get involved with local 'trouble makers' who will try to create problems bringing dis-credit on the Cadet Force, just don't get involved.

KNOW WHO's WHO IN YOUR COMMUNITY

This will bring you and your unit into close contact with the community in which you live.

You will meet new people in a variety of situations, some may be employers, others local councillors, professional people like doctors, solicitors or accountants.

It will all present opportunities for them to get to know you, your unit and the Cadet Force and of course for you to get to know them.

GENERAL INFORMATION

ANNUAL CAMP KIT CHECK LIST	
COMBAT TROUSERS	
COMBAT JACKET	
SHIRTS - TWO	
JUMPER	
BUNGEES (6)	
BRASSARD	
BERET	
BELT- WORKING	
BOOTS AND CLEANING KIT	
THICK SOCKS (AT LEAST 3 PAIRS)	
SPORTS KIT (INCLUDING SWIM KIT)	
TROUSER ELASTICS (TWO SETS)	
KNIFE, FORK, SPOON AND MUG	
CIVVIES	
WASHING KIT (INCLUDING SHAMPOO & SOAP)	
HAIR GRIPS, SCRUNCHIES, HAIRNETS, MAKE UP ETC.	
TOWELS (I LARGE, I HAND)	
PILLOW SLIP	
UNDERWEAR	
WASHING POWDER/LIQUID (WRAP TO PREVENT LEAKS)	
POCKET NOTEBOOK AND PENCILS	
NEEDLE AND COTTON	
STRONG PADLOCK AND 2 KEYS	
WEBBING	
TORCH	
SCISSORS AND STRING	
POCKET MONEY	
PERSONAL FIRST AID KIT	
ANY MEDICATION YOU MAY NEED	
YOUR FFI (Free From Infection) FORM (Duly Signed)	
GIRLS - YOUR "MONTHLY STUFF"	
BOYS - IF YOU SHAVE - YOUR SHAVING KIT.	

GENERAL INFORMATION

Example of Free From Infection Form (FFI) Reduced in size

Billet No .... Pl ....

Administration purposes

Name .... Age ..... Date of Birth ....

Address ....

.... Post Code ....Tel No ....

Next of Kin: Name .... Tel No ....

Address ....

Other Contact: Name .... Tel No ....

Address ....

Does the above named have any known conditions
eg, Asthma, allergies etc
....
Are they allergic to penicillin .... or Surgical Plasters ....
Are they a vegetarian .... Allergic to any particular food ....
Any other allergies..
Name and dosage of prescribed medications the cadet will have
brought with him/her

....

Name of Cadets General Practitioner ....

Surgery Address... Tel No............

This is to certify that my Son/Daughter/Ward has not been in contact
with any infectious disease(s) during the previous two weeks.
I also certify that I have read the above information and answered the
questions correctly.

Signed ....

Dated .... Parent/Guardian (Please delete as appropriate)

GENERAL INFORMATION

SELF TEST QUESTIONS

1. How long ago was the first Cadets Pocket Book published,
2. Are your Officers and Instructors fulltime employed in the ACF.
3. What is the training you do in your first few weeks as a Recruit.
4. When do you get 'Enrolled' and what does it mean to you.
5. How soon can you wear your cap badge.
6. What Regiment or Corps is your Cap Badge
7. At the enrollment ceremony who will have been invited.
8. What are 'sponsors' and what is their purpose.
9. What should the enrollment ceremony mean to other Cadets.
10. What is important to you personally about the ceremony.
11. Your Detachment Commander expect a great deal from you, how many of those 'expectations' can you name.
12. What is your definition of being a 'FULL MEMBER of your Detachment.
13. What is the Cadet Charter, What does it say, can you measure up to it.
14. What do you understand by the term "Movers and Shakers".
15. How does your Detachment support your community.
16. What charity work do you help with.
17. What is the main purpose of the Childrens Act 1989.
18. If you have a bad experience who do you report it to.
19. You will often be briefed on safety procedures, whose telephone numbers should you know.
20. Annual Camp Preparation, there are eleven important points to remember what are they.
21. Why is your FFI Form important for going to camp.
22. As a Cadet, when are you not insured for accidents or injury.
23. What is the form when travelling to camp by coach or public transport.
24. There are some Rules about being at Camp what you should do, make a list of them.
25. Should you use an Annual Camp Kit Check List.

CHAPTER 2

THE ARMY CADET FORCE PAST & PRESENT

THE EARLIEST DAYS

The Cadet Force can trace its' beginnings to 1859. At that time there was a threat of a French invasion. Few units of the British Army were at home; most of them were serving in India after the Indian Mutiny. Due to the threat of a French invasion the Volunteers were formed. History was repeated in 1940 when there was the threat of invasion from the German Army.

THE VOLUNTEERS

The formation of the Volunteers – ancestors of the Territorial Army, saw the start of the Cadets. In 1860 at least eight schools had formed units. Volunteer units formed Cadet Companies. One of these, the Queen's Westminsters, paraded their cadets when Queen Victoria carried out a review of the Volunteers in 1860.

The Cadet movement continued, it was seen as being of great value to the boys who lived in the terrible conditions of the London slums.

OCTAVIA HILL – SOCIAL WORKER

One of the most respected social workers of that time was Miss Octavia Hill. She realized that cadet training was of great benefit to these boys; as a result, the Southwark Cadet Company was formed to introduce the boys of the area to the virtues of order, cleanliness, teamwork and self-reliance. The story goes that she had contacts at the Woolwich Garrison and persuaded them that the boys who were living rough on the streets could be accommodated in the stable haylofts at the Barracks. No doubt there were as many rats and mice there as on the streets, but at least it would be dry and warm; and they got fed regularly!

At the age of 26 she collected rents in Paradise Place, one of the most notorious slum areas in London. She was angry and upset to see families living in such terrible conditions that she decided to make it her

THE ARMY CADET FORCE - PAST & PRESENT

mission in life to find or provide better housing for the poor. Today, as a result of her tireless energy and work there is a thriving Octavia Hill Housing Trust that now has 1300 homes in the London area.

Another passion in her life was the creation of open spaces in built up areas to bring "Healthy gifts of air and joy of plants and flowers". Her public campaigns to save recreational open space accessible to all, led to the creation of the National Trust.

Cadets today can be justly proud that the voluntary spirit of Octavia Hill is part of our history and heritage.

THE OCTAVIA HILL MUSEUM AND SOCIETY

The memory of this lady and her life's work is preserved in the Octavia Hill Birthplace Museum. The museum is organised and staffed by the members of the Octavia Hill Society, who, true to the traditions and spirit of Octavia Hill are all volunteers giving their time supporting the museum and staffing it.

The Army Cadet Force is well represented; a model of an Army Cadet was recently added to the display. Every Cadet should make the opportunity to visit the museum, which is located in the Cambridgeshire town of Wisbech, at **1 South Brink Place, PE13 1JE.** It is always advisable to check the opening times before making a visit.

THE BOER WAR

At the start of the Boer War, about fifty schools had Cadet Corps (the forerunners of the Combined Cadet Force). Many 'Open Units' (forebears of the present Army Cadet Force) had started in the larger cities.

AFTER THE BOER WAR

In 1908, the Volunteers were converted to the Territorial Army, Public Schools and Universities were asked to provide units of the Officer Training Corps. Cadet Corps were formed in schools and 'open units' for those who had left school. The title Cadet Force was introduced and the administration was taken over by the Territorial Army Associations.

All members of the ACF should support the

Octavia Hill
Birthplace Museum.

When you are at
Annual Camp at Wreatham
it is not far away for a visit on one
of your days off.
Located in the centre of
Wisbech, Cambridgeshire, PE13 1JE
You can help the museum by
becoming a member of

THE ARMY CADET FORCE - PAST & PRESENT

Quarter Guard. Christ's College, Brecon, Cadet Corps. 1898.
Annual camps were an established feature of the Volunteer Force
and the custom soon spread to cadet units. Sometimes a camp
would be organised by an individual unit, but increasingly
combined camps became the order of the day. The first Public
Schools Cadet Camp was held at Churn Downs in 1889.
The competitive element in these camps gave a useful incentive to
training, drill and shooting competitions being keenly contested.
Each unit in turn had to provide the camp quarter-guard and
again there was keen rivalry to produce the smartest turn-out.
The quarter-guard of Christ's College Cadet Corps is illustrated.
They wear dark blue field service caps and scarlet tunics with
white collars and cuffs. Trousers are of dark blue serge with a
scarlet welt down the outside seams. The bugler to the left carries
the wing epaulettes of a bandsman. Belts of white buff leather are
worn and the guard is armed with the cavalry version Martini-
Henry rifles.
The Christ's College Cadet Corps was formed in 1895 and
became affiliated to the 1st. (Brecknockshire) Volunteer Battalion,
South Wales Borderers. By 1908 it was down to only 35 cadets
and was disbanded. It was revived in 1916 as a cadet corps but
again disbanded in 1921. Finally, it re-formed in June 1937 as a
unit of the Officers Training Corps.

THE ARMY CADET FORCE - PAST & PRESENT

THE FIRST WORLD WAR

In 1914, the Great War, there was a massive expansion of the Cadet Force. The War Office took over the administration, and continued until 1923 when control and administration reverted to the Territorial Army Associations. In that year, 1923 the government ceased to recognize the Cadet Force taking away all financial support. This was a very difficult period for everyone, but the voluntary spirit that had been its greatest strength in the early days came to the surface. Individuals had to find the funding for everything. The wearing of Regimental badges and buttons was forbidden. It was a difficult and unhappy time for the Cadet Force.

Frimley and Camberley Cadet Corps 1909.

Surrey is a county which has always been strongly represented in the ranks of the Cadet Force. The Frimley and Camberley Cadet Corps was formed in 1908, largely at the instigation of a Miss G. M. I. Reynolds. Acting very much in the tradition of Octavia Hill Miss Reynolds became concerned at the Cadet Corps lack of recreation facilities for older boys in her bible class. Her subsequent efforts led to the formation of a cadet corps.

The uniform illustrated was worn by the corps between 1908 and 1912, yet it has a curiously modern ring. A brown jersey was worn with a contrasting red collar, perhaps not so much a concession to informality as a means of providing a cheap uniform in days when the full cost had to be met locally. The real attraction for boys would be the slouch hat, an item of headgear which the South African War had made popular in both volunteer and cadet units.

THE ARMY CADET FORCE - PAST & PRESENT

The cap badge took the form of the letters F&CCC in brass.
The equipment worn was limited to a brown leather belt with
brass clasp and a white haversack.

There was no lack of initial support for this unit and in 1909 Lord
Roberts became its President. Curiously, official recognition did not
come until 1912. In the same year, the unit became affiliated to the
5th. (T.F.) Battalion Queen's Regiment with appropriate changes
in. uniform and badges.

The corps was fortunate in its location and adapted to the lean
inter-war years better than most. The Royal Military College at
Sandhurst was able to assist during this period with both
instructors and second-hand uniforms. Since that time, the unit
has survived and prospered; today it has close links with the
2ndCadet BN The Queen's Regiment, Surrey ACF.

NATIONAL CADET ASSOCIATION (BNCA)

Trying to keep the Cadet Force alive and at the same time trying to
win back government support, brought about the formation of the
BNCA. By 1932 the BNCA had gained recognition and achieved some
measure of success. It was allowed, under the guidance of the
Territorial Army – to run the Cadet Force.

THE SECOND WORLD WAR

Shortly after the start of the war, (1939-45), saw a massive expansion
of all the Cadet Forces, not only the Army Cadets and the Sea Cadets,
they were joined by the newly formed Air Training Corps. By 1942
the War Office, known today as the Ministry of Defence, took over the
administration of the ACF once again, giving it support beyond its
members wildest dreams. Uniforms were provided free, they had rifles
issued, although they were from the Boer War period! Camps were
set up and assistance given to help run them and train the Cadets.
The War Certificate 'A' parts 1 and 2 were then the Proficiency Tests
for training, with the red star worn on the arm of uniforms similar to
your APC blue stars today.

At one period there were more than 140,000 Army Cadets. The
biggest problem was to find officers and instructors to run the
Detachments, most able bodied men were already in the forces or
committed members of the Home Guard or other Emergency Services,
taking what spare time they had.

THE ARMY CADET FORCE - PAST & PRESENT

Wiltshire Army Cadet Force 1943.

During the early part of the Second World War, existing cadet units maintained their position, though many Cadet Force officers were lost to the forces, Home Guard or Civil Defence.

In April 1941 responsibility for cadets was tranferred to the Home Guard Directorate, with the subsequent provision of increased cash grants, free uniforms and equipment. From January 1942 a massive expansion took place, assisted by Cadet Committees formed in each County area. A new title of 'Army Cadet Force' was introduced, to distinguish army cadets from the Sea and Air Cadet units which were forming. The original target for A.C.F. strength was fixed at 150,000 but by mid 1943 over 170,000 army cadets were serving. The age range was fixed at fourteen years to seventeen years.

Assistance with training came from a variety of sources. The Home Guard did a great deal, providing both instructors and weapons. Equally, local army units often gave help and at a more official level the army provided 'Travelling Wings' of some half dozen officers and N.C.O.'s for instruction and revision sessions. The pre-war Certificate 'A' examination of the O.T.C. was adapted as War Certificate 'A' and became the training aim. Camps were enthusiastically attended and in the summer of 1942 an estimated 100,000 cadets went to camp for a week.

We show a member of the Wiltshire A.C.F. wearing battle-dress. Distinguishing features of cadet uniform included a deep blue

THE ARMY CADET FORCE - PAST & PRESENT

backing to the peak flap of the khaki field service cap, also a printed shoulder title with the words CADET FORCE in black on a khaki background. The cap badge of the parent unit was worn, along with slip-on regimental titles of khaki cloth on the shoulder straps. The red star which denoted a pass in Certificate 'A' was worn on the left sleeve.

The background to the picture is the site of Stonehenge.

FORMATION OF THE ARMY CADET FORCE ASSOCIATION

In 1945 the British National Cadet Association changed its name to the Army Cadet Force Association, having spent some considerable time planning to meet the peace time needs of the A.C.F.

Growing in importance was the role of training for citizenship. An equally important factor was the continuation of National Service and the need to offer some form of pre-service training.

Some shrinkage of the A.C.F. took place immediately after the war and there was a further loss of some 100 school units in 1948 when they opted to join the newly organised Combined Cadet Force.

In 1956 the Amery Committee was set up to report on the future organisation and training of the Cadet. The recommendations have provided the basis for all subsequent training with their equal emphasis on the development of character, the introduction of Adventure Training and leadership, and the acquisition of soldierly qualities.   The ACF were one of the organisations to join the 'pilot' scheme for the introduction of the Duke of Edinburgh's Award in the same year gave a firm direction to much of the thinking in the report. One important recommendation led to the establishment in 1959 of the Cadet Training Centre at Frimley Park.

In 1960 came the centenary celebrations of the Army Cadet Force. Many Parades were held up and down the country when the newly presented Standard of the ACF was on parade.

The Headquarters of the Army Cadet Force Association is :
Holderness House, 51-61 Clifton Street, London, EC2A 4DW.

THE ARMY CADET FORCE - PAST & PRESENT

THE AMERY REPORT

In 1957 a special Government Report (The Amery Report), was published. It concerned the future of the ACF in the immediate post war years. Many changes were made; Frimley Park, the Cadet Training Centre, was founded. The ACFA was one of the youth organisations given massive grants from the King George VI Memorial Trust Fund. As a result of this the Cadet Officer and Instructor courses that are run at Frimley are called the KG VI Leadership Courses.

Cadet training took on a new direction, the war was over and National Service was about to cease. It then became more important to develop the Cadet as a person, more responsible for their actions, guiding and developing them through their training to become good citizens.

THE DUKE OF EDINBURGH'S AWARD SCHEME

It was a happy coincidence that the Duke of Edinburgh's Award Scheme started soon after the Adventurous Training was introduced into the ACF. As a result of this the ACF became involved in the Award Scheme as an operating Authority, right from the start.

Thre are many benefits to be gained by taking part in the Award Scheme. It is recognised world wide for any individual who has achieved an award.

ADVENTUROUS TRAINING INTRODUCED

With the emphasis on this change of direction, Adventurous Training was introduced as a subject in the cadet syllabus. Special grants were made available to County Territorial Army

THE ARMY CADET FORCE - PAST & PRESENT

Associations to set up County Adventurous Training Centres. Many Counties took advantage of this and set up Adventure Training Centres in their counties. Hopefully, many of you still have the opportunity to go on weekend training.

ACF ONE HUNDRETH ANNIVERSARY

1960 was the centenary of the ACF and was marked by the presentation of a Banner to the Force by His Royal Highness the Duke of Edinburgh. Another highlight of the year was a review of the ACF and CCF in the grounds of Buckingham Palace by Her Majesty the Queen and His Royal Highness, the Duke of Edinburgh.

In the period from 1960 to the mid 1980s some counties had enrolled girl cadets, initially as a pilot scheme, now of course they are making an increasing contribution to the success of the ACF.

The Colonel in Chief presenting the ACF Bnner at the Royal Hospital March 1982

NEW RIFLES INTRODUCED

1986 was a special 'milestone' in our history with the introduction of the L98. A1 Cadet GP Rifle made especially for the Cadet Forces.

The L81A2 Cadet Target Rifle was reintroduced to encourage more target shooting in the Cadet Forces. Initially there were some probems which have now been rectified. There is an ever increasing number of teams who compete at Bisley.

THE ARMY CADET FORCE - PAST & PRESENT

1994 saw the replacement of the .303 Bren LMG. This was a much loved weapon by those who were marksmen. It had proved its worth in battle from the North African desert, the jungles of the far East . It was a simple action, easy to strip and clean.

The Light Support Weapon (LSW) is the SA 80 Rifle with refinements making it ideal as the Section Fire Team weapon.

For a number of years cadets spent their pocket money buying 1958 pattern webbing equipment in order to be up to date with the same appearance as the Regular Army Soldier.

To everyones delight 1958 Pattern webbing equipment was eventually issued to all County ACF's. At first it raised a few problems as the Cadet could put so much in all the different pockets and pouches that they were unable to lift it off the ground. This was solved by introducing sets of scales to check that the weight was under the permitted amount - one quarter of their own body weight.

The illustration of the Royal Irish Ranger Cadet on the next page shows him wearing Barrack Dress. Cadets on parade always looked so smart in their Barrack Dress instead of combat kit, however these were withdrawn.

In the year 2002 during an Annual Camp a female cadet was involved in an accident as a result of which she lost her life. As a consequence of this tragic accident questions were asked as to who was responsible for and in charge of the Army Cadet Force.

The short answer was it was unclear at the time and to a great extent each County ACF *did their own thing*.

The Ministry of Defence through HQ Land Command officially took over the ACF in the UK.

At about this time TAVRA's (Territorial Army Volunteer Reserves Assn) were re-named RF & CA (Reserve Forces & Cadet Assn).

Many changes in the movement are being made and it might be said that the ACF is now more professional in its outlook and attitudes. A great deal of finance has been made available to the Counties by HQ Land for Cadet training, improvement to facilities, transport, the supply and maintenance of equipment and uniforms.

Cadet County Commandants are now clear to whom they are responsible, and that is their Regular Army District Commander.

THE ARMY CADET FORCE - PAST & PRESENT

Royal Irish Rangers.

In the pre-war years, the authority of the various bodies controlling British cadets did not extend to Northern Ireland. Therefore, apart from some O.T.C. units, there is little early evidence of cadet activity.

The Northern Ireland A.C.F. was formed in January 1943 and organised into battalions of the three Irish infantry regiments; the Cap badge Royal Inniskilling Fusiliers, the Royal Ulster Rifles and the Royal Irish Fusiliers. After the war, cadet units became affiliated to the newly constituted Territorial Army units and a variety of cap badges were worn.

Strengths rose during the fifties with a greater emphasis on adventure training and the Duke of Edinburgh's Award Scheme. In 1968 the detachments affiliated to the three infantry regiments were re-badged to the new combined regiment, the Royal Irish Rangers. Despite the limitations imposed by civil unrest, the A.C.F. in Northern Ireland is thriving and has a total strength of 108 officers, 129 adult instructors and over 1,700 cadets.

We show a cadet sergeant in barrack dress. Which was dark green trousers in a strong material. A woolly pullover and stable belt. He wears the distinctive dark green bonnet or caubeen of the Royal Irish Rangers, complete with green hackle. The brassard on his right arm carries an A.C.F. flash in white and green, dark green chevrons and various proficiency badges. In the background is Carrickfergus Castle.

THE ARMY CADET FORCE - PAST & PRESENT

DIRECTION OF THE ACF

INTRODUCTION

This Chapter explains how the Army Cadet Force is directed, organised and supported. It is important for you to have an understanding of this to realise how much is done for you, by whom it is done and the need to for you to make an effort to show how much it is appreciated.

The Charter of the ACF combines two mutually supporting themes - firstly as a youth organisation, designed to help you develop as an individual and a citizen, and secondly for you to identify with and understand the Army, as the ACF is modelled on some of the methods used by the Army.

As a national youth organisation the ACF is represented by the Army Cadet Force Association (ACFA).

The ACF is not a part of the Armed Services in any way.

THE ROLE OF ACFA

The ACFA has three main roles, they are as follows:

1. To direct activities outside military training in which the ACF is involved as a Youth Service. National Sporting events. Duke of Edinburgh's Award. National Shooting Competitions. Commonwealth Cadet Forces.
2. To advise the Ministry of Defence on all matters of policy. This is a very important role on your behalf.
3. To maintain the spirit of the Army Cadet Force throughout the UK, to act very much in the same way as a Regimental Headquarters does.

ACTIVITIES OF THE ACFA

As mentioned in the History of the ACF, the Army Cadet Force Association was formed from the BNCA - the volunteers - who "kept the flag flying" when the government of the day was giving them a difficult time.

As far as the "members" of the ACFA are concerned it is in many respects similar to a Regimental Association, keeping them informed of all that is going on, providing insurance schemes for non military activities.

THE ARMY CADET FORCE - PAST & PRESENT

It is a source of information, that is of course, if you keep in touch by joining the Association and paying your annual subscription.

All Officers and Adult Instructors in the ACF are expected to be members of the ACFA, although anyone can join by writing to the Membership Secretary, **ACFA, Holderness House, 5 1-6 1 Clifton Street, London EC2A 4DW. Email: Editor a@armycadets.com.**

ARMY CADET MAGAZINE

As a member of ACFA you will be sent the official magazine of the Army Cadet Force, the ARMY CADET. This always has interesting articles on cadet activities from home and abroad. Ask your Officers or Instructors to show you their copy·

Every cadet Detachment should receive a copy of the Army Cadet Magazine sent direct to their Detachment.

At the end of every year ACFA produces an Annual Report setting out the different activities in which they have been involved and a report on the general "state" of the ACF throughout the UK.

Also listed are the various committees and the members who serve on them, illustrating the close liaison with the Ministry of Defence to give advice and guidance on the future role and policy for the continued success of the Army Cadet Force.

THE MINISTRY OF DEFENCE (MOD)

The MOD provides the military organisation, equipment and facilities for training and the finance via Reserve Forces & Cadet Associations (RF&CA) to run and administer the Army Cadet Force.

Perhaps one of the most important facility provided by MOD is the Cadet Training Centre, Frimley Park, Nr Camberley, Surrey. The majority of Officers and Adult Instructors will have attended courses at Frimley during their cadet careers.

As a senior cadet NCO you could also have an opportunity to be a student at Frimley Park.

The MOD also provides the Annual Camp Locations for all the County Army Cadet Forces and the Combined Cadet Forces.

ORGANISATION

The ACF itself is organized on a County basis, other than in the greater London Area where it is divided into four Sectors. In every county the RF&CA has a County Cadet Committee which is responsible for all cadet business, working through the County Cadet Commandant and Secretary of RF&CA.

The Department of Education and Employment in England and Wales, the Scottish Department of Education and Employment and the Northern Ireland Department of Education also have an interest in the ACF.

The relevant Education Acts have placed on the Minister the general responsibility of seeing that help is given to all voluntary youth organizations.

In the ACF this means that the closest co-operation must exist between the Ministry and the ACF either directly or through the medium of the Standing Conference of Voluntary, Youth Organizations of which ACF is a member.

At County and district levels it means that the same co-operation should exist between County Youth Authority and the corresponding cadet authority. The encouragement, financial help and provision of equipment will, in the case of the ACF be mainly on the sport and citizenship training side.

The ACF is also indebted for help and encouragement to many other adult organizations.

The sporting associations have given solid backing, as have the St John's Ambulance, British Red Cross and the St Andrew's first aid societies, and especially those organizations which have come forward to assist in the development of the Duke of Edinburgh's Award Scheme.

Reserve Forces and Cadet Association (RF&CA)

The RF&CA's on behalf of the MOD look after most of the routine Administrationand Logistics of the ARMY CADET FORCE within their Counties.

We are dependent on their help and the history of the Army Cadet Force shows that we were in the same position way back in the 19th century, when the cadets were a part of the Volunteer Battalions of the day, who were the ancestors of the present day Territorial Army.

The RF&CA's have a full time staff at their own County Headquarters. This usually comprises the Secretary who is a retired senior officer from the services, his deputy - also a retired officer, plus a small Administrative Office staff.

THE ARMY CADET FORCE - PAST & PRESENT

Their work as far as the ACF is concerned is to look after the property provided for us, from the provision of new premises to the maintenance of existing cadet huts and vehicles used by the ACF. This in no way means that we should not help to look after our property, as the money available for this is very carefully controlled through a system of grants.

They keep a "watching brief" on how the administration is carried out by the County ACF Headquarters, checking the different accounts where Public Money is being spent, the control of rations, cleaning and maintenance of uniform held in stock, general expenses and many other activities, so, you can see that they have a very important role to play in the smooth running of the administration of ACF in their County.

CADET TRAINING TEAMS

Regular Army provides Cadet Training Teams to "assist Division/ District/Brigade HQ's in the Training of the ACF" they are to:
1. Run courses for Officers and Adults Instructors.
2. Run Courses/Cadres for Senior Cadets.
3. To assist in the conduct of Adult Initial Training Courses and Senior Cadet Instructor Courses (4 Star).
4. To assist in the conduct of advanced training for Cadets, Adventure and Initiative training, NCO Cadres, Special to Arm. Infantry type training and similar activities.
5. To advise the County Cadet Commandant on training matters. To provide assistance at Annual camps..

Many of the courses are carried out at Annual Camp, when a group of Officers and Adult Instructors undergo a weeks training as a part of their Initial Training Course run by the Cadet Training Teams (CTTs). Many of the teams members are ex-cadets and therefore have a good understanding of how the Army Cadet Force functions.

THE COUNTY CADET COMMITTEE

To assist the RF &CA in 'cadet matters' there is a special County Cadet Committee. The committee members are usually people who have special interest in and experience of the Cadet Forces in general within the County.

As an example, the members of the committee usually comprise of some of the following:

THE ARMY CADET FORCE - PAST & PRESENT

The Secretary of RF&CA, the present County Cadet Commandant, ex-Cadet Commandants of the County. Commanding Officers of TA units who have cadets badged to them, the County Cadet Medical Officer, serving ACF Area/ Battalion/commanders, County Padre, representative of the County Youth Service, Police, Education: Headmasters and Headmistresses Associations. Representatives of the Sea Cadets and the Air Training Corps.

Others may be co-opted for special purposes or dealing with specifice problems where professional help can be of benefit. Generally those representing: Sport, Swimming, Shooting, WRVS, and many others all of who can help in the support of Cadets in the County.

It will be appreciated that the 'spread' of representation will have a wide influence on the direction of your County, preserving the reputation of the Army Cadet Force and maintaining the spirit of all those who serve in it.

ARMY CADET FORCE ASSOCIATION

In carrying out its responsibilities the MOD is assisted in its task by the advice and help of the Army Cadet Force Association. The functions exercised by the ACFA with the approval of the MOD and other Government Departments concerned.

ACFA is the representative body of the ACF and amongst its many 'services' it carries out are the organising of Sports, Shooting at Bisley, D of E Award, First Aid, Bands, production of the Army Cadet magazine. ACFA organises the insurance cover for all cadet activities It goes about its work without making any fuss, yet it has an important role in the promotion of the ACF in many Government Departments and other organisations.

RF & CA STAFF AT COUNTY HQ

In addition RF & CAs employ the full-time staff you will find at your own County Cadet HQ.

The Cadet Executive Officer (CEO) is the senior member of the staff and is accountable for the efficient and proper running of the administration within the county for the Cadet Commandant. This is a very important job and requires a great deal of experience in controlling and accounting for clothing, equipment, weapons, ammunition and on the financial side, for the pay and allowances, rations, Officers Mess and Warrant Officers and Sergeants Mess

THE ARMY CADET FORCE - PAST & PRESENT

accounts. The CEO is assisted by a staff who take on the jobs of **County Quarter Master (QM)** and **Cadet Administrative Assistants.(CAA)** who visit detachments carrying out routine checks of equipment and security, delivering stores and uniforms.

In most county HQ there is a **Clerical Officer** who is responsible for the efficient running of the office, dealing with the requests for courses, orders, statistics and general office routine.

COUNTY (ACF) STAFF (Volunteers)

THE COUNTY CADET COMMANDANT

Like you the Commandant is a volunteer, and may be an officer who has had many years experience in the Cadet Force or is a retired senior officer from the Regular Army or TA.

They are appointed by the MOD on the recommendation of the County Cadet Committee normally serving for a three year term.

As the Chief Executive officer they are responsible for all matters relating to the ACF in the County

As the leader, they will be involved in the initial selection of potential Officers and Adult Instructors, and their training.

The Commandant will also be be watching the quality of training that the cadets are receiving and the results not only in APC passes, but how, as a result of the many activities the Detachment takes on in support of the community, encouraging the cadets to understand the importance of voluntary work as a part of turning them out as good citizens.

The Cadet Commandant's time is more directed at building an efficient and enthusiastic team of the right people, who put into practice the policies agreed by the County Cadet Committee.

The County Commandant will have been sponsored by the County Cadet Committee, and appointed by the MOD.

In addition to his/her responsibility for Training and Discipline, which is a responsibility to MOD through the normal military channels, he/she is, of course, expressly nominated as the Commanding Officer of the ACF within his/her County.

THE DEPUTY COUNTY CADET COMMANDANT

Like the Commandant they are appointed by the MOD on the recommendation of the County Cadet Committee. They will 'stand in' on occasions when the Commandant is not available. Very often they

THE ARMY CADET FORCE - PAST & PRESENT

take on special responsibilities for the Commandant, such as Discipline of the officers and instructors, planning Special Projects such as fund raising on a large scale, setting up audit boards, organizing `special event' days at Annual Camp and many more.

THE PADRE

The Padre's role is multifunctional. He/She has the obvious responsibility for the religious wellbeing of all cadets, adults and officers of the county/sector regardless of their religious denomination. If you need a 'listening ear' the Padre will provide it; they are there for you at any time - you do not have to go through the 'chain of command' to speak to them. They often help out when there is a shortage of officers or adults. Talk to your Padre whenever you get a chance - they know the right people!

THE COUNTY ADJUTANT

The role of Adjutant in the ACF county is in many instances multivarious. He or she answers directly to the County Commandant. They are usually experienced Cadet Officers who have the ability to forsee problems and take the necessary action to prevent it happening. Their main occupation is the control and when required to discipline junior officers for 'minor acts of indiscipline'. Traditionally the giving of 'extra duties' is the form of punishment such as visiting the Guardroom in the small hours of the night! Invariably they are not popular, but it is worth keeping on their right side!. They act as the "eyes and ears " of the Commandant.

THE COUNTY TRAINING OFFICER

This job is normally taken on by a senior officer who has had a great deal of experience in training cadets at all levels. Working in close contact with the Commandant, the Training Officer is responsible for ensuring the Commandants Training Programme is met.
They will pay special attention to new Detachments, help new or inexperienced officers and instructors. They are often responsible for arranging adult training, Cadet NCO's Promotion Cadres, and monitoring the APC testing of cadets within the County. They play a large part in drawing up the Annual Camp plans under the guidance of the Cadet Commandant and work in liaison with the CADET TRAINING TEAM (CTT).

THE ARMY CADET FORCE - PAST & PRESENT

COUNTY SHOOTING OFFICER

He/she will ensure that potential 'good shots' have access to coaching and range days.

The Shooting Officer also ensures that Companies/Detachments are aware of the various shooting competitions and leads a team of 'coaches' to assist Cadets in the County Shooting Team to shoot in the National Competitions at Bisley

THE COUNTY SPORTS OFFICER

Every Detachment should practice some form of sporting activities. The competition between Detachments for the County Championship Cup and all other sporting activities would be the sort of job the County Sports Officer would be responsible for organising. If these competitions are not run then it makes it difficult for a County Team to be picked from the best players.

DUKE OF EDINBURGH'S AWARD OFFICER

S/He is appointed by the Cadet Commandant as the County D of E Officer. His/her role is to give assistance to Areas and Detachments who have cadets already enrolled in the scheme or helping those who wish to do so, and the training of Officers and Adult Instructors in how to run the scheme with their own cadets in the Detachment. Remember, that if you are a Dof E Award holder at the Gold level it is a very valuable asset when you are going forward in your chosen career

COUNTY PUBLIC RELATIONS OFFICER

The County PRO is responsible for the promotion of the ACF in the County and is the main link with all types of media, newspapers, TV and local radio.

They make sure that all items of information are correct so as not to give the wrong message to the public. It is therefore important that any 'hot news' is sent direct to him/her and not communicated to any other sources. Every Detachment should have the telephone number of their PRO clearly shown on their Detachment Notice Board.

COUNTY VOCATIONAL QUALIFICATIONS OFFICER

The County VQO is the Officer who advises Officers, Adult Instructors and Cadets on the VQ Scheme full information on the scheme can be accessed on : www.vqaward.org

THE ARMY CADET FORCE - PAST & PRESENT

THE COUNTY RSM (Regimental Sergeant Major)

The RSM works closely with the Adjutant in maintaining the policies of the Cadet Commandant.

The job of RSM is always seen as setting the standards that make a good County ACF. He/she is the senior Rank amongst the Non Commissioned Officers and is held responsible for the conduct of the members and the running of the Sergeants Mess.

The standard of behaviour, dress and discipline set by the RSM is expected to be followed by all Adult Instructors and Cadets.

He /she does not like anyone wandering across his/her parade ground. If you must cross the parade ground - march smartly.

ARMY CADET LEAGUES

The Army Cadet Leagues are organised in some Counties across the UK. They have nothing at all to do with the control or direction of the ACF in their respective Counties.

The best way to explain their role is to call them a 'Supporters Club' for
the Cadets of their County.

Most Leagues are open to membership from any of those who are interested in supporting their Cadets, some are ex-members of the ACF who continue the friendships formed while in the ACF and many others are also members of ACFA.

Any money they do raise is invested and goes into their funds. The interest the funds earn is then made available to provide Detachments with items that the Ministry of Defence do not. Such as sports equipment of all types, helping those Cadets who find it difficult to raise the funds to buy a pair of boots, or who cannot find their Annual Camp fees, etc.

They do not fund any requests to the full amount and expect you to raise half of the costs of what ever project is on hand.

If you have a Cadet League in your County and you can help support them by raising funds, so much the better as some cadet in need of help will benefit from your efforts.

THE ARMY CADET FORCE - PAST & PRESENT

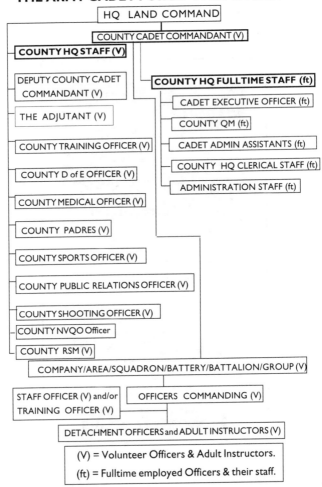

HQ LAND COMMAND

COUNTY CADET COMMANDANT (V)

COUNTY HQ STAFF (V)

DEPUTY COUNTY CADET COMMANDANT (V)

COUNTY HQ FULLTIME STAFF (ft)

THE ADJUTANT (V)

CADET EXECUTIVE OFFICER (ft)

COUNTY QM (ft)

COUNTY TRAINING OFFICER (V)

CADET ADMIN ASSISTANTS (ft)

COUNTY HQ CLERICAL STAFF (ft)

COUNTY D of E OFFICER (V)

ADMINISTRATION STAFF (ft)

COUNTY MEDICAL OFFICER (V)

COUNTY PADRES (V)

COUNTY SPORTS OFFICER (V)

COUNTY PUBLIC RELATIONS OFFICER (V)

COUNTY SHOOTING OFFICER (V)

COUNTY NVQO Officer

COUNTY RSM (V)

COMPANY/AREA/SQUADRON/BATTERY/BATTALION/GROUP (V)

STAFF OFFICER (V) and/or TRAINING OFFICER (V)

OFFICERS COMMANDING (V)

DETACHMENT OFFICERS and ADULT INSTRUCTORS (V)

(V) = Volunteer Officers & Adult Instructors.

(ft) = Fulltime employed Officers & their staff.

THE ARMY CADET FORCE - PAST & PRESENT

SELF TEST QUESTIONS

1. What are the TWO supporting themes of the ACF.
2. What are the THREE roles of ACFA.
3. How can you become a member of ACFA.
4. How can you get the Army Cadet Magazine.
5. Who sponsors the Cadet Kit Shop
6. How can you get the Cadet Kit Shop Catalogue.
7. What does MOD stand for.
8. What does ACFA stand for.
9. What does RF&CA stand for.
10. What does RF&CA do for the ACF in the County.
11. What is the County Cadet Committee.
12. Name THREE people who might be on the County Cadet Committee.
13. What is the 'CEO' and who is it in your County.
14. What is the CEO responsible for in the County.
15. Who appoints the County Cadet Commandant.
16. How long is the Commandant's normal "Term of Service".
17. What is your County Commandant's rank and name.
18. What do you know about Frimley Park.
19. Who is your County DofE Officer.
20. What is the Cadet Training Team, what do they do.
21. Who is responsible for training in your County.
22. Name those who are members of the Commandants County Staff.
23. What is the name of your County Padre.
24. What is the name of your County Shooting Officer.
25. What is the name of your County PRO.
26. What is the name of the CO of your Affiliated TA Regt/Corps.
27. What is the Army Cadet League, and what do they do.
28. Where will you find the Membership Secretary of ACFA
29. What is the name of your County RSM.
30. What is the role of an Adjutant, who does he/she answer to.

Chapter 3

PERSONAL TURNOUT & DRILL

CLOTHING

Unlike many youth organisations, your uniform is issued to you free of charge. This costs a great deal of money to provide all Cadets with uniforms and carry stocks for exchanges. Please take care of it; keep it clean, pressed and in good repair. You will have been given instruction on its care in basic training.

"Sloppy Uniform, Sloppy Cadet"!

THE BRASSARD

The Brassard is worn in Jersey and Shirt Sleeve Orders only.

The Brassard is difficult to keep clean; it can be dry cleaned, but has to be treated with care. The ironing/pressing can be done in several ways, check with your Detachment Adults on the correct method for your County.

Badges of Achievement

The following badges and insignia may be sewn on. **Do not stick them on with glue.**

- Badges of rank and chevrons in white tape
- APC (ACF) Star badge at top right
- Not more than four Proficiency/Skill at Arms badges taking precedence from top left

Exchanges: You have ripped your combats on the weekend training exercise or your lightweights are at 'half mast'? There is a system for exchanging uniform, find out what to do about it.

PERSONAL TURNOUT AND DRILL

THE BRASSARD

The brassard is a separate detachable sleeve shaped to the contours of
the upper arm from the point of the shoulder to just above the elbow.
It is secured at two points, at the point of the shoulder and at the
lower end of the upper arm.

It is difficult to keep clean, it
can be dry cleaned, but has
to be treated with care. The
ironing/pressing of the
Brassard can be done in
several ways according to
the instructions that a
County may give.
Brassard - Badges of
Achievement.
The simplest method is to
lay it out flat and carefully
iron it with a WARM IRON,
not to scorch it. It is worn in
Jersey and Shirt Sleeve
Orders only and the
following badges and insignia
may be sewn on to it.
EmbroideredACF shoulder
titles County insignia or
tartan patch Badges of rank,
and chevrons in white tape.

Not more than 4 embroidered proficiency/Skill at Arms badges taking
precedence from the top right, where the APC(ACF) star will be sewn,
to top left to bottom right to bottom left.

THE BACK OUTSIDE COVER OF THIS BOOK ILLUSTRATES THE
BADGES OF ACHIEVEMENT YOU MAY EARN AS A MEMBER OF
THE ARMY CADET FORCE

PERSONAL TURNOUT AND DRILL

Hints for Pressing Uniform

- Check the label; do not get your iron too hot.
- When ironing trousers or skirts, use an old tea towel (not terry toweling) as a pressing cloth. If using a steam iron, do not damp the cloth.
- Place the cloth on the item you are ironing, apply the iron.
- Don't be tempted to apply any substance to your trousers in order to have a 'permanent' knife-edge crease – it can go horribly wrong.

REMEMBER: DO NOT WEAR YOUR UNIFORM WITHOUT PERMISSION FROM YOUR DETACHMENT COMMANDER UNLESS YOU ARE ON CADET DUTIES

EXTRA ESSENTIAL KIT

BOOTS

A pair of black regulation boots. Make sure they fit you correctly, too small; they will hurt and damage your feet too large; you will keep falling over.

Care and Cleaning of Boots

There are different ideas about how clean your boots should be. It is most likely that you will only have one pair and they will have to be worn for all your Cadet activities. It is almost impossible to wear them on exercise one day and have them fit for a Drill Competition the next! Most Counties have a common sense approach; they plan their activities to give the Cadets time to smarten their boots for a special parade.

What is most important is to make sure they fit you comfortably and are kept in good repair. The laces should be removed to thoroughly clean and polish your boots, make sure you lace them with the laces straight across the eyelet holes, not crossing over them. Should your boots get wet, do not dry them in front of a fire or over heat. It will make the leather hard and brittle, thus letting water in. It helps to stuff newspaper inside to absorb the wet/damp, replacing it after a couple of hours with dry paper. Always carry a spare pair of laces.

PERSONAL TURNOUT AND DRILL

Socks: Do not make the mistake of wearing 'normal' socks with your boots. You will soon find that they rub your feet, perhaps even cause blisters. Good thick wool or cotton mix boot socks will help cushion your feet and absorb moisture. It is suggested that you have a minimum of two pairs. If you are on exercise and space is limited, a pair of socks will last for two days (if they do not get wet), by turning them inside out for the second day.

DESIRABLE KIT

Although not essential, the following list could solve some Birthday present problems!

Webbing: Most Detachment stores have supplies of '58 pattern webbing, the newer issue can be purchased through the Cadet Supply Department and other retail outlets, but it is quite expensive.

Rucksack: Ensure that it is comfortable to wear and is not too big for your height.

Knife, Fork and Spoon set: Useful to have, particularly if they all fit together

Mess Tins: Ensure that you mark them with your name or a distinguishing mark.

Sleeping Bag: As good a quality as you can afford. Make sure that it is washable.

Sleeping Bag Liner: Very useful particularly if you do not have your own sleeping bag.

Bungees elastic supports for bivies.

Compass: A Silva or Sunto Compass (mils) and a Pathfinder Protractor/Romer

PERSONAL TURNOUT
MALES

- Face clean and shaved if necessary
- Hair not over the collar or ears, sideburns not below bottom of ears.
- Clothes clean, washed
- Personal hygeine, washing, clean nails, clean socks in good condition.

PERSONAL TURNOUT AND DRILL

FEMALES

- **Hair:** If your hair is long enough to put up NEATLY, then do so. Try to keep your hair from 'falling' as it can be a problem on exercise or the ranges. Do not wear fancy hair slides, bobbles or fancy scrunchies.
- **Earrings:** ONE pair of plain studs. It is advisable to remove them whilst on exercise, to prevent loss.

General
Body Piercing

It is your personal choice whether you have body piercing. However, for your safety, these should be either removed whilst in uniform, or covered securely with a sticking plaster. There is a real danger of these piercings being caught or becoming infected whilst undertaking most cadet activities.

Rings: One signet ring is acceptable, but 'Rings on every finger' does not look right when in uniform. There is also a possibility they may slip off during an exercise or getting caught when weapon cleaning.

Neck Chains and Bracelets: Should not be worn when in uniform, unless they are Medic Alert or similar.

COMPLIMENTS
Saluting – Origin and information

The salute with the hand, the present arms and salute with the sword were methods by which a person paying a compliment could show the person to whom the compliment was paid that no offence was meant. They were all gestures symbolic of loyalty and trust.

- You will be trained how to salute smartly and correctly
- It is discipline that you salute smartly when you meet an Officer
- If an Officer fails to return the salute, it is bad manners on their part.

PERSONAL TURNOUT AND DRILL

THE QUEENS COMMISSION

All compliments derive their origin from the Sovereign, to whom the highest compliment, the Royal Salute, is paid. All Officers of the Army Cadet Force hold the Queens Commission, and when an Officer is saluted it is in recognition of the Queens Commission held in trust by that Officer.

Ask one of your Officers to bring their Commission Paper along for you to see. It is written on parchment paper, signed and sealed by Her Majesty The Queen.

When Compliments are paid:

THE NATIONAL ANTHEM

When on parade, stand to attention, **only** Officers and Warrant Officers salute, NCOs will if in charge of a party.

When **not** on parade, but in **uniform,** all ranks **will** salute. When not on parade, and in **plain clothes**, all ranks will stand to attention. If a hat is worn, it will be removed (**Females do not remove hats**).

**THE
UNION
FLAG**

STANDARDS GUIDONS AND COLOURS

As a squad on the march you will give an 'Eyes Left' or 'Right'.
As an individual, you halt; face passing Standards, Guidons or Colours.

ARMY CADET FORCE BANNER

The Banner, presented by HRH The Duke of Edinburgh, is dedicated, but not consecrated; it does not rank as a Colour, Standard or Guidon. It will be accorded the respect of a Colour except that:
1. Individuals or parties of Cadets passing will not salute it.
2. When Banner passes, individual or parties stand to attention.
3. When taken over, individual taking it will salute first.

PERSONAL TURNOUT AND DRILL

BADGES OF RANK

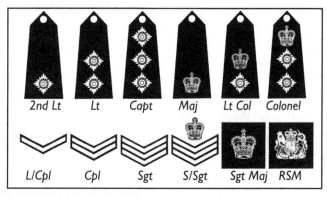

| 2nd Lt | Lt | Capt | Maj | Lt Col | Colonel |

| L/Cpl | Cpl | Sgt | S/Sgt | Sgt Maj | RSM |

PAYING COMPLIMENTS –

Saluting to the front: Common Faults.
1. Body and head not remaining erect, shoulders back.
2. Allowing the Right elbow to come forward.
3. Right hand not straight, not in the correct position, wrist not straight and thumb not straight.
4. Allowing the Left arm to creep forward.
5. Left fist not clenched with the thumb in front and in line with seam of trousers. Arm not tight in to the side.

As an aid to good saluting, remember your right hand – with the palm flat, thumb on top, travels the "Longest way up" and the "Shortest way down". Having saluted, clench your fist, smartly cutting your arm down to your side, keeping the thumb to the front ready to align with the seam of your trousers.

PERSONAL TURNOUT AND DRILL

INTRODUCTION TO DRILL

Through history, British Army Drill has been the foundation upon which discipline; teamwork, pride and pageant have all taken equal part.

In the days of the 'Brown Bess' musket, when in battle, the infantry formed a square in their three ranks in order to give effective firepower.

This action was carried out as a drill, taught and practiced on the barrack square. The discipline required to 'hold the line' was the difference between defeat and victory. Drill parades were hard and rigorous, with harsh violence dished out by the instructors.

Times have changed, the Regular Army still rely on drill to build team spirit and to train the soldiers' mind to respond to orders given in the quickest possible time.

When you are first introduced to Drill Commands, you may find that your reactions are slow and mistakes easily made. Fortunately your initial lessons are all completed at the 'Halt' i.e. stood still. It is difficult enough to stand still, especially when there is a fly walking down your nose – no matter, stand still! Once you have mastered the initial movements and been taught how to march without your arms moving in the wrong order, you will suddenly find it all comes together, your squad starts to move as a team. It will probably feel even better when you take part in a Civic or Cadet Sunday Parade. You will be with the rest of your Detachment, smartly turned out and marching behind a band. It might sound odd to some of you who have not attended such Parades, but it gives you a real 'Buzz' and dare it be said, pride in your Detachment and the Army Cadet Force. (Particularly if your family and friends are watching!)

DRILL – INTRODUCTORY WORDS OF COMMAND

Used for Squad Drill Good instructors give INTRODUCTORY words of command giving warning of what the next word of command is to be.

Many instructors do not do this; the result is the squad turning in different directions at the same time!

Before moving a squad in any direction, the instructor indicates what direction they intend to move them by using an INTRODUCTORY

PERSONAL TURNOUT AND DRILL

word of command, before giving the actual command to execute the order. As a member of the squad, this does give you the time to work out the direction of your next move.

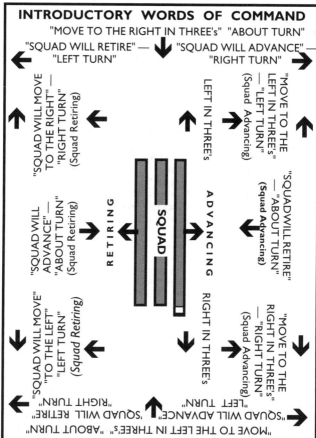

PERSONAL TURNOUT AND DRILL

Look at the diagram. Turn it sideways as if you were standing in the center of the front rank of the 'squad', facing the same direction as the arrow pointing to 'ADVANCING'. The words of command you should be given to move the squad in any particular direction are as shown in the diagram. Suggest you enlarge this page by photocopy or scan and put it up on your bedroom wall - you will be ace at Drill.

CHANGING DIRECTION - WHEELING ON THE MARCH

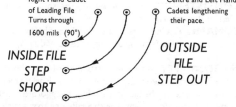

Right Hand Cadet
of Leading File
Turns through
1600 mils (90°)

Centre and Left Hand
Cadets lengthening
their pace.

INSIDE FILE
STEP
SHORT

OUTSIDE
FILE
STEP OUT

The term "Step Short" means reduce the length of your pace, "Step out" means slightly lengthen your pace.

By doing this while Wheeling you keep your Dressing in each file as it changes direction.

A common fault when giving the "Left or Right Wheel" is for the command to be given sharply, when in fact it should be drawn out - "WHEE-EEL", allowing the files to slowly change direction, keeping their dressing in three's. You must glance out of the corner of your eyes to check your dressing, not turning your head.

MARCHING AND DRESSING OFF

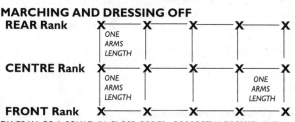

REAR Rank X——X——X——X——X

ONE
ARMS
LENGTH

CENTRE Rank X——X——X——X——X

ONE
ARMS
LENGTH

ONE
ARMS
LENGTH

FRONT Rank X——X——X——X——X

DIAGRAM OF A SQUAD IN CLOSE ORDER, CORRECTLY DRESSED AND COVERED OFF FROM LEFT TO RIGHT, AND FROM FRONT RANK - TO REAR.

PERSONAL TURNOUT AND DRILL

TEACHING DRILL

The aims of Drill are:

1. To produce a Cadet who has self respect, is alert and obedient
2. To provide the basis for teamwork

Drill is exacting and strict attention to detail must be observed. You will need the following qualities to become an excellent Drill Instructor.

1. PATIENCE. Never lose your temper.

2. ENTHUSIASM. You must fire your squad with a will to achieve.

3. CONSISTENCY. Set yourself and the squad a high standard and do not deviate from it.

4. HUMANITY. Understand the squad's problems; praise readily, do not become over familiar or humiliate individual members of your squad.

5. PERSONALITY. As a drill instructor you must impress your squad – always have them under control, lead by example:

When demonstrating, be accurate; never exaggerate a drill movement. If the movement is with a rifle use that article and nothing else.

Never use bad language and sarcasm; it is the sign of a poor instructor. Ensure that your words of command are clear, DO NOT do as some drill instructors, create your own 'drill language', it is bad practice.

THE WORDS OF COMMAND

All words of command must be clear and powerful; the way in which they are given affects the reaction that they inspire. Words of command are divided into three parts:

1. INTRODUCTORY. This tells the squad what movement they are about to carry out, e.g. "MOVE TO THE RIGHT IN THREES".

2. CAUTIONARY. The drawn out and loud reminder to the squad, e.g. R –I – G – H – T.

3. EXECUTIVE. The high-pitched sharp command "TURN".

Sometimes there is no need for an *INTRODUCTORY* word of command, e.g. **"SQUAD – SHUN"**. Occasionally there is no *CAUTIONARY*, E.G. **"FORWARD"**.

Timing of Words of Command

The table at the end of this chapter shows on what foot the executive word of command is given.

PERSONAL TURNOUT AND DRILL

The cautionary word of command should be consistently drawn out over about the equivalent of **Four paces** in quick time. There should be a pause between it and the executive word of command.

There should be a pause between it and the executive word of command of:

1. **At the Halt** – the regulation pause.
2. **In Quick Time** – about four paces
3. **In Slow Time** – about three paces.

DEVELOP YOUR WORD OF COMMAND

The following information will help you develop good voice control. Practice whenever you can.

Explanation. Many drill instructors end up with sore throats after a prolonged drill practice. This may well be because they do not use their lungs correctly.

It is important to breathe in through your nose and take your breath 'right down to your stomach'. In other words, learn to breathe deeply. When giving a word of command, 'push' the air out.

Do not forget to stand to attention when giving commands. Standing with your feet apart or leaning backwards may result in straining your groin. KEEP YOUR WEIGHT FORWARD AND YOUR FEET TOGETHER.

Have your head up, looking directly at your squad; when giving the word of command AIM your voice straight over the squad.

Giving Words of Command.

Giving a Cautionary or preliminary word of Command you have to pitch your voice on the same note to ensure that it does not 'tail away' at the end. It must be short and sharp, "SQD". Then comes the Executive word of command, equally short and sharp, "SHUN".

It is most important to develop the correct method of delivering commands; nothing is worse than a poor drill instructor. If you really cannot do it properly, leave it to someone who can.

Words of Command.

They must be pronounced CLEARLY. It is not just a sound. A quick tightening of the stomach muscles so that the word comes out quick, short and higher in pitch than the Cautionary produces the Executive

PERSONAL TURNOUT AND DRILL

word of command. Ensure that there is a pause between the Cautionary and the Executive. Failure to do this may result in the squad anticipating the word of command, thus the whole purpose of drill is lost – and chaos will reign!

Note: Use your mouth; the wider open it is, the louder the sound!

To summarise:

Power: plenty of air into the lungs.

Pitch: Hold your head high and pitch the word of command high over the   Squad.

Punch: Given quickly by tightening the stomach muscles.

Pronunciation: Make your words CLEAR. LOUD and AS AN ORDER.

Communication Drill

1. First demonstrate to the squad all words of command at the halt, including rifle drill.
2. Then "conduct" the squad while they give elementary words of command; insisting on clarity and power from each cadet.
3. Divide the squad in to two ranks, place them about 25 metres apart, with 5 paces interval between each cadet.
4. Each cadet should now drill his/her opposite number 25 metres away without regard to those to the left or right of them.
5. After no more than ten minutes, change the ranks, so that the cadets in both ranks have a chance of controlling their opposite number.

Mutual Drill

Form the squad into three ranks and explain the introductory word of command and which is the DIRECTING FLANK.

Call out each member of the squad in turn to drill the squad and then call out another member of the squad to watch and be prepared to comment on his/her performance.

Note:

1. Be patient and make encouraging comments.
2. When correcting, be sure you address your remarks to the whole squad, they can all learn by one cadet's mistakes.

PERSONAL TURNOUT AND DRILL

AIDS TO BETTER DRILL

Calling out the time

All cadets in their early stages of training should call out the time of
their Drill movements so that:

Every member of the squad has the regulation pause fixed in their
head.

The squad learns to act together, building team spirit.

The squad should call out the words for a given movement.

They must learn to be still when calling out **"TWO THREE"** for the
regulation pause.

When you can see your cadets improving, select individuals to call out
the time for the whole squad. It helps to build the confidence of the
more junior cadets.

TIMING AND PACE

All Instructors should know the rates of marching, measured in the
number of paces taken in a minute, the length of the pace being taken,
measured in inches/mm and the timings of both foot and arms drill.
The recognised measurements are set out below.

 However, it must be remembered that these are for grown adults
NOT Cadets, therefore some allowance must be made as and when
required.

RATES OF MARCHING

RATE	PACES TO MINUTE
1. Quick Time (normal)	116
2. Quick Time (Recruits)	140
4. Slow Time (Normal)	65
5. Slow Time (Light Infantry and Green Jackets Regt)	70
6. Double Time	180

RATE OF MARCHING	LENGTHS OF PACE
1. Quick and Slow Time	30 inches (76 cm)
2. Stepping Out	33 inches (84cm)
3. Stepping Short	21 inches (54cm)
4. Double Time	40 inches (102cm)
5. Side Pace	12 inches (31cm)

PERSONAL TURNOUT AND DRILL

DEFINITIONS

Alignment – A straight line on which a body of Cadets is formed or is to form.

Covering - The act of placing yourself directly behind another body.

Depth - The space occupied by a body of Cadets from front to rear.

Distance - The space between Cadets or bodies from front to rear.

Dressing - The act of aligning oneself with and covering others within a body of Cadets.

File - (a) Either two or three Cadets of different ranks who are covering each other, or (b) A body of Cadets in two ranks facing a Flank.

Single File – Cadets one behind another on a frontage of one at normal marching distance.

Blank File - A file in which there is no center and rear Cadet, or no centre Cadet, due to the inequality of numbers within a body of Cadets.

Flank – Either side of a body of Cadets as opposed to its front or rear.

Directing Flank - The flank by which a body of Cadets takes its dressing.

Frontage - The extent of ground covered laterally by a body of Cadets, measured from flank to flank.

Interval – The lateral space measured between Cadets or bodies of Cadets on the same alignment.

Line – Cadets formed in the same alignment.

Markers – Cadets employed to mark points on which a movement is to be directed, or by which a formation or alignment is to be regulated.

Order (Close or Open) - The distance between ranks in line, which is either thirty inches or sixty inches depending on circumstances.

Rank – A line of Cadets side by side. (i.e. 'Front Rank').

Supernumerary Rank – the extra rank, fourth rank in three ranks, or third in two ranks, formed by the senior NCOs of a body of Cadets.

A Squad – Means a sub – unit formed for Drill and is used throughout to avoid explanations.

A REGULATION PAUSE. Refers to the short pause between two movements of drill, which is the equivalent of two marching paces in quick time, i.e. Forty movements to the minute.

PERSONAL TURNOUT AND DRILL

TABLE FOR TIMING WORDS OF COMMAND

WORD OF COMMAND	QUICK TIME (WHEN GIVEN)	SLOW TIME (WHEN GIVEN)	WHAT THE SQUAD CALL OUT	REMARK
"HALT!" (Marching)	On the Left foot	Left foot passes right.	"ONE, TWO"	
"QUICK (or SLOW) MARCH"	"QUICK!" and "SLOW!" both given on the left foot. "MARCH" both on the Right foot (ON SUCCESSIVE FEET)			
"RIGHT—TURN!" (incline)	As Left Heel Strikes ground	Right foot about to touch ground		"LEFT -TURN vice -versa
"ABOUT—TURN!"	As Right Heel strikes ground	Just before the Right foot reaches ground	Quick Time)"IN", LEFT, RIGHT, LEFT, FORWARD (Slow Time) "ONE STOP, TWO STOP, THREE STOP, FORWARD!"	
"MARK - TIME"	Over complete Left pace.	Over complete Right pace	(Quick Time) "IN"	
"HALT!" "FORWARD" (Marking Time)	Left knee fully raised	Right Knee fully raised		

PERSONAL TURNOUT AND DRILL

TABLE FOR TIMING WORDS OF COMMAND

WORD OF COMMAND	QUICK TIME (WHEN GIVEN)	SLOW TIME (WHEN GIVEN)	WHAT THE SQUAD CALL OUT	REMARKS
"CHANGE STEP!" (Marching and Marking Time)	"CHANGE!" on the left foot. "STEP!" on the right foot. (On successive feet)		(Marching) "LEFT, RIGHT LEFT!" (Marking time) "LEFT, LEFT, RIGHT!"	
"BREAK INTO QUICK TIME, QUICK - MARCH!"		"QUICK!" on the left foot. "MARCH!" on the right foot. (On successive feet)		
"BREAK INTO SLOW TIME, SLOW - MARCH !"	On right foot.			
"OPEN (CLOSE) ORDER!"	Over complete right pace.			
"SALUTING! EYES RIGHT" (Marching)	On LEFT foot	On RIGHT foot	(Quick time)" ONE, TWO, THREE, FOUR, FIVE, DOWN, SWING!"	
"SALUTING!" 1. To the front marching 2. As on sentry.	On the Left foot			

Note: For all movements of foot and arms drill at the halt in which there is more than one part the squad will call out "ONE! TWO, THREE, ONE!" Moving only as they call "ONE!"

PERSONAL TURNOUT AND DRILL

SOME GUIDING PRINCIPALS FOR PARADES

A parade should always start with an inspection of all who are on it.
Strict observance of rank should be shown; therefore an Officer, Adult
Instructor or a Cadet, when they wish to either join or leave the
parade, should report to the senior rank and ask permission to do so.
Cadets should not walk across a parade ground when drill, in which
they are not taking part, is taking place.

Those who are to command it should plan the form and purpose of a
parade beforehand.

At the end of a parade all ranks "Dismiss" to show respect to the
senior rank present.

Having been dismissed from a parade, march smartly off the parade
ground without stopping for a "Chat".

"Always be five minutes early rather than five minutes late".

SELF TEST QUESTIONS

1. What are the origins of paying compliments – Saluting?
2. How do you tell if a squad is advancing or retiring?
3. On what foot is the HALT given?
4 What does a DIRECTING FLANK mean?
5. Given the preliminary word of command, "Squad will retire", is the
    squad 'advancing' or 'retiring'?
6. When wheeling in a squad who 'steps short' and why?
7. What do you understand by a "INTRODUCTORY" word of
    command?
8. At "Close Order" what is the distance between ranks?
9. Marking time, the HALT is given when the knee is …..?
10. What six qualities are required of a good Drill Instructor?
11. What is meant by "Words of Action"?
12. What are the three stages in giving a Word of Command?
13. What is Communication Drill?
14. Cautionary Words of Command should be drawn out – Why?
15. What is Mutual Drill carried out for?
16. What are the reasons for calling out time in Drill?
17. What do you understand about "Dressing"?

PERSONAL TURNOUT AND DRILL

18. What are Markers called out for?

19. What causes a "Blank File" in a squad?

20. What do you understand by a Regulation Pause?

21. Leaving or joining a parade, what should you do?

22. What is important about the position of your head when giving a command?

23. What have the Four "P"s to do with drill?

24. What does "Keeping your Dressing" mean?

25. What does it mean when you are given the order, "By the Left"?

26. How much does your uniform cost you when you join the ACF.

27. Which shoulder do you wear your brassard.

28. How are the badges fixed on the brasard.

29. How do you lace up a pair of boots - crossing over or straight across.

30. What is the best way to dry out very wet boots.

31. What are the best type of socks to wear with your boots.

32. List the items of kit that are desirable to have.

33. Name the important points on Personal Turnout, male/female.

34. When are compliments paid and by whom.

35. When the National Anthem is played who salutes.

36. What is it relating to "the longest way up and shortest way down"

37. When saluting at the 'halt' what is the position of the left thumb.

38. When do you step short

39. What is the 'Aim' of drill.

40. Words of command are divided into three parts. What are they.

41. Why do some drill instructors finish up with sore throats.

42. In Quick Time what is the normal number of paces per minute.

43. What is the advantage of a Drill Squad calling out the time.

44. What is a 'Regulation Pause' and how long is it.

45. When' on parade' what will an inspecting officer be looking for.

Chapter 4

FIELDCRAFT

Introduction

Fieldcraft is the one subject that always gets you and your 'mates' to turn out in strength, especially if it says on the programme that it is an Escape and Evasion exercise, and if it's at night - so much the better. We are not suggesting that all cadets still like playing 'cowboys and Indians', but may be Field Craft could be described as organised cowboys and Indians!

If you live in a city/town you are at some disadvantage to see Field craft in action, however, if you are able to get into the countryside or live in or near it, you will be aware that the wild life 'get a living' off the land by being experts in the use of their skills of: stealth, patience, speed and fitness, stamina, planning and cunning and being natural experts at camouflage and concealment.

NATURAL SKILLS

Fieldcraft is their prime skill in catching their food and to be good at Fieldcraft you could do no better in many ways than to study wildlife at every opportunity.

Observe how a cat stalks its quarry, how the Sparrow Hawk hovers patiently, observing the right moment to drop in on the Field Mouse; the Fox who uses the hedgerows to move from one field to another, see how well a Rabbit is camouflaged against the ground, all of these examples are types of Individual Field Craft skills exercised for the purpose of either defence or attack.

In your case, having knowledge of Fieldcraft brings together and practices some of the skills required to achieve your APC 1 to 4 Star not only as an individual, but also as a member of a team or section.

As Cadets you should normally work only at SECTION LEVEL, and for you to understand where a Section 'fits into' the organisation of an Infantry Battalion we set out on the next page a diagram showing the outline organisation of an Infantry Battalion and how the Section fits into it.

FIELDCRAFT

Outline Organisation of an Infantry Battalion

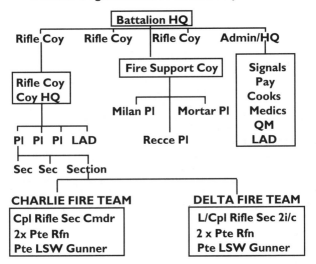

SECTION ORGANISATION

The normal fighting strength of a Section in the Regular Army is two NCO's and six men, but it can operate with one NCO and five men.

The Rifle and the LSW are the main weapons of the Section. The Riflemen can be divided into smaller groups to provide better "fire and movement" capability.

The LSW provides support for the movement of the Section especially in the assault.

FIELDCRAFT

INDIVIDUAL FIELDCRAFT

Once you have an understanding of the need to imitate the skills that wild life practice to survive in the field, then you will be on the way to attaining an acceptable standard of Individual Fieldcraft. You need to be mentally alert, physically fit, and have a lot of practice and patience to develop the natural ability to react instinctively in any given situation, both as an individual and as a member of a group.

As an NCO Fieldcraft gives you the opportunity to control and direct your section under field conditions. You must be expert at Individual Fieldcraft to command a Section.

METHODS OF JUDGING DISTANCE

WHY JUDGE DISTANCE: if you can judge distance you will know the approximate area in which to look when given an order. If your sights are not correctly adjusted, your shots will probably miss the target.

USE A UNIT OF MEASURE

100 metres is a good unit, The Range is marked out at 100 metre intervals. A Full Size Football pitch is about 100 metres long. DO NOT USE THE UNIT OF MEASURE METHOD OVER 400 METRES IF YOU CAN'T SEE ALL THE GROUND BETWEEN YOU AND THE TARGET.

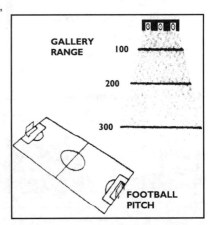

GALLERY RANGE

100

200

300

FOOTBALL PITCH

FIELDCRAFT

JUDGING DISTANCE

When you know what 100 metres looks like, practice fitting your Unit of Measure between you and your target.

REMEMBER

AIDS TO JUDGING DISTANCE

APPEARANCE METHOD

By noting what a person looks like at a set distance, you can then use the Appearance Method

Common objects may also be used for this method.

FIELDCRAFT

Things seem closer

Further away

Things seem closer .. In bright light, if they are bigger than their surroundings, if there is dead ground between you and them, if they are higher up than you.

Further away ... With sun in your eyes, in bad light. When smaller than surroundings. Looking across a valley, down a street or along a path in a wood, if you are lying down.

AIDS TO JUDGING DISTANCE - KEY RANGES

If the range to one object is known, estimate the distance from it to the target.

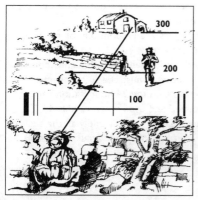

BRACKETING

Calculate mid-distance between nearest possible and furthest possible distance of target.
Nearest - 100
Farthest - 300.
Mid-distance - 200.

HALVING

Estimate the distance halfway to the target then double it:
$100 \times 2 = 200$

FIELDCRAFT

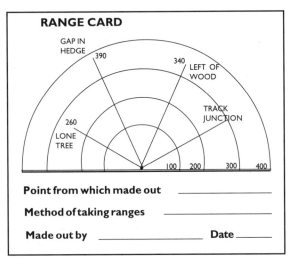

THE SMALL ARMS RANGE CARD

Range Cards are to be prepared whenever a position is occupied for more than 30 minutes or more.

Section and Platoon Commanders are responsible for ensuring the Range Card is made out accurately.

A Range Card must be made out for every position and should be passed on to the next occupant who must check its accuracy.

A printed Range Card is available on the 24 hour Ration Pack boxes, these should be retained and used when required.

When making out your Range Cards you will apply all the skills of Judging Distance and as a result improve your accuracy better than most.

FIELDCRAFT

PERSONAL CAMOUFLAGE AND CONCEALMENT

The enemy is looking for you so - don't make it easy.
Merge with your surroundings

TOO MUCH **JUST RIGHT** **TOO LITTLE**

LOSE YOUR SHAPE
Make sure nothing
shines.
Blend in with your
surroundings - if
they vary, so must
you.

AVOID SKYLINES

Stand back from
windows - merge into
the shadows - don't
lean out you will be
seen.

FIELDCRAFT

Don't use isolated cover - it stands out.

SOMETHING IS SEEN BECAUSE ITS:-

Shape
Shadow   } **FAMILIAR OR STANDS OUT**
Silhouette

Surface
Spacing   } **DIFFERENT FROM ITS SURROUNDINGS**
Movement

SEEING IS .... Noticing details.

EASY TO SEE   DIFFICULT TO FIND
SHAPE ...... Disguise your shape - including equipment
and weapons.

FIELDCRAFT

SHADOW .... Keep in the shadows

SILHOUETTE .... Don't skyline

SURFACE..... Don't differ from your surroundings.

FIELDCRAFT

SPACING... Keep spread out - but not equally spaced.

MOVEMENT .... Move carefully - slowly when concealed - sudden movement will attract attention.

Look through cover - if possible -not round it .
You **MUST SEE** without being **SEEN**.

FIELDCRAFT

TARGET RECOGNITION

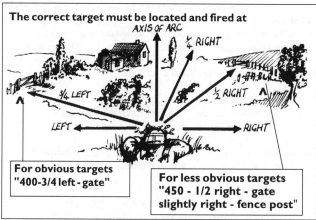

The correct target must be located and fired at

For obvious targets
"400 - 3/4 left - gate"

For less obvious targets
"450 - 1/2 right - gate
slightly right - fence post"

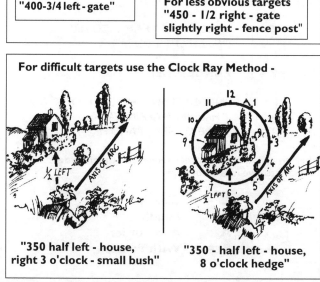

For difficult targets use the Clock Ray Method -

"350 half left - house,
right 3 o'clock - small bush"

"350 - half left - house,
8 o'clock hedge"

FIELDCRAFT

FIRE CONTROL ORDERS.

When the Section comes under fire the Section Commander will give the order 'TAKE COVER'.

The drills for this are covered later, however there will come a time when the Section Commander will need to take control of the fire power of the Section to concentrate it on the target, this is achieved using a **Fire Control Order.**

You must learn how to do this instinctively so that you can:

    a. Re-act to the Fire Control Order correctly.

    b. Give an order yourself if no one else can see the target.

To give a correct Fire Control Order you have to follow tha set sequence, it will help you if you remember it by the "Key Word" **GRIT**, as follows:-

G =	WHICH **FIRE TEAM** IS TO FIRE ("*No 2 SECTION, DELTA*").
R =	**RANGE** IN METRES "450"
I =	**INDICATION** WHERE TO LOOK ("*HALF RIGHT GAP IN WALL*")
T =	**TYPE** OF FIRE ("RAPID FIRE")

When giving this type or order remember it is an **order** therefore to give it as an **order:** -

C =	**Clearly**
L =	**Loudly**
A =	**As an order**
P =	**With Pauses**

FIELDCRAFT

TYPES OF FIRE CONTROL ORDER

The details of the Fire Control Order you get depends on the
Type of Target to be engaged.

> **BRIEF Orders -**
> *"Sights down quarter right rapid fire".*
> **FULL Orders - "***Delta - 450 left-house
>   doorway- bursts-fire".*
> **DELAYED Orders.**
> *"No 2 Section-300-quarter right-small wood -
> when enemy appears - rapid -fire".*
> **INDIVIDUAL Orders**
> *"No I Section 300 - slightly left - small bushes -
> enemy in that area - watch and shoot".*

MOVEMENT IN THE FIELD

When close to the enemy you do
not want your movements to be
seen-therefore use cover.
Remember to - Use the hedges and
walls for cover.

Leopard Crawl

Crawl on the inside of your knees
and your elbows. Useful for moving
behind very low cover. Move by

using alternate elbows and knees, rolling your body a little as you
bend your knees.
Keep your heels, head and body down, you must observe at all
times.

Over page is
shown the
Leopard Crawl
with a rifle.

LEOPARD CRAWL

FIELDCRAFT

Leopard Crawl — with a rifle.

Hold your Rifle with the right hand on the Pistol Grip and the left hand on the Hand Guard.

The Monkey Run

This is a normal "hands and knees" crawl. Useful to move behind cover about two feet high.

You can move quite fast, but it does make a noise.

Moving slower and to prevent twigs cracking as you move, put your knees on the spot where your hands have been.

Keep your "rear end" and head down, but continue to observe. With a rifle hold it at the point of balance, make sure that no dirt gets into the muzzle.

The Walk

The Rifle is held in the ALERT position, ready for instant action. You must adopt a positive and alert attitude, observing in all directions.

Don't walk on the flat sole of your boots, use the edge so as to walk quietly. It helps to keep your balance if you slightly bend your knees as you move.

FIELDCRAFT

The Roll

The quickest way of getting off a skyline or crest of a hill.

Protect your Rifle, hold closely into your side. Keep feet together and your body straight.

MOVEMENT AT NIGHT

Always move quietly.

Movements used during daylight are not suitable at night- they have to be adapted.

The Ghost Walk

Lift legs high, sweeping them slowly outwards. Feel gently with toes for safe place for each foot, put weight down gently. Keep knees bent. Use the left hand to feel the air in front of you from head height down to the ground checking for obstructions, trip wires, booby traps or alarms etc

The Cat Walk

Crawl on hands and knees. Search ground ahead for twigs, move knee to where hand has searched.

The Kitten Crawl

It is quiet-but slow. It is very tiring.

Lie on your front, search ahead for twigs, move them to one side.

Lift your body on your forearms and toes, press forward and lower yourself on to the ground.

NIGHT NOISES

At night you hear more than you see. Stop and listen.

FIELDCRAFT

Keep close to the ground, turn your head slowly and use a cupped hand behind the ear.. Freeze if you hear a noise.

MOVING AT NIGHT - REMEMBER

Keep quiet .... have no loose equipment. Move carefully ... use the ghost walk, cat walk or kitten crawl.

Clear your route ... dry vegetation will make a noise.

Use available cover ... flares, thermal imaging and night observation devices will turn night into day.

Keep to the low ground ... you split your party at night at your peril.

LISTENING AT NIGHT

If the enemy is about - keep an ear close to the ground.
The closer you are to the ground, the more chance you have of seeing the enemy on 'skyline'.

USE ALL YOUR SENSES AT NIGHT - ESPECIALLY YOUR SENSE OF SMELL - A 'WHIFF' OF COOKING OR SMOKE OR EVEN BODY ODOUR CAN GIVE YOURS OR THE ENEMY POSITION AWAY.

NIGHT VISION

We can see in the dark - but REMEMBER our eyes take 30 minutes to get used to the dark.
We see less than in daylight.
We see shapes - not detail.
We see skylines and silhouettes.
We may see movement.

FIELDCRAFT

YOUR EYESIGHT

Your eyes have two sets of cells, one set for daylight (CONES) in the centre of your eyes, the other set for darkness (RODS), which are around the CONES.

The night cells work when the day cells are affected by falling darkness.

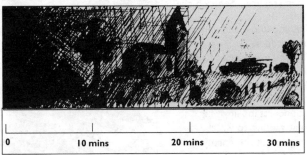

| 0 | 10 mins | 20 mins | 30 mins |

With constant practice night observation can be improved. If you have a cold, headache or are tired it can reduce your night vision. You will find that there is a limit to the time you can concentrate effectively on any given point or your vision becomes blurred.

Most Army unit use Thermal Imaging (night sights) that "turn darkness into daylight" in as much that they pick out an object giving out heat (body heat), The SUSAT sights on the SA80 Rifle/LSW (an optical sight) has advantages similar to that of binoculars for night observation.

BRIGHT LIGHT RUINS YOUR NIGHT VISION

If caught in the light of flares take cover at once in open ground.
If in a wood - FREEZE.
If you see a flare, quickly close one eye to protect your night vision, use the other eye to look about you taking advantage of the light, but do not move suddenly as this will give you away.

FIELDCRAFT

DUTIES OF A SENTRY

A sentry is the eyes and ears of the unit.

If the job is done well, the unit will be safe and secure.

When you are a Sentry make sure:-

That you know and understand your orders.

That you know what to do if your post is approached by a person or vehicle.

That you ask questions if you do not understand anything.

What ground to watch.

Direction of the enemy.

Signal for defensive fire.

Names of prominent landmarks.

Where neighbouring posts are.

About patrols that maybe in the area, or coming through your post.

SENTRIES AT NIGHT IN THE FIELD

At night sentries work in pairs.

Sentries must know:-

What to do if anyone approaches their post.

What ground to watch.

The Password.

FIELDCRAFT

Sentries close to the enemy must know :-

Direction of the enemy.

Name of land marks.

Where neighbouring posts are.

Signal for defensive fire.

About patrols that may come in or out through their post or near them.

HOW TO CHALLENGE.

When you see movements which you think may not be your own troops - alert your Section Commander.

Say **'HALT' HANDS UP.**

'Advance one and be recognised'. "Halt".

Give the challenge half of the password - quietly, so that only the first man can hear it.

ACTION - Allow friendly troops through, know how many and count them through - one at a time.

FIELDCRAFT

Section opens fire at enemy troops.
NOTE Be aware of a common trick
which is for the enemy to approach a
sentry, listen and learn the first half of a
PASS WORD then fade away.
An inexperienced sentry may allow this
to happen. The same enemy then
approaches another sentry and
challenges them before they can
challenge them.
Again the inexperienced sentry might
then give the reply then allow the
enemy into the position.

So be careful and never allow anyone into your position unless
you can positively identify them, when in doubt call for help.

USE YOUR SENSES.
What are your senses, how can they help in Fieldcraft?
On a patrol or on duty as a sentry you will use your **EYES** and
EARS, and your **TOUCH** when feeling your way through woods
or difficult cover.
Your sense of **TASTE** may not be used, but your sense of
SMELL — depending upon the SMELL — may remind you of
taste. SMELL — Body smell or the smell of cooking, or anything
else that drifts on the air and can give yours and the enemies
presence away.

> *"time spent in reconnaissance
> is seldom wasted"*

FIELDCRAFT

SECTION BATTLE DRILLS

These notes are for a Section organised as **FIRE TEAMS.**

DRILL No 1. BATTLE PREPARATION.

a. Personal camouflage.

b. Check weapons.

c. Check ammo.

Section Commanders Orders

a. Ground ref points.

b. Situation Enemy forces. Friendly forces. Pl formation and Task.

c. Mission - the section mission.

d. Execution Section formations Team for which Flank and Route to take.

e. Service support - Info passed down from Pl Commanders orders.

f. Command & Signals; any info passed down from Pl Commander.

REFERENCE POINTS & ANTICIPATORY ORDERS.

In the 'Advance to Contact' the Section Commander will look out for :

1. New reference points for fire orders.

2. Place where the Section can take cover if it comes under effective fire.

DRILL No 2 - REACTION TO EFFECTIVE FIRE.

The drill to be adopted is: On the order of the section commander - "TAKE COVER", DASH - DOWN - CRAWL -OBSERVE -SIGHTS - FIRE.

DRILLS No 3 - LOCATION OF THE ENEMY

Location of the enemy is usually difficult, failure means casualties and section not be able to move and may lose the initiative as result. Three stages in this drill:

a. Observation - look in area from which thump came from.

b. Fire - fire order to couple of riflemen to fire at likely target.

c. Movement - Section Commander orders rifleman to move while remainder of section observe.

FIELDCRAFT

DRILL No 4 WINNING THE FIRE FIGHT

As soon as the Section Commander knows the enemies position a fire order must be given to bring sufficient weight of fire on the enemy to neutralize them. (See Fire Control Orders)

DRILL No 5 - THE ATTACK BATTLE ORDERS

Will always be one of the following depending on the number of stages in the attack. They will be as brief as possible.

Orders for a one stage attack, that is when the riflemen go straight into the assault.

Orders for a two stage attack, that if when the LSW's must move to another position before the riflemen assault.

Orders for a three stage attack in which the fire teams move alternately, and finally the riflemen assaults. LSWs give covering fire.

The Advance

a. The section Commander will lead the riflemen in the assault.

b. All movement in the open by either group must be covered by the LSW..

c. When rifle group gets into fire position after a bound, the LSW must move forward to a new position automatically.

d. The section 2i/c who is the LSW controller, watches the Section Commander, listens for orders ,and watches riflemen to give them covering fire at critical moments.

The Assault and Fighting through the Objective

The assault goes on as fast as possible.

Riflemen fire from the shoulder or the "on guard" position.

LSW fires as long as possible during the assault, then switches it's fire across the objective in front of riflemen.

DRILL No 6 REORGANISATION

When objective cleared of enemy the Section Commander must regain close control over men and position, ready to beat off counter attack. Reorganisation must beswift and efficient, if not all that was gained will be lost.

The Section Commander will:

1. Allot fire tasks to each member of section.

2. **Post sentries.**
3. **Check on casualties and ammunition.**
4. **Arrange re-distribution of ammo.**
5. **Supervise re-digging of shell scrapes.**
6. **Send prisoners and captured kit to rear.**
7. **Report to Platoon Commander for orders.**

CHOOSING A ROUTE.

If you have to advance across country, check that you know where to make for. Then decide on the best route.

REMEMBER

Routes must be planned ahead.

You must move in bounds or stages from one observation point to another.

You must check your direction - are you keeping on course.

Always use a compass

Must not be seen but should be able to see the enemy.

If you have to take a chance choose a route which offers the risks early in your approach rather than later on, since you will have If If you have to advance across country, check that you know the If you have to If you have to advance across country, check that you know where to make for. Then decide on the best route.

SECTION AND PLATOON FIELD SIGNALS

Field Signal are a silent means of communication between members of the section and platoon.

They should be used whenever possible and be constantly practiced, even when going about normal duties it is as well to use them, so as they become second nature to everyone.

Very often there is a need to attract the attention of those who are to receive the signal, especially if the Section Commander wants to tell several members of his section at the same time.

Watch and Listen

This does not absolve you as a member of the section from watching out for signals, as there may be times when an audible signal is not practical for obvious reasons.

There are four recognised methods of attracting attention, they are:-

FIELDCRAFT

1. A **SINGLE** whistle blast - during fire contact only.
2. Snapping forefinger and thumb.
3. Knocking butt of weapon with knuckles.
4. Silent whistle.

Whistle BLASTS are often used to indicate situations, they are as follows:-

1. **SHORT BLASTS - ALARM** - air attack, NBC attack, etc.
2. **LONG BLASTS** indicate "STAND DOWN".

FIELD SIGNALS

The following pages set out the normal Field Signals used by the Infantry. We have not put the name of description of the signal with it, but have numbered them and listed the description etc — you will learn them better this way.

Key and Description of Field Signals

1. READY TO MOVE. Move hands as if cranking handle.

2. DEPLOY. Arm extended below shoulder level, waved slowly from side to side, hand open. If deployment to either flank is wanted, commander points to flank, after completing signal.

3. ADVANCE or FOLLOW ME. Arm swung from rear to front below shoulder.

4. HALT or REST. Arm raised until the hand is level with shoulder. Indicate length of halt by number of fingers. Point to 'rest area'.

5. GO BACK or TURN ABOUT. Hand circled at hip height.

6. CLOSE or JOIN ME. Hand placed on top of head, elbow square to the right or left, according to which hand is used. Point to RV area.

7. DOUBLE. Clenched hand moved up and down between thigh and shoulder.

8. SLOW DOWN (APC). Arm extended to the side below shoulder, palm downwards, moved slowly up and down, wrist loose.

9. LIE DOWN or DISMOUNT (APC). Two or three slight movements with the open hand towards the ground (palm downwards).

10. AS YOU WERE or SWITCH OFF (APC). Forearm extended downwards, hand open, waved across body parallel to ground.

11. ENEMY SEEN or SUSPECTED. Thumb pointed towards ground from clenched fist.

FIELDCRAFT

12. NO ENEMY IN SIGHT or ALL CLEAR. Thumb pointed upwards from clenched fist.

13. LSW. Clenched fist raised to shoulder height.

14. SCOUT GROUP. Clenched fist with forefinger upright.

15. RIFLEMEN. 'Victory' sign - fist and second finger extended and open in 'V' remainder of fist clenched.

16. LIGHT MORTAR. Weapon held vertical. Imitate loading mortar rounds.

17. LAW/MAW. Weapon placed on shoulder and held like a LAW/MAW.

18. SECTION CMDR. Two opened fingers held against arm to indicate Corporal's Stripes.

19. PLATOON CMDR. Two opened fingers held on shoulder to indicate a Lieutenant's stars.

20. GIVE COVERING FIRE. Weapon brought into aim.

21. OBSTACLES. CROSSING. TRACK JUNCTION. Arms crossed. For water obstacle make waves.

22. HOUSE or HUT. Hands folded in inverted 'V'; to indicate shape of roof.

23. RECONNAISSANCE. Hand held to eye, as though using eye glass.

24. ATTACK. A chopping movement with edge of hand in direction attack is required.

25. MOVE UP. Fingers spread, arms swung slowly in direction movement is required.

26. FORM AMBUSH. Hand placed over face, followed by pointing to place of ambush.

27. FREEZE AND LISTEN. Hand cupped to ear.

28. 'O' GROUP. Fingers together, moved in conjunction with thumb to indicate person talking.

29 RIGHT or LEFT FLANKING. A curved sweeping movement of the arm in direction concerned.

30. FIRE & MANOEUVRE. One hand used in a rolling forward action in front of the body.

31. SPACE OUT. Palm of hands held against weapon and moved away several times.

32. ARROW HEAD. Both arms forced backwards or forwards at an angle of 800 mils, depending whether arrow is backward or forward.

FIELDCRAFT

33. SINGLE FILE. One arm fully extended above head.

34. STAGGERED FILE. Both arms fully extended above head.

35. SPEARHEAD. As for arrowhead plus indicating Gun Group to move in at rear.

36. DIAMOND. Arms raised above the head with arms slightly bent so that hands touch to form diamond shape.

37. EXTENDED LINE. Arms raised to the side level with the ground, indicate which side group is to go.

> **THE ONLY WAY TO LEARN FIELD SIGNALS IS TO PRACTICE AND USE THEM ON EVERY POSSIBLE OCCASION**

FIELDCRAFT

FIELDCRAFT

SECTION FORMATIONS

As a member of a Section you move as a part of your Fire Team within the Section.

How you move depends upon six factors

1. The type of ground you are moving across.
2. How far you can see.
3. The likely direction from which the enemy may fire on you.
4. How your Section Commander can best control the Section.
5. The need for the Section to produce the maximum fire with minimum delay.
6. Who controls the Air Space.

SECTION FORMATIONS

Section Formations are used to meet the above factors and are mostly decided upon by the Section Commander, who will change the formations as the Section moves over different types of ground during its advance.

Some of the formations are described on the following pages.

FIELDCRAFT

SINGLE FILE

Good for moving along hedges or ditches or along the edge of woods. Good for control by the Section Commander especially at night. Bad formation to produce fire to front.
Vunerable from frontal fire, especially down
a ditch or sunken road/stream.Not good for observation or passing information to the members of the section.

FILE

Not good for observation or passing information to members of the section. A good formation for control and night movement. Can be used going down a track or either side of a hedge.
Disadvantage — it makes a good target for the enemy.

ARROWHEAD

Best for moving across open country, produces effective fire against frontal attack. Easy to control, has good all round observation. Bad for exposing good target to enemy fire.
Formation used only when crossing open country at night.
Easy to control, has all round observation and protection, each person can see the next, the Section Commander can be at the front or in the middle.

FIELDCRAFT

DIAMOND

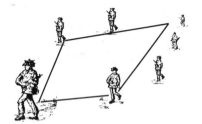

Formation used only when crossing open country at night. Easy to control, has all round observation and protection, each person can see the next and Section Commander can be at the front or in the middle

EXTENDED LINE

Formation used for the "final assault", difficult to control, needs good "field discipline" by members of Section to watch/listen.

REMEMBER

When moving in a Section Formation:-

1.Watch your Section Commander for hand signals.

2.Keep in contact with members of the Section on each side of you — but not too close.

3. Keep quiet and listen for commands and anticipatory orders.

4. Keep in correct position for formation.

5. Be observant.

6. Be ready to change to a new Section Formation.

FIELDCRAFT

CHOOSING A ROUTE

REMEMBER

Routes must be planned ahead. You must move in bounds or
stagesfrom one observation point to another.

You must check your direction - are you keeping on course.

Always use a Compass.

Must not be seen but should beable to see the enemy.

If you have to take a chance, chose a route which offers the risks early
in your approach rather than later on, since you will have less chance
of being seen.

The best route will have places to observe the enemy - without being
seenyourself.

Don't go blindly towards the enemy. Give good fire positions.

You must be able to fire if necessary. Give cover from enemy fire.

Lets you move without being seen.

Not to have impassable obstacles such as marsh land or open ground
or ravines.

Establish and record reference points en route and their map
references. bearings and time/distances to reach them.

FIELDCRAFT

PACING

Pacing is necessary because you must always know how exactly far you have gone when counting a number of your own 'paces'.
You should know your 'Pacing Scale', over different types of conditions, i.e tarmac roads, tracks, grasslands, woodlands etc.
To find your PACING SCALE, put two markers out 100m apart. Walk the distance between them as you would on a patrol, counting the paces as you go.
If it has taken you 120 paces to cover the 100m, then that is your

PACING SCALE.

It follows, to use this scale if you were on a patrol and had to go a distance of 300m, you would have to count out 360 paces.
Under some conditions you can use a specific length of string, tying knots at every 120 paces. Having used the length of string, un-tie the knots and repeat the process on the next 'leg' of your route.
It is always advisable to have a CHECK PACER, remembering to check that your PACING SCALE is the same by day and night.

NAVIGATION

This is the art of moving from one place to another and consists of three important stages that MUST be carried out if you are to be successful, they are as follows:-
1. PLANNING.
2. KEEPING DIRECTION.
3. GOOD PACING.

PLANNING - You must plan your route in advance, using maps, air photos, sketches and information from previous patrols or recces.

KEEPING DIRECTION - Always take several compasses and as many 'pacers'. Always get someone else to check your navigation, at both the planning stage and while you are executing the movement.
It is often hard to keep direction, especially at night, in fog or in close country. When it is necessary to make a detour to avoid an obstacle or seek cover, it is easy for leaders to miss the correct lines of advance.

FIELDCRAFT

AIDS TO KEEPING DIRECTION.

Some of the aids to keeping direction are:-

a. The compass, map and air photographs.

b. A rough sketch copied from a map or air photograph.

c. Keeping two prominent objects in view.

d. Using a series of easily recognisable landmarks, each visible from the previous one.

e. The stars and also the sun and moon if their natural movement in the sky is understood.

f. Memorizing the route from a map or air photograph. Helpful details are the direction of streams, distances between recognisable features coupled with pacing, and the course of contours.

g. Trees in exposed country tend to grow away from the direction of the prevailing wind. Moss may grow on the leeward side of tree trunks.

h. Remembering the back view, patrols and others who may have to find their way back should look behind them from time to time and pick up landmarks to remember for the return journey.

j. Leaving directions marks on the outward journey, these may be pegs, small heaps of stones.

k. If the route is being walked by day by those who are to guide along it by night, they must take note of skylines and objects or features which they will be able to recognize in the dark.

SELECTING OF LINES OF ADVANCE.

Remember the keyword - 'G R O U N D'

G	Ground from the map. Open/close country, Rolling/flat.
R	Ridges, water courses and watersheds (highest) mark on map or talc.
O	Observation good view points.
U	Undergrowth - study woods, scrub, trees, villages.
N	Non Passable obstacles, such as rivers, ravines, marsh land.
D	Defilade covered lines of advance and areas which offer cover can now be selected.

**HAVE YOU CHECKED YOUR
INDIVIDUAL COMPASS ERROR ?**

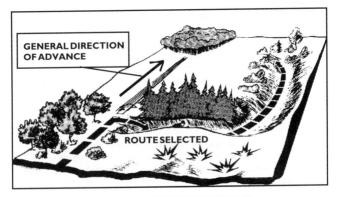

OBSERVATION — SEARCHING GROUND

The skill of searching ground is based upon learning to "scan" an area using an accepted system.

It will test your concentration and exercise your knowledge of "why things are seen" and the principles of Camouflage and Concealment.

In the diagram we have - for the purpose of illustrating to you — drawn lines across the landscape.

In practice you would choose prominent features, landmarks, roads etc., and draw your imaginary lines across the landscape through these reference points.

The landscape is divided into **FOREGROUND, MIDDLE DISTANCE** and **DISTANCE**. You can further divide this by indicating a centre line (again based on reference points), calling left of the line **"LEFT OF ARC"**, and right of the line **"RIGHT OF ARC"** as shown in the illustration above.

Having divided the landscape, the correct method is to scan each area horizontally (left to right or right to left).

View the area in short overlapping movements in a very precise manner, especially any features that are at an angle from your position.

FIELDCRAFT

SEARCHING GROUND

SCANNING

While scanning you may see something move or that requires further
investigation. There may be an area where you may come under
observation from, it would be as well to check that out early.
Weather conditions can give you a clue when searching, frost on
bushes, foot marks will show up clearly, if the weather is hot
camouflaged positions can be given away when leaves or grass dry off
changing colour.
Search across hedges and rows of trees , NOT along them. At all times
consider WHY THINGS ARE SEEN.

FIELDCRAFT

PATROLS

There are three reasons for patrolling:
1. To obtain up-to-date and accurate information.
2. To dominate the ground between a commanders own unit and that of the enemy.
3. To destroy and disrupt enemy forces.

Successful patrolling calls for a high standard of individual training, good team work, initiative and determination on the part of the patrol leader. Patrolling enables the defence to be conducted in an aggressive manner. The foundation of successful patrolling is through preparation.

TYPES OF PATROL.

Reconnaissance Patrols

Patrols of minimum strength for task, usually 1 NCO and 3 men, who gain information by observation and operate by stealth.

They avoid combat except for self-protection or to take advantage of unusual opportunities.

The roles in which a reconnaissance patrol may be employed include:-
1. Collecting topographical information on features, tracks and state of ground.
2. Obtaining details of minefields and the extent of enemy positions.
3. Locating enemy machine gun and defensive fire (DF) areas, where fire is immediately directed on call in case of emergency.
4. Investigating noises made by the enemy, enemy habits and patrol routes.
5. Checking our wire and/or minefields at first or last light.
6. Acting as listening posts, to give early warning of enemy approach and with the ability to call down fire.

Standing Patrols

Minimum strength 1 NCO and 3 men, to gain information of enemy movement, to prevent or disrupt enemy infiltration.

They move into position quietly - try to remain hidden - gain information until required to withdraw or if discovered fight their way out.

FIELDCRAFT

Their main tasks are to:-

1. Watch and listen on likely enemy approaches.
2. Watch over dead ground in front of and between friendly areas.
3. Watch over mine fields and obstacles, for which they should have good communications, so that they can inform the main body.

Fighting Patrols

These are patrols organized for a particular task with sufficient strength and backup to achieve the mission. The strength can vary according to the task to be performed and the expected combat level:

1. Denying enemy patrols freedom of action in No Man's Land.
2. Driving in enemy protective patrols.
3. Interfering with enemy working parties.
4. Distracting enemy attention from other activities.
5. Carrying out raids.
6. Capturing prisoners for identification purposes.
7. Tank hunting.
8. Laying ambushes.
9. Protecting reconnaissance and working parties of other arms.
10. Escorting stretcher parties.

SEQUENCE OF ACTION TO MOUNT CARRY OUT AND DEBRIEF A PATROL.

The success of a patrol depends on good planning beforehand as well as good action during the actual patrol. Compliance with the following by the Patrol Commander ensures that nothing is forgotten.

PATROL COMMANDER

Issues a warning order to include brief outline of patrol task, members of patrol including second-in-command, time and place for briefing and any special administrative arrangements including weapons and equipment. Normally dress and equipment should be as light as possible but must include water and emergency rations in case the patrol is cut off and has to lie up for a period before returning to base. Studies, Air Photos, Maps, previous Patrol Reports and sketches. Selects observation posts for his recce.

FIELDCRAFT

RECCE

Carries out recce from OP's during which they look for:

a. Routes to and from objective (to be different).
b. Landmarks.
c. OP's.
d. Dead ground and covered approaches.
e. Obstacles.
f. Likely places for ambush - by us or by enemy.
g. Enemy positions, likely positions and DF areas.
h. CONSIDERS light and weather conditions, moon, etc.

Makes his Appreciation and Plan, keeping them as simple as possible.
DRAWS A FIELD SKETCH showing distances (in paces), bearings and timings of bounds.
PREPARES MODEL of the area for briefing the patrol. PREPARES HIS ORDERS. MEETS PATROL AT RV.

BRIEFS THE PATROL

By showing members the ground from an OP (individually if necessary) and points out minefield lanes and gaps in wire etc.,
Gives out his orders:
With the aid of a cloth or sand model of ground, under the following headings:

1. GROUND.

Describes, incl. landmarks, obstacles, and "going". Use OP's, maps, air photos, models, etc.

2. SITUATION

a. Enemy Forces. FEBA, ptl activity, routine, sentries, DF, FPF, minefields, wire, trip flares, fixed lines.
b. Friendly Forces. Own positions, other ptls, fire support available, minefields, wire, trip flares, fixed lines. DF, FPF, stand by ptl.

3. MISSION.

To Recce, Fighting - definite task.

FIELDCRAFT

4. EXECUTION Phase I. General Outline.

a. Number of phases - route, action on objective, return.
b. Who taking part - appointments and position in the platoon.
c. Prep Moves - Drop Off Point. Time leaving rehearsal/base area. Method of move. Loading Plan. Route to and ref of DOP. Arcs of obsn/fire. Order of March (OOM).
d. Action if Ambushed. Action at DOP. Time out. Confirmation or orders/detail.

Phase 2. Route Out, to final RV (FRV).

Fmn. Obs drills/action on mines/trip wires/booby traps. Actions on: PW. Cas. If separated from ptl. If lost. Confirm FRV ref.

Phase 3. Action in final RV - on arrival

1. Occupation. Move in. Secure. Fmns, position of grps, sig for FRV.
2. Recce Group - Composition, Tasks. Route. OOM, fmns, arcs. Action on ambush, sig to open fire. Action if FRV gp loc by en.
3. Remainder - Composition, Tasks, Arcs, Actions - on en pre-seen or ambush, sig to open fire, if recce gp loc by en, on return of recce gp or if fails to return. Confirmation or orders/info.

Phase 4. Action on Objective

1. Cover/Fire Gp. Composition, Fmn, posn, routes, tasks, arcs, action if en act first, duration on SP's, Sigs for opening fire. Action if separated from group.
2. Recce/Assist/Snatch. Composition, fmn, task, posn, routes, action on recce/asslt/snatch, sigs for sp fire. Action if surprised, sig net, wire, illumination.

Phase 5. Withdrawal and action in final RV.

Sig to wdr. OOM sequence of gp wdr, arcs, fmns. Action and posns in FRV -pack kit etc. Head check and sig to move out. Actions: if in contact, PW's, if gp fails to return, if FRV gp has moved, if surprised in FRV. Pass on info sketches etc. Confirmation of orders/info.

From/To	Bearing	Distance	Fmn	Ground	RV
(1) Leg 1					
(2) Leg 2					
(3) Leg 3					

FIELDCRAFT

Phase 6. Route Back

Route. Fmns. RV's. Obs. Actions; en pre-seen, ambush, sig to open fire, cas, if lost, if separated. Action on arr at pick up point (PUP). Time in. Confirm orders/info.

Co-ordinating Instructions

Timings. Meals, rest, rehearsals (day/ni), weapons test, inspections, time in/out constraints. Debrief. Action on halts, lights. Fireplan. Rehearsals loc and details. Deception and security.

Summary of Execution.

1. Summary of Timings - Rehearsals, prep of eqpt, inspection, rest, meals test wpns, night rehearsals, final check time out, time in. RV's and refs.
2. Action on white Lts
3. Action on Halts - for obsn/protection.
4. Action to take on Meeting En if:-
    Pre-seen or Ambushed
    On the Route Out .... On the Route In ....
5. Action on Cas
    On Route Out........ On obj......... On the Route In........
6. Action on crossing Obs
7. Action with PW
8. Rehearsals
9. Lost procedure
10. Action on Mines
11. Distr on Ni Vis Aids

5. SERVICE SUPPORT

Ammo. Feeding. Dress and Eqpt. Special Eqpt - radio spares, etc. Wpns type and distribution. Rats, meals before during and after, water. Med, Fd dressings, stretcher, med pack, casevac method. PW handing on/after capture. Tpt to DOP/from PUP. Confirm orders/info.

FIELDCRAFT

6. COMMAND AND SIGNAL

Chain of command 1i/c, 2i/c and 3i/c and conditions for taking over cmd. Location of ptl comd. Sigs, radio, radio checks, other sigs. Password. Use of Radio and restrictions. De-briefing location, who doing. Patrol report. Special instrs on reporting Info.

Rehearsals

Carries out daylight or night rehearsals which must include:

a. **Moving out** and returning through own FEBAS.

Patrol Commander goes forward to contact the sentry. Normal challenging procedure follows.

b. **Formations** and drill for changing formations.

One or more of the three formations = single file, file or diamond - is adopted during a patrol depending on ground and visibility.

c. **Use of Scouts.** Move by bounds ahead and are followed by the Command Group (Patrol Commander, Radio Operator and his protector).

d. **Movement.** Every member is allotted his specific task, movement must be silent, frequent halts to observe and listen, when approaching the enemy position and also at night. When halted sink down to the ground level, avoiding a jerky movement, and make use of the skyline. Make use of the previously prepared signal to move - a silent "touch" signal - to ensure that no-one is left behind.

e. **Action on objective.** Nearby RV. This is an RV to which the patrol goes after completing the task, it must be easy to find and indicated to all members of the patrol during the approach to the objective.

f. **Firm Base.** If a patrol has to move a long way it may leave a party between its own and the enemy position, this forms a "firm base" from which remainder of patrol carries out main task and to return afterwards.

On arriving near the objective, the Patrol Commander will:-

1. Search the area, especially the RV or Firm Base for unexpected enemy.

2. **Make a brief Recce**, Appreciation and Plan, brief the patrol members concerned

g. **Action on Lights.** If time allows get away - otherwise, freeze, close
one eye to preserve night vision. If a trip flare move from area
quickly as possible, get down and observe.

h. **Encounter drill**.

Action will depend on the task and circumstances. It may be desirable
to avoid action and move away as quickly as possible. If this is
impossible an immediate assault is the alternative.

If ambushed, scatter and move individually to previously arranged RV.

i. **Crossing Obstacles**

1. On encountering an obstacle, Commander goes forward to recce it,
decides whether to cross or go round.

2. Requirements of obstacle crossing drill are:-

(a) Silent movement.

(b) Posting a man to guide others over.

(c) At all times at least one man ready to fire his weapon or throw a
grenade if the patrol is surprised.

j. **Casualty Evacuation**

1. All casualties must be brought back.

2. Improvise a stretcher.

3. If on the way out, the patrol may have to pick up the casualty on
its return or summon help.

k. **Prisoners**

1. If a fighting patrol takes a prisoner they must be brought back
whether or not this was the task of the patrol. - prisoners are
valuable sources of information.

2. If a prisoner cannot be taken with the patrol, they may be put
under guard and collected later either by the sane patrol or by
another one detailed or summoned by radio for this purpose.

l. **Carries out Final Inspection**

a. Dress and equipment light as possible, but include emergency
rations and water.

b. Dress and equipment to be properly fitted and silent. Jumping up
and down will show whether it is satisfactory.

c. No documents will be taken which can afford useful information to
the enemy if captured.

"TIME SPENT IN RECONNAISSANCE IS SELDOM WASTED"

FIELDCRAFT

LEADS PATROL OUT THROUGH FEBA.

a. **Navigation**. Previous study of air photos and maps etc. use of landmarks. By compass bearing and counting paces -especially at night. "Legs" to be measured to the nearest 50 paces from map. If the patrol becomes dispersed, RV at the end of the previous leg. Avoid prominent cover, e.g. edges of woods, tracks, hedges, defiles - likely places for enemy ambushes or standing patrols.

b. **Fire Support.** Pre arranged or called for by radio -

(1) To distract enemy.

(2) For support on objective.

(3) To help the patrol extricate itself in emergency.

DE-BRIEFED ON RETURN.

Verbal report followed by a written report.

On the next page is shown the layout of a Patrol Report.

This is produced as guidelines for you to use when preparing a report, and includes many of the factors that should be taken into consideration.

This serves as a reminder of the vast amount of valuable information and activities that a Patrol Commander is expected to deal with.

This is a standard format use as a Patrol Report and you would be well advised to make a copy of it, study it in readiness for when you have to do a report.

POST EXERCISE ADMINISTRATION

On the completion of all exercises, stores have to be returned. Rotten chore, it is probably the last thing you wish to do, **BUT** - Kit must be cleaned, dried and checked then inspected for damage and deficiencies; any found must be reported to the Quarter Master. Thus ensuring that damaged equipment is not re-issued.

Note: it is always advisable to check kit when you draw it from the stores - especially if you are signing for it. If damaged, make sure that it is noted on your form 1033.

FIELDCRAFT

PATROL REPORT

Date   **Destination of Patrol**

Aim

Maps

Size and composition of Patrol

Task

Time of Departure   **Time of Return**   **Routes**

Out and Back

Terrain - (Description of the terrain - dry, swampy, jungle, thickly wooded, high brush, rocky, deepness of ravines, rivers/streams/canals, width/ depth, condition of bridges as to type, size and strength, effect on armour and wheeled vehicles.)

Enemy - (Strength, disposition, condition of defences, equipment, weapons, attitude, morale, exact location, movements and any shift in dispositions. Time activity was observed, co-ordinates where activity occurred.

Conditions of Patrol -including disposition of any casualties)

Conclusions and Recommendations - (including to what extent the mission was accomplished and recommendations as to patrol equipment and tactics)

Date _____ **Time** _____ **hrs**

Signature of Patrol Commander _____

ADDITIONAL REMARKS BY INTERROGATOR

Date _____ **Time** _____ **hrs**

         Signature.

FIELDCRAFT

AMBUSHES

INTRODUCTION

Ambushes are usually carried out as a part of patrolling activity. It requires close team work, skill, intelligence, fitness, cunning and discipline.

An ambush is a surprise attack, by a force lying in wait, upon a moving or temporarily halted enemy. It is usually a brief encounter, conducted at comparatively close quarters.

When well prepared and executed it can cause heavy causalities and serious loss of morale amongst the enemy; however poor planning, preparation and execution may result in failure, and serious losses to the ambush party.

TYPES OF AMBUSH

a. **DELIBERATE** - with time to plan in advance.

b. **IMMEDIATE** - In response to 'hot' information, to 'contact' the enemy, with no time for recce.

AMBUSH SITES

The best places for an ambush site include:-

a. Known enemy routes.

b. Known admin/supply/water points, food or ammo dumps, approaches to villages.

c. Where the terrain changes - edge of woods or forest, where a valley has steep sides. Where a river crossing is shallow etc.

d. Approaches to own bases or positions, also on route out of your own positions - if enemy follows you back.

PRINCIPLES OF AMBUSH

a. Good intelligence to ensure contact and success.

b. Thorough planning and preparation, planned Recce, ambush well rehearsed.

c. Security - careful Recce - not to betray ambush site.

Be prepared for an attack on yourselves.

d. Concealment - good track discipline, no signs of your whereabouts, good camouflage and concealment.

e. Good control and communications - all know the plan in detail, signals, plan for springing ambush. Must be kept simple, and thoroughly rehearsed.

f. Discipline -ambush only successful if everyone alert, no noise, restricted movement, fast re-action to signals, weapons always ready to fire.

g. Safety - all weapons in "made safe" state while on the move. No firing at individuals - even when minimum distance of 50 metres between muzzle and the enemy.

THE DELIBERATE AMBUSH

The ambush parties are sub-divided into smaller groups, each with their own leaders. Normally the groups are as follows:-

a. THE AMBUSH GROUP - covers the chosen place for the ambush and springs the ambush. Group contains Ambush Commander and the LSW teams(s). Four men to ambush a section. A Section and Platoon HQ to ambush a Platoon.

b. CUT-OFF/STOP GROUPS - serve to give warning of enemy approach, cut off their lines of retreat or help to take care of a counter attack from a flank. For a section ambush the group would consist of two men. A platoon ambush would be a section strength.

PLANNING - prior to occupying an ambush position the following sequence of planning events must be carried out:-

Recce. Issue preliminary orders in the base camp. Preparation and rehearsals in the base camp.

Move to the ambush area.

Final Recce by Amb Cmdr and Cut Off Grp Cmdr's.

Amb Cmdr issues final orders if required.

Occupy ambush position.

RECCE - Amb Cmdr should - if possible - carry out recce of amb site before giving orders. He may be limited to air photographs, maps, patrol reports or sketches made.

Must try to put himself in enemy position/point of view, he must select/confirm:-

a. Ambush area, positions of the Ambush Group and cut off Groups, detailed siting of GUN GROUP(s), booby traps, trip flares etc.

b. Check positions for each group for: concealment, approach routes, good fields of view and fire and of the enemy approach route.

c. The withdrawal routes for all groups.

d. The final RV, and routes to and from it.

ORDERS, PREPARATION, REHEARSALS & MOVE OUT.

ORDERS - Like all Patrols the information given and the quality of the orders must be very thorough and detailed, using a model of the area and leaving sufficient time for preparation and rehearsals.

The orders for an ambush follow the same sequence and detail as Patrol Orders, but need to have extra details under the 'EXECUTION' phase, as follow:-

ACTION ON ARRIVAL AT FINAL RV/FIRM BASE

Entry order of march. Positions and arcs of fire - describe these, also cover in rehearsals. Sentries if necessary. Action if surprised. Action if recce party does not return within.... minutes. Confirmation of orders, timing, refs, RV's etc.

ACTION IN AMBUSH AREA

Order of march. Method of entry. Positions. Laying of communication cord. Arcs to be covered.

Sig for 'Ambush Set'. Time ambush to be set by ..... hrs.

ACTION ON APPROACH OF ENEMY -

Warning signal from Cut Off Groups. Signal to stop. Search party if required.

WITHDRAWAL TO RV/FIRM BASE - Signal for withdrawl.

Order of march. Action at final RV/Firm Base - reorg, check numbers, weapons, re-distribute ammo, prepare to move out.

Thorough preparation is essential for success and should include the following:-

Cleaning and testing of all weapons. Testing and checking special equipment, ropes, night viewing aids, boats or rafts, safety and medics. Radios and spare batteries. Camouflage of clothing and equipment.

REHEARSAL - If for a night ambush, then rehearsals should be held in the daytime and also at night.

They must:—

Show where each group and those who are within them are in relation to each other.

FIELDCRAFT

Test signals/communications.

Cover alerting, and springing of the ambush.

Practice withdrawal to Firm Base/Final RV.

MOVE TO AMBUSH AREA - Ambush party move to the Final RV/ Firm Base and take up defensive position and wait for the Amb Cmdr and the Cut Off Team Cmdrs to do their final recce.

FINAL ORDERS Only need for confirmation or last minute changes that need to be made as a result of the final recce. This could be more likely and important by night than day and could include:-

a. Description of the ambush area, enemy approaches and counter attack routes.

b. Individual tasks if they vary from rehearsals.

OCCUPATION SEQUENCE

Having completed his recce and returned from any Final Orders briefing, Ambush Cmdr will remain on the position, sending Cut Off Team Cmdrs back for remainder of party. If a platoon operation, sentries would be taken forward, posted and remain in position throughout the move to the ambush area.

Cut Off Team followed by Assault Group move into position, Ambush Cmdr places himself in central position for control and near to LSW Team.

SETTING UP AMBUSH - Once all groups in position, Cut Off Team start laying communications cord/cable to Ambush Cmdr. Set up trip flares, booby traps etc are set.

AMBUSH SET - When Ambush Cmdr receives signal from all groups that everyone in position, gives the 'Ambush Set' signal. After this signal no one leaves their position, Care to make no movement or noise. Get into a comfortable position for the time you are waiting for the ambush to be sprung.

SPRINGING THE AMBUSH - On sighting the enemy, Cut Off Team alerts Ambush Cmdr of their approach and direction using communication cord, alerts remainder of the force. All prepare for ambush, carefully moving into aim . Ambush Cmdr waits until as many of enemy are in ambush area. Gives signal for springing ambush. This signal usually a burst of fire from the LSW , a shot from commanders weapon or setting off a trip flare. It is NEVER the commander shouting 'FIRE'.

AFTER SPRINGING AMBUSH THE FIRE FIGHT - short and sharp. Cmdr gives 'STOP' or 'CEASE FIRE'. pause while all check for: movement of enemy. Enemy counter attack. Enemy moving back to collect casualties, thinking ambush has withdrawn.

WITHDRAWAL - On receiving withdrawal signal, all groups withdraw to Final RV, in order as rehearsed. Minimum time spent there, check all present, check no **enemy follow up, re-call sentries and move off by return route.**

PATROL HARBOUR

A patrol harbour is a position taken providing security when a patrol halts for a period. A form of advanced base from which it can service and send out Partrols Some of the reasons are:
1. To avoid detection.
2. To lie low while a recce is made prior to the formation of a plan and issue of orders.
3. A base from which operations can be mounted, e.g., attack, ambush, reconnaissance, or establishing OPs.
4. Provides an RV for small groups..
5. Provides secure base for admin halt after long periods on patrol

Triangular Harbour Drills

A patrol harbour is set up as a Triangular (three sided) defence position by a platoon or adopted by a smaller patrol.
The triangular harbour ensures the following:
1. All round defence, an LSW at each corner.
2. Mutual support ,in that an attack from any side is covered by two LSWs.
3. Ease of command /control with PL HQ in the centre.
4. Ease of administration simple, compact layout.
The procedure for moving into a triangular harbour at platoon level is divided into five stages:

FIELDCRAFT

Stage I Selection harbour location.

From map, air photographs, aerial reccce or on the ground. Site must be confirmed by recce, and area secured before occupied.

When selecting site you must consider:

1. Mission. The harbour must give the patrol best chance to achieve task.

2. Location. Choose site:

a. Which can be easily defended.

b. Dense vegetation, provide cover from air/ground.

c. Away from human habitation or areas or used by civilians.

d. With access to water.

e. With good routes in and out.

f. Where communications are good.

3. Avoid the following:

a. An obvious position.

b. Ridge lines or crests which may be used as routes.

c. Roads, tracks, etc.

d. Wet areas, steep slopes and small valleys.

Stage 2 - Occupation.

Essential to have swift/efficient occupation of a harbour. A well practiced routine is essential. Carried out using hand signals without noise. Many different 'drills' can be used, an example is set out below:

a. Platoon stops just short of the chosen site. It should break track and set up an ambush on its previous route to engage any patrol following or tracking the platoon.

b. The platoon commander and reccee party (i/c sections, and a guide go forward to recce harbour in detail. The Pl Sgt stays in command

3. On the site of harbour, tasks are as;

a. Pl Cmdr selects Pl HQ and the location of the 6 and 12 o'clock positions.

b. The Pl Cmdr and Sec Cmdrs allocate the section areas, and the LSW positions.

c. The perimeter wire is laid setting out the triangle for the when the platoon occupies the harbour.

d. When recce finished, a Sec Cmdr and guide sent to up main body. Platoon led to the harbour site in single file.

FIELDCRAFT

e. Sections are met and each man is shown their position and arc to cover.

f. This ensure that an LSW is at each corner of the triangle, noise kept to a minimum the track plan is understood

g. When in position, each man removes their pack and adopts a fire position.

Section commanders should sites own positions centrally, having in view the platoon commander and own 2IC.

Pl Cmdr checks the perimeter to ensure liaison between sections Sec Cmdrs meet him at his corner LSW position; minor adjustments to layout of harbour made at this stage.

Stage 3 - Clearance Patrols.

1. On a signal from the platoon commander, each section sends out a clearance patrol to cover their own section's arc. The rest of the section remain 'stood to'.

2. The section commander or 2I/C and one or two men move out through the neighbouring section's LSW position. They go out to the limit of visibility and sound, then turn and move along their own section's frontage. This drill ensures that the section arc is fully covered. The clearance patrol then returns through their own section's LSW position. In this way all tracks into the position are covered by an LSW position.

3. Clearance patrols are to detect and report to Pl Cmdr:

a. Signs of recent enemy activity.

b. Possible approach routes enemy may take.

c. Unexpected obstacles , (mines, contaminated ground and ravines).

d. Streams and and dry river beds. High Ground.

e. Possible ERV locations.

4. If initially thorough recce patrols have been carried out, on occasions it might not require Clearance Partols immediately after the occupation, easpecially at night.

Also if there is not much time between occupation and last light, Pl Cmdrs may do without clearance patrols.

However, if the patrol stays in its harbour during the next day, clearance patrols must go out at first light.

FIELDCRAFT

Stage 4 - Sentries. When clearance patrols finished, sentries to be posted.

Points to remember are:
a. Sentries should be posted beyond the limit of noise from the harbour (to avoid distraction and to alert the platoon before any enemy hear the harbour).

b. One sentry per section posted in depth will normally be enough.

c. The sentries to act as early warning of enemy approach. They should be armed with rifles but fire only in self defence. Their withdrawal route back to the harbour should be via the LSW position and be clearly understood by all.

d. Communication between sentries and the LSW positions must be established. This should include use of communication cord.

e. Sentries are located outside the harbour only during work routine.

f. By night, sentries will normally consist of staggered double manning of the corner LSWS. The double manning provides continuity at the sentry position, allows one sentry to fetch the relief and reduces the chances of a sleeping sentry.

Stage 5 - Work Routine. Once sentries are posted, work begins to strengthen the harbour. Tasks include:

1. Preparation of stand-to positions and fields of fire, construction of shell scrapes and the positioning of warning devices (e.g, trip flares).

2. Preparation of a path to allow silent movement round the position. Shell scrapes should be on the outside edge of the path. Soldiers would live in and fight from their shell scrapes. Wire would be laid just inside the shell scrapes to mark the path and prevent accidental movement outside the harbour at night. This is lowered during daylight hours.

3. Laying of communications cord from sentries to LSW positions and/ or section commanders, and from section commanders to platoon commander.

4. Positioning of shelters. These are erected over shell scrapes at last light and taken down before first light. They may be erected in poor weather at the platoon commander's discretion.

FIELDCRAFT

5. Confirmatory orders by the platoon commander to establish an operational and administrative routine. The points are as for routine in defence and include:

a. Future operations (i.e., patrols).

b. Alarm and stand-to system (and its rehearsal).

c. Orders for opening fire and defence of the harbour.
   Location of platoon ERV.

d. Sentry roster.

e. Re-supply.

f. Sleeping and feeding.

g. Track discipline.

h. Staggered cleaning of weapons.

j. Latrines these should be within the perimeter of the harbour or outside within the sentries arcs.

Security

The platoon commander must ensure:

a. Sentries are correctly posted and briefed.

b. Good communications with sentries to ensure early warning of enemy approach.

c. All round defence is maintained.

d. Good battle discipline is maintained. Points to include:

1. Correct camouflage.

2. No lights, smells or unnecessary noise.

3. Webbing worn and weapons carried at all times. Kit not in use to be packed away.

STORES & EQUIPMENT

If you have the responsibility for drawing/collecting kit from the Stores you will have to sign for it' on a form 1033. This means that you have taken on the responsibility of ensuring it is not misused, damaged, or goes missing. It is a good idea to check that the kit you draw is in good order /correct amount before you sign. When returning the stores they will be checked.

Once the check is complete, ensure that the stores copy of your form is either signed as 'stores returned' or destroyed in front of you.

The above applies for everything you sign for.

WARNING

SAFETY - FIRING BLANK AMMUNITION
With all field training when blank
ammunition is in use, *NEVER* aim
directly at anyone.
**DO NOT AIM AT ALL IF THEY ARE LESS
THAN 50 METRES AWAY FROM YOU.
DO NOT FIRE BLINDLY IN THE DARK
-YOU HAVE BEEN WARNED -
THINK BEFORE YOU SHOOT.**

SELF TEST QUESTIONS

1. To be good at Fieldcraft you need to have what.
2. For what reason do you use: Unit of Measure. Key Ranges. Bracketing.
3. Who makes out a RANGE Card, what for and when.
4. When carrying out Personal Cam what do you have to remember.
5. What is "Isolated cover", would you use it.
6. Why are things seen, what must you remember about "smell".
7. What is important about Shape, Shadow, Silhouette.
8. How do you indicate a DIFFICULT target.
9. What is the "Key Word" for fire control orders and what does it mean, and how do you give an order.
10. How many types of Fire Control Orders are there and what are they.
11. Give a method of moving at night.
12. How long does it take for your eyes to get used to the dark.
13. When an illuminating FLARE 'goes up', what do you do.
14. When do sentries work in pairs.
15. Name the Duties of a Sentry.
16. What is the correct CHALLENGE a sentry should give, when and how should it be given.

FIELDCRAFT

17. How many members are there usually in an Infantry Section.
18. What is Fire Team within the Section.
19. How many Sections are there in a Platoon.
20. What helps you to listen at night.
21. What is the "drill" if you come under effective fire.
22. A Sentry close to the enemy must know — What.
23. What is the sequence and headings used by a Section Commander giving his orders
24. Give the three important points to consider when "choosing a route".
25. How do you work out your own PACING SCALE.
26. Give six methods to help you Keep your Direction when on a Patrol.
27. Give the meaning of the Key Word : G R O U N D and explain its use.
28. How do you split up an area you are going to SCAN and SEARCH.
29. Name two types of Patrols and the role that they play.
30. In daylight, you must not fire a blank at anyone less than, how many yards away, and at night what is the rule.
31. How should orders be given.
32. What should you remember by the letters C.L.A.P.
33. Where will you find the Cut Off Group.
34. Give three reasons for having Patrols.
35. Give the three important stages of Navigation.
36. What do you understand by a Three Stage Attack.
37. As a Sentry how loud do you shout to challenge anyone approaching your post.
38. Outline what you would expect the info a Patrol Report would give.
39. When would an interrogator be used.
40. How many types of Ambush are there and what are they called.
41. Setting up an Ambush site what would you look for.
42. What is a Patrol Harbour used for.
43. What is the role of a Clearance Patrol

Chapter 5
MAP AND COMPASS

INTRODUCTION
We are fortunate to have excellent maps of this country produced
by the Ordnance Survey.
The Military Survey, a specialist branch of the Royal Engineers,
undertakes the provision of maps, charts, hydrographical, and other
geographical products for all three of the armed services. The ACF
use the maps made available by the MOD.

RELIABILITY OF MAPS
A map is literally a "Bird's eye view" of the ground drawn on paper.
It is accurate only at the time it was drawn. Today, maps are
produced from aerial photographs, which ensures their accuracy.
In just a few years, the shape of a landscape can change, villages may
disappear under a reservoir, new roads may appear, and whole
woods may disappear. For practical map reading purposes this will
not affect the accuracy as far as you will be concerned, any map
produced within the last few years may be relied upon unless
specifically stated otherwise.

CARE OF MAPS
Maps should be treated carefully or they soon become useless.
When using outdoors, it is advisable to fold the map to the area
required and place it in a map case or plastic bag to protect it.
When planning routes, place a transparent film over the map; writing
directly on to the map ruins it for further use. Ensure you learn
how to fold a new map correctly; it will prolong its useful life.

WHAT YOU WILL FIND ON MAPS

Marginal Information
On most maps you will find a part set aside for 'marginal
information', find this as soon as you unfold your map, it provides

MAP & COMPASS

useful information and guidance on how to interpret the detail on the map.

Until you have been map reading for some time, you will constantly refer to this section – until you have a good understanding of what all the symbols or CONVENTIONAL SIGNS mean.

The reference number and scale of the map is to be found at the top of the map.

The index giving adjoining sheet numbers is usually shown near the bottom right hand corner of the map. You will need this info if the route you are planning "Goes off the map".

Most maps now use metres as the "Unit of Elevation", this scale is to be found in the margin at the bottom of the map as "ELEVATION IN METRES".

THE GRID SYSTEM

The British National Grid System divides the whole country into large squares which are sub – divided and finish up as the GRID LINES printed on maps that you would normally use.

Grid Lines are used to 'pin point' a specific spot on the map by using the numbers of each line as shown in the margins around the outside of the map. Maps are printed with the North at the top of the sheet, one set of GRID LINES run up and down the map (North and South), the others run across the map (East and West). It is important that you are able to find a point on the map and then be able to go out and find it on the ground. It is vital to be able to indicate on the map the exact place where you are standing on the ground.

To assist in the accurate use of the grid system it is advisable to obtain a Pathfinder Protractor/Romer, it provides two of the different scales of GRID SQUARES found on Ordnance Survey maps. The Romer is made of rigid plastic that you place on the GRID SQUARE of the map and read off the figures as described below, to the exact pinpoint position.

FOUR AND SIX FIGURE REFERENCES

When giving a reference there are a few simple rules to remember:

1. FIRST, count the figures along the BOTTOM of the map, from **left** (West), to **right** (East); these are called **"EASTINGS"**.

2. Next, count the figures up the side of the map from the bottom (South) to the top (North) these are called **"NORTHINGS"**

MAP & COMPASS

3. A reference must always contain an even number of figures.

4. GRID REFERENCES are

always given with the **"EASTINGS"** value first, followed by the **"NORTHINGS'** value. The example given in the diagram shows a black square that can be given the reference as square 8040 (*'A four figure reference'*)

This square could represent a whole square kilometre of ground, not exactly a 'pinpoint' location on a map or ground.

Should you use a four-figure reference you must add a feature such as a cross roads, a church or prominent physical feature to indicate exactly where you mean within the four-figure square.

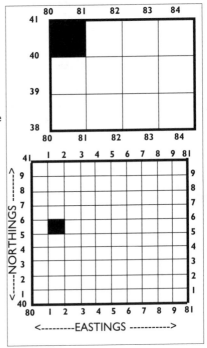

To get an exact position, the square can be further sub-divided into 10 squares in both directions. The bottom diagram illustrates this sub-division the black square is 'square 1- 5' these figures when added as explained below make up a *'six figure reference'*.

The first two figures of the EASTING value followed by the sub-divided square figure, then the two NORTHING value figures, followed again by the sub-divided figure to make up a six-figure reference of 801405

MAP & COMPASS

SETTING A MAP

The first and essential task on the ground with a map is to **'Set it'** or **'Orientating the map'**. It means aligning your map with the features on the ground. Until you have mastered this, you will not get the enjoyment out of map reading.

Setting your map using a Silva type Compass

Lay your map out flat, then find the MAGNETIC NORTH ARROW – usually in the margin of the map as shown at 'A' in the diagram.

Lay the base of the compass on the map with the DIRECTION OF TRAVEL ARROW, ('B' in the diagram), in line with the MAGNETIC NORTH. (See diagram 'line-up').

Carefully turn the map and compass round – watching the compass needle swinging until the **RED MAGNETIC END** of the

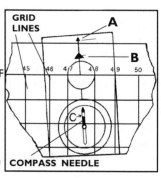

compass needle 'C' coincides with the DIRECTION OF TRAVEL ARROW 'B' and the MAGNETIC NORTH ARROW 'A' on the map. Your map is now **'Set'** or **'Orientated'** in relation to the ground.

MAP & COMPASS

FIRST THINGS - FIRST - ALWAYS SET - ORIENTATE THE MAP

SETTING A MAP WITHOUT A COMPASS
BY CAREFUL OBSERVATION

This can be easy, once you have identified exactly where you are on the map, and if you are standing on a straight road, line up the road on your map with the road you are standing on.

Make certain that the map is pointing in the right direction, i.e the right way round.

If not on a road, you will need to find other objects on the ground such as a road/track junction, church, prominent hill top or farm buildings.

You must also find the same objects on your map, using them as shown in the diagram by turning your map to set or orientate it in relation to the ground

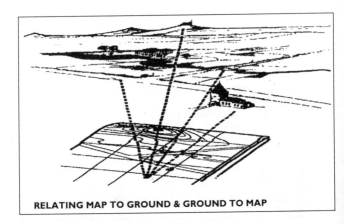

RELATING MAP TO GROUND & GROUND TO MAP

MAP & COMPASS

THE SILVA COMPASS

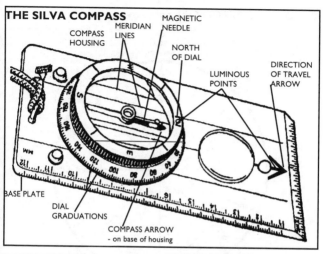

COMPASS HOUSING

MERIDIAN LINES

MAGNETIC NEEDLE

NORTH OF DIAL

LUMINOUS POINTS

DIRECTION OF TRAVEL ARROW

BASE PLATE

DIAL GRADUATIONS

COMPASS ARROW
- on base of housing

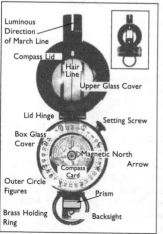

Luminous Direction of March Line

Compass Lid

Hair Line

Upper Glass Cover

Lid Hinge

Setting Screw

Box Glass Cover

Magnetic North Arrow

Compass Card

Outer Circle Figures

Prism

Brass Holding Ring

Backsight

THE PRISMATIC COMPASS

This is the compass that the Army uses. It is a very accurate instrument and therefore costly to make.

Not issued to cadets, but we include it for interest only.

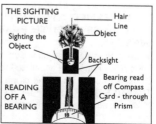

THE SIGHTING PICTURE

Hair Line

Object

Sighting the Object

Backsight

READING OFF A BEARING

Bearing read off Compass Card - through Prism

MAP & COMPASS

CARDINAL POINTS of the compass.

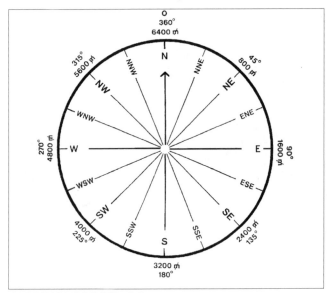

CARDINAL POINTS of the compass.

There are 32 points of the compass, but only 16 of them are normally used in map reading for the description of direction.
These 16 are the four Cardinal Points and 12 intermediate points as shown in the diagram above.

The **INTERMEDIATE POINTS** are combined with the Cardinal points, e.g. **SE** is **SOUTH EAST, NNW** is **NORTH NORTH WEST** etc.

These points describe direction only to within one sixteenth of the full circle. For more accurate indication of direction it is necessary to use sub-divisions of the circle using **'mils'** or **'degrees'**.

The **MILS SYSTEM** divides the circle of the compass into 6400 MILS, the zero being the North Point.

MAP & COMPASS

The MILS system is used by the Army to give greater accuracy than degrees. Cadet Forces work in Degrees - 360 degrees in a circle. The four quadrants or quarters of the circle are each 90^0, and so the East, South and West points fall at 180^0, 270^0, 360^0 degrees respectively, as illustrated on the previous page.
The symbol normally used for Degrees is the ^{0} as shown above.

NORTH POINTS

There are THREE NORTH POINTS

1. **TRUE NORTH** – the actual direction of the geographical North Pole
2. **GRID NORTH** - the direction of the vertical GRID LINES on a map. For all practical purposes, TRUE and GRID are the same.
3. **MAGNETIC NORTH** – the direction towards which the compass needle is attracted is the **MAGNETIC NORTH POLE** – see the diagram.

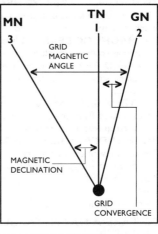

ANGLES BETWEEN NORTH POINTS (GMA)
Grid Magnetic Angles

This is sometimes called the **magnetic variation**; it is the angle between GRID NORTH and MAGNETIC NORTH; it depends on two factors:

1. **TIME:** as the position of the Magnetic North Pole moves slightly eastwards, so the GMA (Grid Magnetic Angle) changes. This is called the **ANNUAL MAGNETIC CHANGE** and must be taken into account when converting MAGNETIC BEARINGS to GRID BEARINGS and vice versa.

2. **PLACE:** The GMA **(Grid Magnetic Angle)** also varies from one part of the country to another. These two factors are included in the marginal information on a map.

MAP & COMPASS

MAGNETIC DELINATION

This is the angle between MAGNETIC and TRUE NORTH as shown on the diagram on the previous page.

GRID CONVERGENCE

This is the angle between GRID NORTH and TRUE NORTH which can in practice, be ignored since for practical map reading purposes TRUE NORTH and MAGNETIC NORTH are the same.

BEARINGS – TYPES OF BEARINGS

There are three kinds of bearings according to the North point from which they have been measured:

1. **A MAGNETIC BEARING** is one taken with a compass (an accurate compass needle always points towards MAGNETIC NORTH)
2. **A GRID BEARING** is one measured on a map with the Silva compass used as a protractor or using your Pathfinder Protractor/ Romer.
3. **A TRUE BEARING** cannot be measured direct, it must be calculated from the other two. However this can be ignored for practical map reading purposes.

NOTE: INDIVIDUAL COMPASS ERROR (ICE)

The accuracy of each compass is subject to error, it is important that you should check your own compass to establish the INDIVIDUAL COMPASS ERROR by checking it against other compasses. Having done so, make a note of the ICE on a small sticky label stuck on to the base of your compass. **Don't forget to allow for it!**

TO TAKE A MAGNETIC BEARING

1. Point the compass direction of march arrow at the object.
2. Turn the compass housing until the red arrow is under the needle.
3. Read off the MAGNETIC BEARING on the compass housing.

MAP & COMPASS

To use your Silva compass for a **BACK BEARING,** keep the compass on the bearing you have taken (as '**X**' to '**Y**' in the diagram), rotate the **COMPASS HOUSING** through 180⁰ (180 degrees) The compass is now **SET** to march on the **BACK BEARING** (in the direction of '**Y**' as shown in the diagram) of your original **FORWARD BEARING.**

To retrace your route – (from '**Y**' to '**X**') march on the bearing given as your **BACK BEARING.**

This is a very important skill, easily learned with your Silva Compass.

Using Forward and Back bearings is one of the best methods of preventing yourself from getting hopelessly lost;

remember practice makes pefect

**FORWARD AND
BACK BEARINGS**

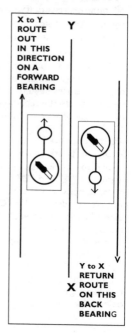

X to Y
ROUTE
OUT
IN THIS
DIRECTION
ON A
FORWARD
BEARING

Y

Y to X
RETURN
X ROUTE
ON THIS
BACK
BEARING

MAP & COMPASS

FIND YOUR POSITION BY COMPASS - RESECTION

There may be times when you need to find your exact position both on the map and on the ground. This could be as a result of being "dropped-off" on an exercise or if you were unfortunate enough to crash land in wild country. You could find your position by using a compass and following the instructions set out below.

You will need to refer to the diagram on this page.

1. Set/orientate your map. Select TWO prominent objects or features which you can be sure of identifying on the map. These objects/features need to be a good distance away, more than 1000 metres and also be separated by an angle of approximately 10 o'clock to 2 o'clock - see diagram opposite.

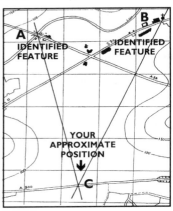

2. On the "plastic" cover of your map, mark the objects/feature at **"A"** and **"B"**. From the position at which you are standing, (call it **"C"**) take a bearing on to each of the objects/features in turn, writing down the bearings. As this has to be accurate, don't move from your position and take a further two bearings on both of the objects/features. Add together the three bearings to each object/feature and divide by three to get the average bearing to each. It is important to do this as accuracy is essential.

3. These are COMPASS Bearings, therefore they are MAGNETIC Bearings.

As you are to use them to 'plot on a map', they have to be converted from MAGNETIC to GRID Bearings.

MAP & COMPASS

NOTE: You will always be best advised to draw a small diagram - until you become familiar with working with bearings - showing the NORTH POINTS as shown on page 5.14, this will remind you to make an allowance for the GMA (Grid Magnetic Angle).

The current GMA is approximately 100 mils ($6°$) This is the figure that you would subtract from the MAGNETIC BEARING.

REMEMBER: "MAG TO GRID - GET RID"

4. Check the resulting bearing and adjust it to the nearest 25 mils. Remember the settings or divisions on the compass card of a Silva or Light Weight Compass are 25 mils.

5. Now set up the GRID BEARING on your compass for bearing **"A"**. Use a wax pencil with a fine point , put the point on **"A"** . Hold it in a vertical position, place the long edge of the compass against the pencil with the DIRECTION OF TRAVEL ARROW pointing in the direction of **"A"**, and the NORTH ARROW pointing approximately to the top of the map.

6. Using the pencil still in a vertical position, pivot the compass about the pencil point until the NORTH ARROW points exactly towards the top of the map, with the edge of the compass or any of the red setting lines on the compass base parallel to the nearest GRID LINES on the map.

7. Hold the compass firmly in this position while you draw a line along the side of the compass.

Repeat the same procedure from point **"B"**.

Where the two lines you have drawn from **"A"** and **"B"** cross each other is your calculated position on the map/ground. Now work out your exact six figure GRID reference of your location.

> *"ONLY WITH CONSTANT USE AND*
> *PRACTICE WILL YOU LEARN TO*
> *TRUST YOUR COMPASS"*

MAP & COMPASS

IDENTIFYING A FEATURE

Set/orientate your map, use the edge of your protractor or a pencil, place it on the map with the edge running through your position, swing it across the map until it lines up with the feature you can identify on the ground. The feature should be easy to pick out, provided it is not too far away and that it is on your map!.

This like so many Map Reading skills need constant practice until you carry it out as a "drill" and second nature.

After a while you will be able to locate and identify features by just looking across the map.

In setting your map, no matter what method you use, it is the constant relating and comparison of the map and ground which will build a good foundation for your navigational skills.

We remind you that this skill above all will go a long way to prevent you getting lost on your DofE Expedition.

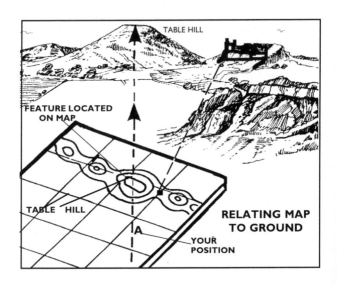

MAP & COMPASS

GRID MAGNETIC ANGLE
(GMA) in UK
GMA = 8 degrees,15' West
or145 mils West in
June 1980
Annual change approx
10' East MN GN GMA
145mils, 8 degrees

REMEMBER
"Grid to Mag - ADD"
"Mag to Grid get RID"

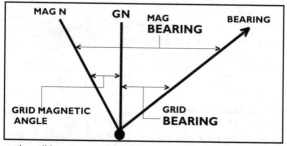

Remember all bearings are measured in a clockwise direction from the NORTH point. A MAG bearing will always be GREATER than the GRID bearing taken, by the amount of the GRID MAGNETIC ANGLE.
Therefore to convert GRID to MAG ADD the GRID MAGNETIC ANGLE.
To convert a MAG bearing to a GRID, SUBTRACT the GRID MAGNETIC ANGLE.

MAP & COMPASS

TO MARCH ON A BEARING

Having converted your GRID BEARING to a MAGNETIC BEARING, set the graduated circle on you compass to read the MAGNETIC BEARING at the DIRECTION OF TRAVEL line.

Then turn the whole COMPASS until the NORTH end of the NEEDLE coincides with the NORTH ARROW and is par allel to the MERIDIAN LINES on the COMPASS HOUSING, holding the COMPASS in front of you march in the direction indicated by the LINE OF TAVEL ARROW.

So long as the compass needle and the NORTH ARROW are kept together, the DIRECTION OF TRAVEL ARROW will remain on the required bearing.

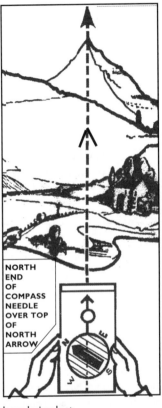

NORTH END OF COMPASS NEEDLE OVER TOP OF NORTH ARROW

BACK BEARINGS with a SILVA COMPASS

When marching on a bearing - especially at night - over some distance you may often have a doubt in your mind that you may go wandering off course and finish up being lost.

The ability to use your compass and to **trust it** by taking a back bearing on to the point from which you started, will prevent you getting into difficulties.

The simplicity of the Silva compass makes the use of back bearings an easy navigational aid.

MAP & COMPASS

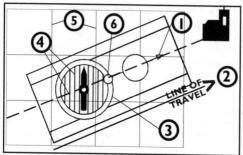

TO TAKE A GRID BEARING
One of the most common uses of taking bearings is to take one from the map to find the bearing to march on.

With your SILVA compass or your protractor it is quite simple to do.
Note: IGNORE THE COMPASS NEEDLE

1. Place the long edge of the compass along the desired line of travel, making sure that the DIRECTION OF TRAVEL ARROW on the compass *POINTS IN THE DIRECTION YOU WISH TO GO. (1)*

2. Turn the COMPASS NEEDLE HOUSING so that NORTH on the housing rim points to NORTH on the map. You will notice that the MERIDIAN LINES on the COMPASS are parallel to the GRID LINES *(5)* on the map – or they should be! *(4)*

3. Read the number of mils/degrees against the DIRECTION OF TRAVEL LINE; this is the GRID BEARING. *(6)* Having taken a GRID BEARING from the map, you must take into account and make allowances for the GRID MAGNETIC ANGLE (GMA).

HILLS AND VALLEYS

The method of showing how the ground is shaped in terms of hills and valleys (termed as **RELIEF**), appear as thin brown lines on the map and are called **CONTOUR LINES.** They are described as "An imaginary line joining all points of equal height above sea level".
You must check the information at the bottom of the map near the scale diagram to find the **"Contour Interval",** that is the height between each contour.
The following information will give you a better understanding of how contour lines can give a three dimensional view of the area covered by the map.

MAP & COMPASS

UNDERSTANDING AND INTERPRETING CONTOURS

Firstly, you must understand that contour lines follow the same height round hills.

They do not immediately provide a picture of the shape of the land, but with practice you will begin to interpret the shape of the land in your mind.

SPURS AND RE-ENTRANTS

A **SPUR** projects out from the landmass, a **RE-ENTRANT** is exactly the opposite, a shallow valley running up into the mass. It is not always possible to tell which is the top of the slope and which is the bottom without being able to find the contour figures. When the contour figures can be read with both the map and the figures the correct way up you will be able to tell if the ground is rising or falling.

A general idea of which way the slopes run can be obtained by looking at other features; particularly lakes, ponds, rivers, streams and railway lines. A stream running near a set of contours indicates at once which is the bottom of the slope.

Features such as railways, villages and large woods are more likely to be found at the bottom of a hill than at the top.

CONVEX AND CONCAVE SLOPES

A **CONVEX** slope is one that 'bulges' outwards, a **CONCAVE** slope is one that curves inwards. Standing at the top of a CONVEX slope you would not be able to see all the way down to the bottom, because the outward slope would obscure

your view. It is important to recognise that this is 'dead ground', and as such can hide obstacles.

When standing on the top of a CONCAVE slope There will be a clear view down to the bottom (unless it is heavily wooded).

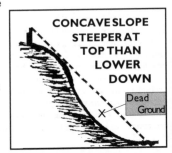

CONCAVE SLOPE STEEPER AT TOP THAN LOWER DOWN

Dead Ground

MAP & COMPASS

CONTOUR VALUES

If you had several paths around a hill, each one keeping at the same level, and were walking round one of them, you would find that where the paths were near to each other the ground would be steep between the paths. Where the paths are some distance apart, the ground will slope gently; the further they were apart, the less the slope would be.

CONVEX SLOPE BULGES OUT AT TOP

STEEPER AT THE LOWER END

MORE ABOUT CONTOURS

On gentle slopes the CONTOURS are far apart, on steep slopes the CONTOURS are close together. If the ground is broken and rugged there will be many **SPURS** and **RE-ENTRANTS**, a path would be constantly turning in and out. Irregular, sharply turning contours shows broken and rugged country. Where the slopes are smooth, the path will curve gently, bending out as it follows the line of a SPUR and swinging in at a RE-ENTRANT. On gentle slopes the contours appear as smooth flowing curves.

Contours may appear to wander about all over, but if you follow them they naturally come back to where they started from; the only exception is when you find a cliff face with a sheer drop, then all the contour lines are so close together they appear to be one.

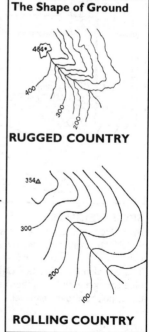

The Shape of Ground

464•

400

300

200

RUGGED COUNTRY

354△

300

200

100

ROLLING COUNTRY

MAP & COMPASS
UNDERSTANDING VERTICAL INTERVAL (V.I.)

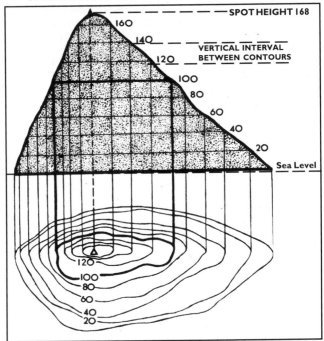

SPOT HEIGHTS

Apart from contours, height is shown by **SPOT HEIGHTS**
which is marked on a map by a dot and number ● 168. This is the
exact height in metres or feet above sea level.

You will also find **TRIG POINTS**, shown on the map as a small
blue triangle with a number next to it ▲ 576, this again is the
exact height above sea level.

MAP & COMPASS

Every curve or bend in a contour indicates a SPUR or a valley, a rise or fall in the ground, just as it does on the side of a hill. Remember - the distance apart the contours are still indicates the steepness or flatness of the ground.

Each contour is drawn at a specific height above sea level and each one is the same vertical height above the one below. The difference in height between the contours is called the **VERTICAL INTERVAL (V.I.) See illustration on previous page.**

These heights are written into the contour lines at intervals along their length. On Ordnance Survey maps figures showing the height of contours are always printed so that they read facing up the hill. It is useful to remember this so that you may quickly find out which direction the ground is sloping.

Check the information in the margins of the map to find out if the VI (Vertical Interval) is in Feet or Metres.

Whenever you are 'out and about' look at the ground in the area and draw imaginary contour lines around the hills and valleys. Make a rough sketch and then get a map of the area and see how accurately you have interpreted the ground.

Practice as much as you can, interpreting contours correctly is important when you are planning the route of an expedition, or trying to find a different route out of a difficult area.

MAP & COMPASS

Contours and the shape of ground

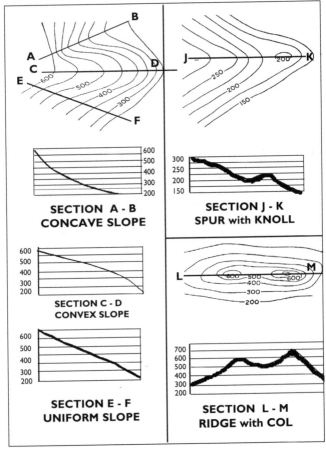

SECTION A - B
CONCAVE SLOPE

SECTION J - K
SPUR with KNOLL

SECTION C - D
CONVEX SLOPE

SECTION E - F
UNIFORM SLOPE

SECTION L - M
RIDGE with COL

MAP & COMPASS

KNOW YOUR CONTOUR PATTERNS

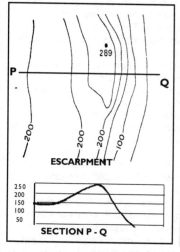

ESCARPMENT

SECTION P - Q

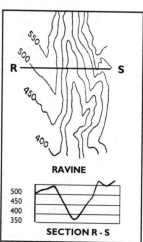

RAVINE

SECTION R - S

1. Contours close together mean steep slopes.

2. Contours far apart mean gentle slopes.

3. When contours are evenly spaced the slope is uniform, thes slopes have small undulations and pockets of dead ground.

4. When the spacing of the contours, reading from high ground to low, decreases, the slope is convex. Convex slopes mean short visability; dead ground becomes very close.

5. When spacing of contours, reading from high to low, increases, the slope is concave.

Concave slopes mean good visibility and little dead ground.

6. Wandering contours at various distances apart and never close, mean undulating ground. Important to note the general direction of the fall in the ground.

7. Gently curving contours indicate an area of country of rounded slopes. As the ground becomes steeper the contours come closer together; as it becomes more rugged the curves disappear and the contours take on 'jagged' shapes.

5-22

MAP & COMPASS

SCALES AND MEASURING DISTANCE

The scale of a map is the relationship between the actual distance measured from one point to another on the ground and the distance between the same two points on a map. The way that the 'scale' of a map is expressed is by the **Representative Fraction.** It used to be expressed in words, "one inch to a mile" or "four miles to one inch".

The **Representative Fraction (RF)** is the standard method used on all continental maps and wherever the metric system is used.

Most British maps are now expressed in metric. It is simple to use if you remember that the RF is 1/X, one unit of distance on the map represents X units of distance on the ground. For example, a scale of 1/50,000 means that one inch/centimetre/metre on the map represents 50,000 inches/centimetres/metre on the ground.

The essential connection is that the SAME unit of measurement applies both to the map and to the ground measurement. A distance of 2cms on a 1/50,000 map therefore represents 2 x 50,000 cm on the ground = 100,000cm = 1000 metres.

All maps are printed with graphic linear scales, usually in the centre of the bottom margin, from which any horizontal distance may be measured on the map in kilometres and metres, or in miles and yards.

A linear map scale is always shown in the form of a diagram, you will notice that the zero mark is set from the left of the scale by one major division, which is then subdivided into ten (or other suitable) sub-divisions usually not longer than about 4mm each.

SCALE   1 : 50 000

2 Centimetres to 1 Kilometres (one grid square)

| 2 | | 1 | | 0 | | 1 | | 2 |

Kilometres

| 1 Kilometre = 0.6214 mile | 1 Mile = 1. 6093 Kilometres |

Miles

NOTE: The above diagram is NOT to scale, but to illustrate the scale found on a 1: 50 000 map. Any measurements falling between these sub-divisions must be estimated.

MAP & COMPASS

PACING

Pacing is necessary because you must always know how exactly far you have gone when counting a number of your own 'paces'.

You should know your 'Pacing Scale', over different types of conditions, i.e. tarmac roads, tracks, grasslands, woodlands etc.

To find your PACING SCALE, put two markers out 100m apart. Walk the distance between them as you would on a patrol, counting the paces as you go.

If it has taken you 120 paces to cover the 100m, then that is your

PACING SCALE.

It follows, to use this scale if you were on a patrol and had to go a distance of 300m, you would have to count out 360 paces.

Under some conditions you can use a specific length of string, tying knots at every 120 paces. Having used the length of string, un-tie the knots and repeat the process on the next 'leg' of your route.

It is always advisable to have a CHECK PACER, remembering to check that your PACING SCALE is the same by day and night.

You will have to make adjustments according to the terrain, weayher, wind, temperature, rain etc.

	ROUTE CARD							
				Date_____				
Produced by____ Start Point Grid Ref _____ ETD _____								
Date finish____Finishing Point GridRef_____ ETA _____								
	From		To		Bearings			Remarks
Leg	Location	Grid Ref	Location	Grid Ref	Grid	Mag	Distance	Landmarks Hazards
			Example of headings and layout of a Route Card - reduced in size.					

MAP & COMPASS

LINEAR MAP SCALE

How To Measure Distance

Make a mark on the straight edge of a piece of paper, put the mark on
the point you wish to measure from and make successive marks along
the edge of the paper as y you follow the route from your starting
point to the final point.

This is easy if you just wish to measure along a straight road, but if it
means going round corners you will have to pivot the paper and
make several marks as you progress.

The total distance is recorded along the edge of the paper.

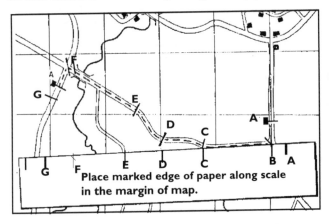

Place marked edge of paper along scale
in the margin of map.

Lay the paper along the scale on the map, with the right hand, tick
against one of the major divisions, so that the left hand tick lies against
the sub-divisions to the left of the zero mark. The total distance is
then the number of major divisions plus the distance to the left of the
zero.

With practice this is quite an accurate method of measuring distances.

MAP & COMPASS

MOVING ROUND OBSTACLES

Obstacles are often found on a route and in order to keep a really
accurate direction you should go round them by plotting a series of
right angles and measuring by paces as illustrated in the diagram, **200 x
500 x 200**

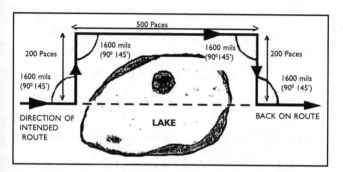

FINDING TRUE NORTH FROM THE SUN USING A WATCH

When you do not have a map or
are map reading without a
compass, it can help if you are
able to find the rough direction
of TRUE NORTH or SOUTH.
The method explained will give
you an approximate direction —
not accurate enough for reading
bearings or other measurements.

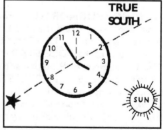

INFORMATION – as the sun rises in the EAST, and moves (in the
Northern Hemisphere) through the Southern sky, setting in the
WEST, the position of the Sun, when visible, is always a rough guide to
the direction of NORTH.

MAP & COMPASS

A watch, when set to Greenwich Mean Time (GMT) for UK (or to local time for other areas some distance EAST or WEST of Greenwich may be used.

If summertime or other artificial time is in local use, your watch should be adjusted to Greenwich Mean Time (GMT) or to the local standard time.

METHOD – lay your watch flat, with the HOUR HAND pointing to the Sun.

In the NORTHERN Hemisphere, TRUE SOUTH will then be midway between the hour hand and twelve o'clock on the watch – see the diagram.

In the SOUTHERN Hemisphere, lay your watch with twelve o'clock pointing to the Sun.

TRUE NORTH then lies midway between the hour hand and twelve o'clock.

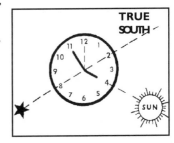

When the Sun is high up in the sky, this method cannot be used with any success. In any case the result is unlikely to be accurate to better than five degrees.

FINDING TRUE NORTH – by the stars (Northern Latitude)
In latitudes less than 60° the **POLE STAR** is never more than about 40 miles away from the **TRUE NORTH**.

The position of the **POLE STAR** is indicated by the "pointers" of **The Great Bear or Plough – see diagram.**

All stars revolve round the POLE STAR and the Plough may be either below it low down near the horizon and "right way up" or above it in the sky and "upside down" or in any position between.

If the Plough is obscured or below the horizon, **Cassiopeia** which is shaped like a **'W'** and is on the opposite side of the POLE STAR from the Plough, may be visible; the POLE STAR is the nearest bright star within the arms of the 'W'.

Above 60° the POLE STAR is too high in the sky to be a good guide to NORTH.

MAP & COMPASS

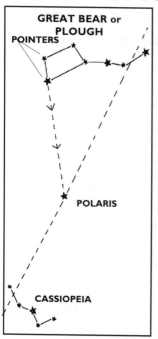

GREAT BEAR or PLOUGH

POINTERS

POLARIS

CASSIOPEIA

At the NORTH POLE it is vertically overhead.

The only way to learn night navigation is to get out in the dark, identify the constellations shown in the diagram on the left and practice moving in different directions by using stars and then checking with your compass. As with all map reading and compass work –
PRACTICE MAKES PERFECT

ROUTE CARDS

The purpose of a ROUTE CARD is to ensure that you plan the route you are taking and from the start become aware of the distances you are proposing to travel, the obstacles that you will encounter, either overcoming them or taking action to find a route round them. RV's and the locations for your campsites, approximate timings. Always ensure that you give a copy of your Route Card to a responsible person to ensure that if there is an emergency the rescuers know where to start looking.

The illustration of the route card on the next page is self-explanatory; you need plenty of space in each column to write your information. Never be short on detail, it is better to have more information than you need rather than not enough. List mobile phone numbers and names

If you are in a group, ensure that each member of the group has a good copy of the route card, again we stress that it is important to ensure that you leave a copy with someone you will be in contact with during your expedition.

Remember, always include your CHECK POINTS and the **expected TIMES** that you will be there on your Route Card.

MAP & COMPASS

On the previous page the hands on the diagram of a clock face are pointing to a quarter past eight.

If it was in the morning (Ante Meridian - **AM** - before noon), you would call it 0815 hours.

If it was in the evening, (Post Meridian – **PM** - after noon), you would call it 2015 hours.

The importance of using the 24 hour clock system cannot be ignored as it avoids any confusion over timings and is explicit in its meaning. The Armed Services use what is know as the date/time group, which includes the date as two figures in front of the time.

Examples: 122200 June would be 2200hrs on the 12th of June, i.e. 10pm in the evening of the 12th of June.

This system is used when timings cover several days,
e.g. START Exercise 170600 END Exercise 201000
The Exercise will begin at 6am on the 17th and end at 10am on the 20th.

As with any new skill, make use of the 24 hour clock when giving the time - practice makes perfect!

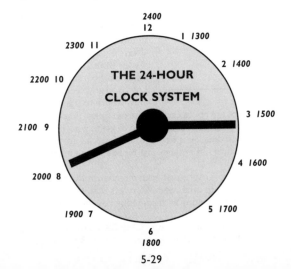

MAP & COMPASS

ORIENTEERING

Orienteering is like a car rally on foot, and as a sport has become well established in the UK. It can be over a mile or two or made to cover a vast area. It can be a morning's fun, last a day or several days. "Tough" orienteering can include crossing mountains, or be "improved" by including rafting or even canoes. It can take the form of a 'Treasure Hunt', or finding 'escaped prisoners'.
It will depend upon the imagination of your instructors to make it fun.

It is a highly competitive sport testing your map reading skills and your ability to think quickly on your feet. You need to be physically fit and have determination to safely navigate around a set course laid out by the organisers. The 'event' is judged by the shortest time it takes competitors to navigate and complete the course with the most correct points scored. Your progress is recorded on a Control Card that contains spaces for the individual checkpoint marks.

HOW IT IS ORGANISED

A **MASTER MAP** of the area in which the orienteering is to take place will be set up for all competitors to see. Normally you will be given a list of **MAP REFERENCES** that are the **CONTROL POINTS.** You will be issued with your own map in a plastic cover or case. You are given time to plot the CONTROL references on your map from the Master Map, and then when it is time for you to begin, set out for your first CONTROL.

CHECK POINTS OR CONTROLS

The CHECK POINTS or CONTROLS, which make up the route, are usually marked in some way to distinguish between them. In some Forestry Commission areas these markers are diamond shape painted red and white, fixed to posts each one being separately numbered.
In competitions moveable CONTROLS are put out before the competition. This allows the organisers to use different areas and different courses. To prove you have been to the CONTROL you have to make a note of the number or symbol carved into the top of each post or use a special punch called a Swedish marker punch on

MAP & COMPASS

your event card. These will be checked on your return, time penalties are added for incorrect CONTROL marks.

The Controls are not easy to find, more often than not they can only be seen from a close distance, usually less than 30m, therefore accurate map reading is essential if you are to find them.

It is a good idea to chose an easily identified point like a track junction near to the CONTROL (this is called an ATTACK POINT) and then pace the distance on a bearing to the CONTROL.

EQUIPMENT

To Orienteer safely you normally require: Map and Map Case (or plastic cover), Compass (Silva type), Pen/Pencil, and Whistle.

CLOTHING

The type of clothing you wear depends on the time of year, the location of the course, the type of country and how long the event is to last. Check with the organisers, some will refuse entry to competitors inadequately dressed for the area. If you really enjoy the sport and wish to make it a hobby you may wish to buy special kit. Remember, experienced Orienteerers take only what they need.
The following list may be useful.
Wool or cotton shirt or vest
A lightweight waterproof cagoule
Long trousers/track suit bottoms to protect legs against thorns, nettles bracken, etc.
Cotton or wool socks
Strong walking/running shoes (spare laces)
A towel for when you return to base
A change of clothing and shoes, (you may be very wet and dirty).

KEEPING DIRECTION

To Orienteer successfully you must be able to keep going in the correct direction. This can be achieved in two ways:
I. USING A COMPASS. This will always tell you where NORTH is and by SETTING the compass you can find the direction in which you want to go. This is only useful in open country like moor land.
2. USING THE MAP. This is perhaps the best method since it is hard to get lost if you use your map correctly. The compass is only used to orientate the map, (point the map North). Once the map is

MAP & COMPASS

orientated always use known features to get you to your destination.
This involves planning your route in advance and in a number of
short, easily navigated "legs". If there is a leg with no easily identified
features, trust your compass.

GETTING LOST

Even the best navigators can sometimes get lost, however this is not
usually the disaster it may seem, since it is not too difficult to find
yourself again.

If you do get lost, **STOP AND THINK IT THROUGH.**

1. Don't panic – a cool head is needed.
2. Use the compass and orientate your map, try and trace your
   route.
3. Try to identify the ground around you and match it to the map. If
   you succeed, then you are no longer lost, plan your route
   onward.
4. If you cannot identify the ground, then try and re-trace your route
   to the previous Checkpoint.
5. If this also fails, set your compass and walk toward a road or other
   easily identifiable line on the ground then stay there until found.

The map is usually a large scale, (1:10000 or 1:15000 scale)
representation of the land, the information around the margin of the
map will tell you what the colours and symbols mean. Study your
map and identify everything.

Colours on the SPECIAL ORIENTEERING MAPS are used to
indicate the speed at which you can MOVE, not the TYPE OF
GROUND, for instance an area shaded dark green might indicate
ground which would be very difficult to move through, usually
known as "FIGHT" because you would have to fight your way
through it, whereas a light green area could indicate close woodland
or very rough ground through which you would walk.

White may indicate where you could run, perhaps grassland or very
mature woodland where the trees are well spaced.

MAP & COMPASS

THE ORIENTEERING MAP

The map is usually a large scale, (1:10000 or 1:15000 scale)
representation of the land, the information around the margin of the
map will tell you what the colours and symbols mean. Study your
map and identify everything.

Colours on the SPECIAL ORIENTEERING MAPS are used to
indicate the speed at which you can MOVE, not the TYPE OF
GROUND, for instance an area shaded dark green might indicate
ground which would be very difficult to move through, usually
known as "FIGHT" because you would have to fight your way
through it, whereas a light green area could indicate close woodland
or very rough ground through which you would walk.

White may indicate where you could run, perhaps grassland or very
mature woodland where the trees are well spaced.

Because of it's scale, the orienteering map shows great detail and will
accurately position depressions in the ground, holes and mounds,
earth walls and embankments which would normally not be shown.
Learn these new symbols as soon as you can, identifying them on the
ground could be the difference between being lost and finishing the
course. You must know exactly where you are at all times, you will
only achieve this by checking your map and always keeping it
orientated.

NAVIGATION TECHNIQUES, CHOOSING A ROUTE

When you chose your
route try and find the
best way of getting to
the first CONTROL by
selecting a good, easily
identifiable **ATTACK
POINT** like a track
junction and then plan
your route to this
ATTACK POINT

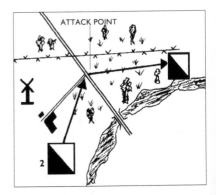

MAP & COMPASS

using easily followed features like tracks, fence lines, forest edges and streams. These features are known as **COLLECTION POINTS** because as you move around the course you can 'collect them'. Attempting to go directly to a **CONTROL** is not a good idea since they are easily missed.

Continue to plan your route round the course in the way described, chose a route that has as many **COLLECTION POINTS** on it as possible. Remember to periodically check your route with your compass.

Try to avoid bogs, dense forest and very steep hills, as these will either slow you down or prove to be impassable. It will often be better to go round an obstacle, even if the distance covered is greater, it may well be easier and faster. To help you decide, remember the following:

The Short Hard Route versus The Long Easy Route; swim across a lake or go around it: climb up and over a mountain or go round the valley. Remember to periodically check your route with your compass.

A good runner will typically take the following amounts of time to complete 400 metres over differing terrain:

a. Path – 2 mins.

b. Heath land – 4 mins

c. Open Forest – 6 mins

d. Thick Firs - 10 mins or more.

The Steep Short Route versus The Long Flat Route

When orienteering in hilly country you will often find that the course has a number of **CONTROLS** at opposite sides of a steep hill or valley. You must then make the decision whether or not it will be quicker to go over the top or to 'contour' round. To help you make your choice, a 25-metre height gain will be the equivalent to 100 metres on the flat.

AIMING OFF

Sometimes the **CONTROL** you are aiming for is on a linear feature such as a track or stream at right angles to your line of approach. This will mean that the **CONTROL** may be difficult to find if you aim straight for it since if you miss it, you will not know for sure whether it is North or South, for example.

Simply AIMING OFF to one side o the **CONTROL** can overcome

MAP & COMPASS

this problem, let us say the North, then when you reach the stream/track you will know that the **CONTROL** is to the South. This will cut down time spent searching for the **CONTROL.**

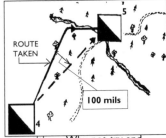

Many ACF Counties run their own competitions, some Districts organise 'finals'. The Regular Army organise the cadet forces annual orienteering competition. Why not try and arrange a 'challenge' at your Detachment, Cadets v. Adult Instructors. You may even win!

ON MAPS

The majority of maps in your Detachment will be Ordnance Survey 1:50000 scale.

Most Military Maps used onAnnual Camps, and at weekends on military land will be produced as1:25000 scale (some are 1:50000 so do check them)

You will find that the actual sheet size of some maps are large and difficult to handle. They require careful folding to leave exposed the area you are working on. Keep them in a plastic cover or a proper Map Case to keep them clean and dry.

Points to note

1. The marginal information is usually at the bottom of the map, and the information includes extra items, such as "No Go' and 'Out of Bounds' areas.

2. "No Go" areas are subject to frequent change in some areas, so ensure that your map is the latest issue before you start planning routes.

3. Remember that contour lines that appear to be further apart are NOT, it is a larger scale map than the 1:25000; don't be caught out and find you have a steep climb instead of a gentle slope.

4. Because of the larger scale, there will be far more information given; this may be rather confusing for a while.

Remember as always "practice makes perfect"

MAP & COMPASS
TERMS USED IN MAP READING

BEARING The angle, measured clockwise, that a line makes with a fixed zero line. It may be a True Bearing, measured from True North - a Magnetic Bearing measured with a compass from Magnetic North, or a Grid Bearing measured from Grid North.

COL (SADDLE): The low land or ridge, connecting two hilltops.

CONTOUR: An imaginary line on the surface of theground at the same height above mean sea level throughout its length. Contour line are drawn a map to show the shape of the ground.

CREST: The highest part of a hill or range of hills.

DETAIL: All the topographical information on a map.

ESCARPMENT: The steep hillside formed by a drop in land level, usually at the edge of a plateau.

GRADIENT: A slope described by a percentage, mostly used on roads to indicate a steep hill.

GRID: Lines drawn on the map forming squares as a basis for a system of map references.

LEFT or RIGHT BANK: The appropriate bank of a stream or river when facing DOWN stream.

LOCAL MAGNETIC ATTRACTION: Attraction of the compass needle due to presence of metal or magnetic iron ore. NOT to be confused with Magnetic Variation.

MAGNETIC VARIATION or DECLINATION: The angle between True North and Magnetic North.

MAGNETIC NORTH: The point in far north of Canada, to which a compass needle points.

MERIDIAN: A true north and south line.

ORIENTATING a MAP: Placing it so that its True North line points True

MAP & COMPASS

North (or Magnetic or Grid North line points to Magnetic or Grid North), also called "Setting the Map".

PLATEAU: A raised plain, usually quite flat, above a level of the land

PLOTTING: Transferring to a map bearings and other measurements.

RAY: A line drawn from the position of an observer to fix the direction of an object.

RE-ENTRANT: A shallow valley running into a hill, usually between two spurs, found where a stream runs off a hillside.

RE-SECTION: The process of finding a position by taking bearings on two identifiable points and plotting them on a map, also by fixing a position by observation of at least two previously fixed points.

SPOT HEIGHT: A point on a map whose height has been found by survey methods, identified on a map by a dot with figure against it.

SLOPES (Concave and Convex): Convex "bulges out", Concave "caves in".

SPUR: A hill feature or low ridge, running out from a hill or high ground, often found between two re-entrants.

TRIG POINT: A concrete pillar with a brass mounting used by Ordnance Survey for their survey work. The correct name is a Triangulation Point. Marked on a map by a small triangle with the height above sea level shown next to it.

TRUE NORTH: The direction of the North pole from that point.

VERTICAL INTERVAL (V.I.) The difference in height between two adjacent contours.

WATERSHED: The line, usually mountain range where waters divide to flow in different directions.

Deception using a large scale maps

A tip to remember when using large scale maps, contour lines close together indicate steep sloping ground, but due to the scale you may be misled as to the severity of the slope on the ground

---

MAP & COMPASS

GLOBAL POSITIONING SYSTEM

GPS is a simple concept involving a complex system of ground stations, satellites and receivers. The first GPS satellite was launched by the Americans for military use by the in 1989.

For the civilian user, GPS accuracy has improved greatly over the years. Refinements in technology and removal of selective availability by the US government mean that the average user can now pinpoint their position to within 20 yards. However, GPS is still only a navigational aid; it does not work indoors because a clear view of the sky is needed.

Now, 24 satellites (soon to be 30), orbit the earth every 12 hours from a distance of 11,000 miles, sending signals to a GPS receiver to compute velocity, time and position. The receiver must lock on to four of the satellite signals to compute a 3-D position fix for accurate reading.

A typical GPS device consists of a 12 channel parallel receiver, an antenna, internal memory, and a LCD screen. Many sizes and configurations are available. GPS planning programs contain so much information that is has become virtually impossible to get lost, with over a million waypoints (latitude/longitude coordinates) that translate into markers on a GPS unit. There are web – enabled packages that provide up to date weather and construction warnings along your route, hiking trails, hospitals and much more. Some of the more sophisticated programs include spoken and voice – activated commands for use with multimedia laptops and PDAs.

GPS technology is similar to the internet in that both were created by the United States Government for government use. In the near future, GPS will be part of our everyday life; un – manned vehicle navigation may be closer than we think!

If you are planning to buy a GPS, do some research before you buy; consumer GPS units are produced by several manufacturers, PC software manufacturers are integrating GPS support into many of their trip – planning and mapping programs.

MAP & COMPASS
PATHFINDER PROTRACTOR/ROMER
IMPROVE YOUR MAP READING TRAINING & SKILLS

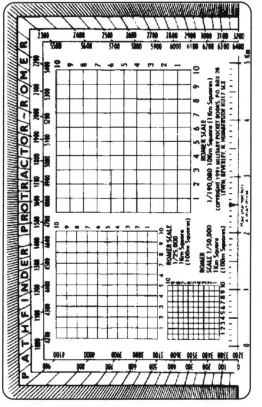

Available from Military Pocket Books Ltd
PO Box 28, Leven, Beverley E Yorks HU17 5LA

MAP & COMPASS

SELF TEST QUESTIONS.

1. Who produces maps for the Army.
2. Where will you find the Map Sheet number.
3. What is the Grid System used for.
4. Do you normally use a four or six figure reference to pin point a item.
5. On a map sheet where is North.
6. What is a Romer used for.
7. What is to Orientate a map for.
8. Where do you find Meridian lines on a Silva compass.
9. How can you set a map without a compass.
10. Name eight Cardinal Points.
11. How many North's are there.
12. What do you understand by the GMA.
13. What is Grid Convergence.
14. How many types of Bearings are there, and what are they called.
15. What is I.C.E, and what do you do about it.
16. Taking a bearing, which two arrows on a compass do you "line-up".
17. Taking a Grid bearing, what do you do with the compass needle.
18. Complete the sentence: "Grid to Mag Add, _ _ _ _ _".
19. What is the reverse of a forward bearing.
20. What use has a contour line, give a definition.
21. Concave and Convex slopes, which "bulges" out, which has good visibility.
22. Where are you most likely to find a re-entrant.
23. What type of ground will you find if contours are close together.
24. What is the name given to the height between contours.
25. It says; "one unit of measure on the map, equals X on the ground". Explain what is this about.
26. When finding North with a watch (that has hands) which hand is pointed to the sun.
27. Without a compass, how would you find North on a clear night.
28. You are to make out a Route Card, give the headings required to do so.
29. When do you use a Master Map.
30. When Orienteering, why do you "Aim Off
31. What is the scale of most MILITARY maps you will be given to use on military training areas,.

Chapter 6

SKILL AT ARMS

SAFETY RULES FOR HANDLING WEAPONS OF ANY TYPE AT ALL TIMES

1. Whenever you pick up a weapon or have a weapon handed to you **ALWAYS** carry out the **SAFETY PRECAUTIONS**, whether it is your own or someone elses, **ALWAYS** examine it to ensure that it is **NOT** loaded.

2. **NEVER** point a weapon at anyone - even in fun.

3. **ALWAYS** handle a weapon so that it points in a **SAFE** direction, so that there is no danger if a round is accidentally fired.

4. **NEVER** rest the muzzle of a loaded weapon, or a weapon 'made safe' against your body. Similarly, do not hold a weapon with your hand or hands placed over the muzzle.

5. Weapons will **NEVER** be carried in **VEHICLES** either loaded or in a "made safe" state.

6. **YOU** will **NOT** fire any weapon until such time as you have been fully trained, exercised and tested to be capable of safely handling the weapon.

7. When handing over a weapon to someone else, **SHOW/ PROVE** to them first that it is in a **SAFE** and in an **UNLOADED STATE**.

8. When anyone hands a weapon to you - **NO MATTER WHO THEY ARE - INSIST THAT FIRST, THEY SHOW/PROVE IT.**

9. **ALWAYS WEAR HEARING PROTECTION WHERE LIVE OR BLANK FIRING IS TAKING PLACE.**

SKILL AT ARMS

THE AIR RIFLE

GENERAL INTRODUCTION

Skill at Arms and Shooting is perhaps the activity that is most popular with the Cadet. A great amount of skill is required for this vast subject with great competitive interest generated in this sport, both as an individual and a team member .

This Chapter is to get you started in Skill at Arms. Once you have mastered this initial training you will then be ready to progress on to instruction with the L98 GP Cadet Rifle.

It is not possible to cover the subject of Skill at Arms and Shooting in this Pocket Book, but another Pocket Book The Cadet Forces Skill At Arms and Shooting covers the whole subject.

The air rifle is the ideal weapon for all Cadets as an introduction to shooting, without undue strain or fear from recoil and noise until you have mastered the principles of marksmanship and have been instructed in the safe handling of a weapon.

Like any other weapon an air rifle must be inspected to ensure it is unloaded. To do this the rifle must be broken open.

SAFETY

An Air Rifle is just as dangerous as any other weapon and can cause serious wounds if handled without due care.

Safe handling is a question of good habits and for this reason air rifles must be handled in accordance with the normal rules for handling weapons.

SKILL AT ARMS

SAFE HANDLING

To make a safety inspection of an air rifle it must be **BROKEN OPEN.**

1. Pick up the air rifle, point the muzzle in a safe direction, grasp the small of the butt firmly with the RIGHT hand, keeping the fingers clear of the trigger and tuck the remainder of the butt under your forearm. Grasp the barrel with the LEFT hand as near as is comfortable towards the foresight block.

2. Press firmly and sharply down with the LEFT hand and simultaneously force upwards with the RIGHT hand. The rifle should now break open so that the breech can be inspected.

3. Look into the breech and ensure no pellet is loaded: look through the bore and ensure it is clear.

4. When satisfied that the rifle is unloaded, close the rifle keeping the muzzle pointed in a safe direction.

Note: It is unnecessary to fully cock the action to inspect the rifle: furthermore it is **very harmful to the piston head to cock and release the action unless a pellet is to be fired.**

5. Some new Cadets have difficulty in cocking the action in the lying position. It may therefore be necessary to provide and 'assistant' to do this for you. The assistant will kneel on one knee on the right hand side of the firer (left hand side for left hand firers), take the rifle from the firer and, keeping the muzzle pointed in the direction of the target, break it open, cock the action, bring the barrel up to the for inspection position and hand the rifle back to the firer for them to load.

AIR RIFLE BROKEN OPEN

SKILL AT ARMS

LOADING THE AIR RIFLE PELLET

AIR RIFLES – A NOTE OF CAUTION

If you have access to an air rifle outside the Cadet Force, make sure that you are responsible and careful about where you use it. Broken windows, injured wild life and domestic pets are serious enough, but there have been instances involving injury to people; in one case, a young boy lost the sight in one eye. **DO NOT TAKE RISKS – MAKE SURE YOU ARE IN A SAFE AREA.**

PERSONAL DECLARATION

It is an important part of Rifle Range Safety Rules and Procedures that **ALL PERSONNEL** when leaving the range area for any reason will make a Personal Declaration to the Officer in Charge of the Range or someone deputised by them.

You will find reference to this declaration in other parts of your Pocket Book, it cannot be repeated too often, it must become 'Second Nature'.

How it is conducted: usually you will be fallen in as a squad at Open Order. An Officer or Adult Instructor will make a statement concerning the importance of the Declaration, and what to do if you find a round in your possession later.

You will then find that an Officer or Adult Instructor will stand in front of each of you in turn; you will then make the following declaration:

SKILL AT ARMS

"I have no live rounds or empty cases in my possession, Sir/Maam"
You may be asked to turn out your pockets and/or show that your
pouches are empty by having them inspected.

All staff - Officers and Instructors will make the same declaration to the
Range Officer before leaving the Range. These Range Safety Procedures
are strictly observed and anyone who ignores them is always severely
dealt with, no matter what rank they are.

SHOOTING STANDARDS

Your Rifle shooting towards your APC is based on your ability to fire
a 'Group', this will be fully explained as your training progresses.
Firing with an Air Rifle at 5.5 m (6 yards) your scores to be achieved
against the Group sizes are as below.

Group Size	13mm	19mm	25mm	32mm
Score	25	20	15	10

ARMY CADET FORCE

INSPIRE - TO ACHIEVE

**PERSONAL RECORD
OF TRAINING,
ACHIEVEMENTS
& CONDUCT**

If this book is found please hand it to
the Cadet named inside or to the ACF
Detachment or any Police Station.

'Switched on' Detachment
Commanders ensure that
all their Cadets have a
copy of this
'Little Green Book'.
If your Detachment
Commander is not
switched on, help
yourself.
Log on to the website
below for full details.

**"A SECURE ORDER" SITE
www.milpkbk.co.uk**

INTRODUCTION TO THE GP RIFLE

The L98. A1 CADET GP RIFLE - to give its full name - is the first rifle ever to be designed specifically for the Cadet Forces in the UK. It's appearance is almost identical with the Regular Army's SA80 Rifle.

The SA80 is has a flash eliminator, which the Cadet Rifle does not have, and of course when the SA80 is fitted with the SUSAT SIGHT, it looks very different from the CADET GP RIFLE

GENERAL DESCRIPTION OF THE 5.56mm CADET GENERAL PURPOSE RIFLE.

The GP Rifle is a magazine fed, bolt operated, single shot weapon, which has been modelled on the British Army 5.56 (SA80 Rifle).
It **MUST** be fired from the RIGHT shoulder.
The magazine holds 30 rounds. The rifle is easy to learn and use, good to handle and fire, and is very accurate.
The "kick" or recoil is light, making it ideal for all trained cadets to handle and shoot with.

SKILL AT ARMS

SAFETY PRECAUTIONS.

As with all SKILL at ARMS training the first thing you must learn are the -

NORMAL SAFETY PRECAUTIONS. (NSP)

They will always be carried out at the beginning and end of every lesson, practice or range period, and immediately on returning from a patrol or exercise or duty, and when handing the weapon over to anyone.

To carry out the **SAFETY PRECAUTIONS** with the L98. A1 CADET GP RIFLE the **LOW PORT POSITION** is adopted as shown in the illustration on the left.

1.Hold by PISTOL GRIP, forefinger outside the TRIGGER GUARD.

Point MUZZLE upwards and rest the butt on waist belt or right pouch.Tilt weapon to the right

THIS IS THE POSITION ADOPTED TO CARRY OUT THE FULL ROUTINE OF SAFETY PRECAUTIONS

2. Make sure that theSAFETY CATCH is at SAFE. (S).

3. Cock the RIFLE by gripping the COCKING HANDLE with thumb and forefinger of right hand, now pull AND HOLD IT FULLY TO THE REAR.

4. Pass your LEFT hand under the BUTT,
depress HOLDING OPEN CATCH with fingers of LEFT hand, easing COCKING HANDLE forward until catch stops its forward movement of the carrier.

When done place LEFT hand underneath HAND GUARD, and return RIGHT hand to hold RIFLE by PISTOL GRIP.

NOTE: When LEFT hand is applying HOLDING OPEN CATCH the RIFLE is being held with BUTT against your Waist Belt by pulling back on COCKING HANDLE with the fingers of RIGHT hand, with thumb of RIGHT hand hooked round rear of CARRYING HANDLE.

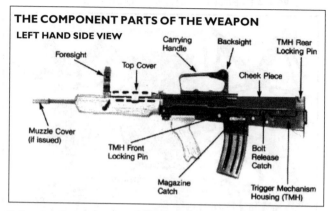

THE COMPONENT PARTS OF THE WEAPON
LEFT HAND SIDE VIEW

Carrying Handle · Backsight · TMH Rear Locking Pin · Foresight · Top Cover · Cheek Piece · Muzzle Cover (if issued) · TMH Front Locking Pin · Bolt Release Catch · Magazine Catch · Trigger Mechanism Housing (TMH)

5. For the rifle to be inspected, push it away from your body, horizontal to the ground and tilting to the left, so as the breech can be inspected.

After it has been inspected adopt the LOW PORT POSITION.

6. On the command "EASE SPRINGS":-

(a) Operate the BOLT RELEASE CATCH with your left hand, letting the working part go forward.

(b) Put SAFETY CATCH to FIRE (F) with RIGHT forefinger

(c) Operate the TRIGGER.

(d) Put the SAFETY CATCH to (S) using left thumb.

(e) Close the DUST COVER with RIGHT hand, folding up and back in its slot.

(f) Put RIFLE in FRONT SLUNG position or if SLING not fitted, Ground arms, rifle laid on its left side - COCKING HANDLE uppermost.

(g) Unfasten pouches and remove MAGAZINES and contents for inspection.

When the inspection has been completed, you put the magazines back in your pouches, FASTEN YOUR POUCHES, pick up your rifle and adopt LOW PORT position.

THE 90 PATTERN INFANTRY EQUIPMENT

A. Rucksack (long or short)
B. PouchSide (rucksack)
C. Waist Belt (all sizes)
D. Main Yoke
E. Additional Yoke (side pouches)
F. Additional YokeStrap (side pouches)
G. Respirator Haversack.

H. Bayonet Frog
I. Left Ammo Pouch
J. Water Bottle Carrier
K. Right Ammo Pouch
L. Utility Pouch
M. ETH Carrier
N. Utility Strap

Belt Order. This consists of, the waist belt, main yoke, entrenching tool (ETH), bayonet frog, water bottle carrier, ammunition pouches, respirator haversack, and if room on belt, the utility pouch.

This order is used for general training, skill at arms, and limited periods in the field. Note it should always be worn when firing on the range.

SKILL AT ARMS

COMPONENT PARTS OF THE WEAPON

RIGHT HAND SIDE VIEW

Ejection Opening
Backsight
Cocking Handle
Dust Cover
Hand Guard
Holding Open Catch
Safety Catch

SELF TEST QUESTIONS

1. Safety Handling of weapons applies to which weapon?
2. Can weapons be carried in a vehicle either loaded or in a made safe state?
3. When will you be alowed to fire a weapon?
4. When do you 'show or prove' a wepon yo someone and why?
5. IF ANYBODY hands a weapon to you, what do you first insist they do?
6. If you fire a 19mm group what would be your score?
7. When is an Air Rifle 'broken open' ?
8. When inspecting why don't you fully 'cock' the Air Rifle?
9. Why do some Cadets have difficulty in cocking the action of the Air Rifle and how is this overcome?
10. Should you have access to an Air Rifle outside your Cadet activity you will be responsible for what?
11. What is a'Personal Declaration" and why and when is it used?
12. How many rounds does the GP Rifle magazine hold.
13. What is the size of the round fired in the L98 A1 GP Rifle?
14. From which shoulder must you fire the GP Rifle from?
15. What reason do you adopt the LOW PORT POSITION.
16. What is the procedure on the command 'Ease Springs' ?
17. Give a list of the component parts of the GP Rifle?
18. Complete the saying; "It's better to be safe than ....

SKILL AT ARMS

Shooting in the Cadet Force 1913.

The provision of weapons for cadet use has often presented problems. The Volunteer Regulations of 1863 authorised the loan of rifles to cadets up to only ten per cent of unit strength. There is no doubt however that cadet units attached to volunteer corps would be able to make use of the additional weapons available.

From 1893, arms were issued to the full strength of a cadet unit, in most cases however these were drill purpose weapons unsuitable for firing. There was thus a continued need for a small number of sound weapons to be retained for range work, again often borrowed from local volunteer units.

At an early stage, the cadet movement acquired from the Volunteer Force a taste for competition shooting, an interest which was both encouraged and organised by the formation of the National Rifle Association.

From 1861, public school units had already competed annually for the Ashburton Shield, now a variety of other trophies appeared and cadets became a recog-nised part of the shooting scene.

The illustration depicts cadets of the Civil Service Rifles, in their distinctive light grey uniforms, at a firing point in 1913. This is obviously competition shooting, a role in which the cadets of the Civil Service Rifles had a fine record. Lee Metford rifles are being used.

Modern cadets use the musketry badges which were worn by the Victorian Volunteer Force before 1887 (i.e.) a single horizontal rifle (second class) with star or crown above the rifle to denote further proficiency. After 1887 the volunteers wore crossed rifles for marksmanship, a practice shared by the cadets of the time.

Available from: Direct from the Publishers:
Military Pocket Books Ltd, PO Box 28, Leven, East Yorks.
HU17 5LX - Tel/Fax: 01964 542828

www.milpkbk.co.uk
"A SECURE ORDER" SITE

Chapter 7

THE DUKE OF EDINBURGH'S AWARD

INTRODUCTION.

The Army Cadet Force was one of the organisations that took part in the Pilot Scheme for this award. Perhaps not surprising as the Duke of Edinburgh was then and still is the Colonel-in-Chief of the Army Cadet Force.

To gain the award is a personal achievement that takes self discipline. The Duke of Edinburgh said that anyone who was determined to gain the award would have to have 'STICKABILITY' to see it through all the way. It is an excellent scheme; many thousands of young people throughout the Commonwealth take part.

THE MAIN PRINCIPLES

1. THE AWARD SCHEME IS ENTIRELY VOLUNTARY.
2. THE AGES ARE FROM 14 TO 25 YEARS OLD.
3. THE AWARD SCHEME HAS FOUR COMPULSORY SECTIONS:

SERVICE - EXPEDITION - SKILLS - PHYSICAL RECREATION

There are three levels of the Award:

BRONZE	SILVER	GOLD

4. The minimum time for completing each level is

Bronze	Silver	Gold
6 MONTHS.	12 MONTHS (6 MONTHS via Bronze)	18 MONTHS (12 MONTHS via Silver)

THE CHALLENGE

Taking part in the Award Scheme it is entirely voluntary at each level. It is an individual effort on your part, your Detachment does not enter a "team", nor are you expected to follow exactly the same elements as other Cadets. You choose what you would like to do and then go for it.

YOUR CONTACT

Find out who is your Detachment or Area/Company Duke of Edinburgh's Award Officer and make contact to enrol in the Scheme.

THE DUKE OF EDINBURGH'S AWARD

There will also be a County Duke of Edinburgh's Award Officer.
You will have to buy your **Entrance Pack** which will include your
Record Book. This is your first commitment to the scheme - your
personal stake in it.
Help will be given to you along the way, but **it has to be your effort.**
As you progress, you will be expected to choose, design and develop
your own programme from the many options available.

ADVANTAGES

The scheme adds an extra dimension, excitement and purpose to
your Cadet career and beyond to your 25th birthday.
The award will bring you into close contact with many other young
people and you will no doubt develop lasting friendships.
The self confidence, awareness, determination and enthusiasm
displayed by successful participants has given Award holders a
deserved good reputation, giving you a distinct advantage when
embarking on you career. Potential employers recognise the scheme
and its objectives and see it as evidence that you have
STICKABILITY.

YOUR OPPORTUNITY

As a cadet you have the advantage to take part in the scheme, whilst
continuing with your cadet career.
This has been made possible by many of the subjects within the APC
Syllabus fitting in with the requirements of the scheme.

Once you have completed your ONE STAR training and are 14 years
old, if you decide to enrol in the scheme you can, with some extra effort,
gain the BRONZE Award by completing APC 2 Star First Aid,
Expedition Training, Shooting/Skill at Arms and Physical Recreation

It must be stressed that it is not compulsory or mandatory for you
to only count ACF related activities towards your DofE award, nor is
the list of activities mentioned in the chart the only ones accepted,
there are a great many more that your Award Leader will be able to tell
you about.
However, any aspect of ACF activity can with some help and
imagination on the part of your instructors, working with the Award
Leader, be brought into a D of E Award programme; this is most likely

THE DUKE OF EDINBURGH'S AWARD

to be the case in respect of the Expedition option in the Silver and Gold Awards.

Your Award Leader will have several leaflets and books that you will be able to read. It is advisable that you do just that before making up your mind to take up the challenge.

All that we can tell you is that if you do join the Award Scheme, and see it through all the way, you will never regret it.

HOW ACF TRAINING MIGHT COUNT TOWARDS THE DUKE OF EDINBURGH'S AWARD

BRONZE AWARD

(normally about APC 2 Star level)

TIME SCALES OF INVOLVEMENT

Service	Skills	Physical Recreation	Expeditions
3 months	3 months	3 months	Plan, prepare for and undertake a 2 day venture
An additional 3 months must be undertaken in any one of these sections			

SERVICE SECTION

Suggestion:

Pass 2 Star First Aid and give practical service for the remaining period. Older Cadets commencing Bronze while undertaking 3 star or higher level, may use Service to the ACF

EXPEDITION SECTION

Suggestion:

To have been trained and passed APC TWO STAR Expedition Training (but see note below). You must have been on at least one practice expedition.

To have learned Map and Compass (Including Route Cards).

The expedition must have a purpose and you will be required to produce a report (oral or written) in some detail of a venture that you have taken part in. This will include sketches, Route Cards, diagrams and how you coped with the challenge.

Note: A Qualifying Venture complying with all the conditions of the Bronze Expedition, will automatically count as passing Expedition Training at 2 star. You may opt to undertake an EXPLORATION, requiring 5 hours journeying, the remainder of the time being spent on work towards your purpose.

THE DUKE OF EDINBURGH'S AWARD

SKILLS SECTION
Suggestion:
This requires you to take up an approved activity from the Duke of Edinburgh's Award Handbook.

You will need to talk to your Award Leader, to help you decide what you are to do. You will be required to take a keen interest in this and study it in some depth, during which time you will become quite an expert in your own right.

Note: Should you wish to take up a skill not listed, then it can be submitted by your DofE Officer through the proper channels for approval. You must wait for approval before proceeding. This applies to all levels of the Award Scheme.

As examples, some of the Military activities are: Skill at Arms & Shooting, Drill, Drumming, Bugling, Forces Insignia, Bands, Marksmanship, Signalling, Model Soldiers etc.

An assessor, who will be a recognised expert in the activity will be appointed to see you through the skill. You will be given an "ideas list" of things you could do to progress in the activity, and you will agree with your assessor how far you can progress in the time allowed (3 or 6 months depending on choice). If you are new to the Skill you will probably start at the beginning.

If you have already had some experience in the Skill, you will start from a point where you will be extending your knowledge. At the end of the period you will be assessed on how well you have done.

PHYSICAL RECREATION
Suggestion:
To choose an activity from the list in the Duke of Edinburgh's Award Handbook and participate for a minimum period. Again you will discuss this with your Award Leader. If there are standards set by the governing body of the activity, you will be expected to try for these.

Note: The Award requires regular participation over 3 or 6 months, which significantly exceeds the minimum period required by the APC. You will need to consider this when choosing your Physical Recreation.

RESIDENTIAL PROJECT
No requirement at Bronze

THE DUKE OF EDINBURGH'S AWARD

SILVER AWARD
(normally about APC 4 Star level)

TIME SCALES FOR INVOLVEMENT

Service	Skills	Physical Recreation	Expeditions
6 months	One Section for 6 months and the other Section for 3 months		Plan, prepare for and undertake a 3 day venture
Direct Entrants must undertake an extra 6 months in either the Service or the longer (Skills or Physical Recreation) Section			

SERVICE SECTION
Suggestion:
You may use your 'Service' in the ACF to qualify for the Silver Award. It is suggested that you work through the following list. If you are opting to spend 12 months on Service (direct entrants), or if you have already completed some of the items, you may need to undertake additional activities from the ideas list.
1. Attend and perform satisfactorily at a Junior Cadet Instructors Cadre
2. Successfully complete the THREE STAR syllabus for the Cadet and the Community
3. Know the history of the ACF, and its organisation in your own detachment, area and county, plus the history of the Regiment/Corps to which you are badged. This must be to a higher standard than required by APC at 2 Star.
4. The total period of involvement in these activities must be at least 6 months and may be 12 months

ALTERNATIVE OPTIONS
1. To gain a recognised adult First Aid qualification from a Voluntary Aid Society, (3 and 4 star First Aid), and give practical service e.g. first aid cover on Detachment Training evenings or camps, training for first aid competitions etc.
2. The Cadet and Community syllabus at 3 and/or 4 star could also be used to count towards Service provided the time scales for the Award are adhered to.
3. Obtain the Community Sports Leaders Award (CSLA) -which also counts for 4 star Cadet and the Community.

THE DUKE OF EDINBURGH'S AWARD

EXPEDITION SECTION

Requirement:
4 Star Expedition standard is required at this level (48 km with two nights out) OR you have the option of undertaking an exploration of 2 nights out, PLUS a project to be carried out, to include 10 hours journeying. Your expedition can be on foot, by canoe, boat, bicycle (or horse). APC 3 star expedition training could be used as a practice for the Silver expedition.

SKILLS SECTION

Requirement:
As for the Bronze Award you must participate in your chosen Skill for a minimum of 3 or 6 months depending on choice
It you are starting the Award for the first time at Silver, then you may opt to follow your Skill for 12 months.
The conditions are the same as for Bronze, but if you are following the same Skill, you will be expected to work further through the ideas list, taking up where you left off. You may, of course, choose a different Skill. Once again you will agree your goals with your assessor.

PHYSICAL RECREATION SECTION

Requirement:
Choose an activity from the Duke of Edinburgh's Award Handbook as at Bronze. It may be the same activity or a different one. It is up to you. Remember that 3, 6 or possibly 12 months will have to be spent on the activity, and you will be expected to try for standards if appropriate.

RESIDENTIAL PROJECT

No requirement at Silver.

THE DUKE OF EDINBURGH'S AWARD

GOLD AWARD
(normally post APC level)

Service	Skills Physical Recreation	Expeditions
12 months	One Section for 12 months and the other Section for 6 months	Plan, prepare for and undertake a 4 day venture
Direct Entrants must undertake an additional 6 months in either the Service or the longer (Skills or Physical Recreation) Section		
Residential Project Undertake a shared activity in a residential setting away from home for 5 days and 4 nights.		

SERVICE SECTION
Suggestion:
You are able to use your cadet 'service' as a qualification at this level, by working through the list. If you have not yet completed items from the list shown for Silver, you should do those first.

1. Attend and perform satisfactorily at the Senior Cadet Instructors' Cadre
2. Carry out tasks of special responsibility or give some specific service to your detachment, e.g. making training aids, organising fund raising events, be responsible for training a specific group of cadets.
3. Hold at least the rank of Corporal for not less than 12 months or if as a Cadet where there is no NCO vacancy, be a 3 Star cadet
4. The period of training and practical service will be at least 12 months, and may be 18 months (direct entrants)

ALTERNATIVE OPTIONS (If not taken up at Silver)

1. To gain a recognised adult First Aid qualification from a Voluntary Aid Society, (4 star First Aid), and give practical service.
2. The Cadet and Community syllabus at 3 and/or 4 star.
3. Obtain the Community Sports Leaders Award (CSLA)

EXPEDITION SECTION
Requirement:
Expeditions at this level are only permitted to take place in specified areas of the country providing suitable "wild country". The expedition may be linked to an exercise to be carried out en-route or some adventurous project.

THE DUKE OF EDINBURGH'S AWARD

As at Silver you may opt for an exploration, and this also requires 10 hours of journeying, the rest of the time being taken up with your project or purpose At Gold level only there is the option of "Other Adventurous Projects" when the venture you want to undertake departs from the normal conditions for an expedition or exploration.

A great deal of preparation is required to ensure correct training is carried out and equipment checked and you have had some practical experience, including at least one practice journey.

The expedition is very much a **team effort,** practising Leadership, Map Reading, Campcraft and First Aid Skills.

SKILLS SECTION - Requirement:

As for the other Awards, you will choose a Skill and agree goals with your assessor, using the ideas list and participate for 6, 12 or 18 months depending on choice. If you have followed the same Skill at Bronze and Silver you may find difficulty in progressing much further. If this is the case you should consider trying a new Skill.

PHYSICAL RECREATION SECTION - Requirement:

Choose an activity from the Duke of Edinburgh's Award Handbook as at Bronze and Silver. Remember that 6, 12 or possibly 18 months will have to be spent on the activity, and be expected to try for standards where necessary.

RESIDENTIAL PROJECT - Requirement:

The intention is for you to undertake a project with a group, most of whom will not be your usual companions. The project should be carried out over a 5 day and four night period. Attendance at many of the normal cadet activities can qualify you for this as long as you are spending time mainly with people you would not normally spend time with.

Annual Camp of 5 days or more, *provided you are separated from your Detachment friends, including during "off-duty" times.*

The Cadet Leadership Course at Frimley and elsewhere. Any of the various Canadian Challenge Courses. MoD Courses or attachments, TA Camps or courses.

In very special circumstances you may be able to carry out your Project over a series of weekends, if you are unable to have a week off. Your Award leader will advise you.

CHART SHOWING HOW ACF ACTIVITIES CAN COUNT TOWARDS YOUR DofE AWARD

	SERVICE	EXPEDITION (ON FOOT)	SKILL	PHYSICAL RECREATION	RESIDENTIAL PROJECT
BRONZE	APC 2 Star First Aid	2 star Expedition Training using DofE conditions	Choose from: Ceremonial Drill Drumming Bugling Signals Shooting Marksman Military Band Piping Map Making Lecturing/Public Speaking Model Soldiers War Games Model Construction Goals to be negotiated with assessor.	Choose from: Team Games Individual Sports Physical Achievement and Fitness Training Other Activities as listed in the Handbook Period of involvement in accordance with individual choice.	No requirement
SILVER	Service to the ACF or APC 3 &/or 4 Star Cadet and the community or APC 3 and 4 Star First Aid, plus practical First Aid or CSAL	3 star Expedition Training (may be used as a Practice Expedition for Silver) and 4 star Expedition Training, or Exploration - could count as a 3 star Expedition			No requirement
GOLD	Service to the ACF or APC 3 and/or 4 star Cadet & Community, or APC 3 and 4 star First Aid (if not used at Silver), or CLSA (if not used at Silver)	Post 4 star training NOTE: Expeditions can also be done by other means, e.g. horseback, sailing, etc			Attendance at: Annual Camp Cadet Leadership Courses. Senior Cadet Course. Master Cadet and MOD Courses. TA Attachments Etc.

THE DUKE OF EDINBURGH'S AWARD
THE PROCESS TO BE FOLLOWED FOR THE SECTIONS OF THE AWARD
SERVICE SECTION

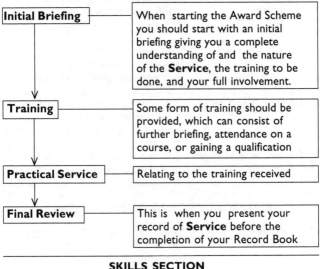

Initial Briefing	When starting the Award Scheme you should start with an initial briefing giving you a complete understanding of and the nature of the **Service**, the training to be done, and your full involvement.
Training	Some form of training should be provided, which can consist of further briefing, attendance on a course, or gaining a qualification
Practical Service	Relating to the training received
Final Review	This is when you present your record of **Service** before the completion of your Record Book

SKILLS SECTION

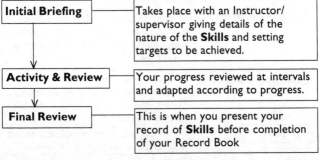

Initial Briefing	Takes place with an Instructor/supervisor giving details of the nature of the **Skills** and setting targets to be achieved.
Activity & Review	Your progress reviewed at intervals and adapted according to progress.
Final Review	This is when you present your record of **Skills** before completion of your Record Book

THE DUKE OF EDINBURGH'S AWARD

EXPEDITION SECTION

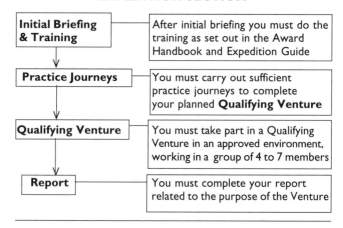

Initial Briefing & Training	After initial briefing you must do the training as set out in the Award Handbook and Expedition Guide
Practice Journeys	You must carry out sufficient practice journeys to complete your planned **Qualifying Venture**
Qualifying Venture	You must take part in a Qualifying Venture in an approved environment, working in a group of 4 to 7 members
Report	You must complete your report related to the purpose of the Venture

PHYSICAL RECREATION SECTION

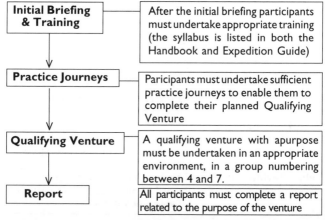

Initial Briefing & Training	After the initial briefing participants must undertake appropriate training (the syllabus is listed in both the Handbook and Expedition Guide)
Practice Journeys	Paricipants must undertake sufficient practice journeys to enable them to complete their planned Qualifying Venture
Qualifying Venture	A qualifying venture with apurpose must be undertaken in an appropriate environment, in a group numbering between 4 and 7.
Report	All participants must complete a report related to the purpose of the venture

THE DUKE OF EDINBURGH'S AWARD

SPORTS AND PHYSICAL FITNESS

As a young person it is important to be as physically fit as you can. It will assist you in your Cadet career, keep you mentally alert and increase your stamina.

Sport and fitness is part of your training, give it as much effort as any other training you do. Participate in Detachment, Company and County sporting events it is part of your commitment to the Cadets. You may not attain a winner's medal, but any Cadet who is prepared to try is a winner.

TEAM SPIRIT

Individual sports, swimming for example, requires encouragement, self-discipline and constant practice. An individual swimmer relies on team spirit to succeed; the coach, fellow swimmers, family support are all involved in the success of an individual.

Taking part in sport or physical training as part of a team is the same. Sometimes a team has to help an individual to shine in order to win the game – TEAM SPIRIT!

THE SPORTS PERSON
A SPORTSPERSON IS ONE WHO:-
PLAYS THE GAME FOR THE GAMES SAKE.
PLAYS FOR THE TEAM AND NOT FOR THEM
SELVES. IS A GOOD WINNER AND GOOD
LOSER;
I.E; MODEST IN VICTORY AND GENEROUS IN
DEFEAT.
ACCEPTS ALL DECISIONS IN A PROPER SPIRIT.
IS CHIVALROUS TOWARDS A DEFEATED
OPPONENT.
IS UNSELFISH AND ALWAYS READY TO HELP
OTHERS TO BECOME PROFICIENT.
AS A SPECTATOR APPLAUDS GOOD PLAY ON
BOTH SIDES.
NEVER CHALLENGES UMPIRES, JUDGES OR
REFEREES - NO MATTER WHAT THE DECISION

THE DUKE OF EDINBURGH'S AWARD

ALWAYS LOOK FOR OPPORTUNITIES TO PLAY ENERGETIC GAMES - ESPECIALLY AT CAMP

If you work hard at your exercises - play games hard and enter into sport with a will and the right spirit — you will not have any fitness problems.
The Army Sports Control Board governs all sporting activities in the Army. Over 50 years ago they drew up their definition of a **SportsPerson**. (See the previous page)

It is just as relevant today, and as difficult to follow, but keep it in mind whenever taking part in sports.

YOUR HEALTH

Unless you are fit and have the stamina to carry out the different types of training throughout your Cadet career, your Instructors will have to make a decision NOT to allow you to take part in some of the activities or exercises because of the risk of you becoming a casualty through being unfit.

Food

Many of us are 'Food Junkies', eating too much sugar, fat and starch - or just eating too much! If you decide to increase your stamina and get your muscles working for you rather than against you, it may well be that your desire to 'binge' disappears!

Medical

Those of you with medical conditions should always check with their Doctor to ensure that they can take part in sports and physical activities. It is perhaps even more important for you to keep fit. As a passing note, some of our top athletes have Diabetes and look what they have attained.
N.B. Make sure that your Adult Instructors and Officers are aware of your medical condition.

THE DUKE OF EDINBURGH'S AWARD

EXERCISE DISCIPLINE

You do not need to join a Health Club or build a 'Home Gym' in your
bedroom, just practice some of the simple
exercises you know already – DAILY. Sit – Ups,
Press Ups, Running on the Spot, Arm Swinging
etc. Do not forget the two-mile speed walk or
run twice a week.

Use the Duke of Edinburgh's Award Fitness Tests
as the measure of your ability.

The Fitness Feeling

Once you have attained a good level of fitness
you will feel great! Alert and ready to take part in other activities. All
you need now is the SELF DISCIPLINE to keep it up.

A WORD OF CAUTION

Remember that you are ONLY INSURED WHEN TAKING PART IN
OFFICIALLY RECOGNISED CADET EVENTS AND ACTIVITIES,
SUPERVISED BY QUALIFIED COACHES AND/OR INSTRUCTORS.

For example, if you have challenged another Detachment to a game of
football, get it made 'official', that way if anyone is injured or property
damaged, it will be covered by insurance.

**RAFTING - COULD
THIS COUNT
AS PART OF AN
EXPEDITION?**

**If you need any help or
information for your
Duke of Edinburgh's Award,
get in touch with your
County D of E Award Officer**

WHERE? WHAT'S

HIS / HER NAME?

THE DUKE OF EDINBURGH'S AWARD

PHYSICAL ACHIEVEMENT TESTS

These may be used to qualify in the physical Recreation Sction of the D of E Award.

Points required to qualify for your APC Star Grades

Basic - 12 points   **One Star - 18 points.**

Two Star - 24 points.   **Three Star - 30 points.**

NOTE: For the Award you are required to undertake all SEVEN events and select SIX to count. A reasonable rest is allowed between each event. Tests may be spread over TWO days.

SCORING MALE CADETS Points Scored					
Events	**1**	**2**	**3**	**4**	**5**
Speed Test Time (secs)	28	26	25	24	23
Ball Speed Bounce Catches 30secs	30	35	40	45	50
Trunk Curl Test Number in minute	20	28	34	40	45
Bailey Bridge Number in 30 secs	12	17	19	21	22
Push-Up hand/foot version No in 1min	15	23	27	34	50
or Push-Up hand/knee moderated version. Number in minute	25	37	44	58	68
Single Leg Squat Thrust. No in 30 secs	40	60	70	76	82
Run Time (mins & secs)	4.20	4.00	3.40	3.20	3.10

NOTE: Score may be counted for either Push-Ups hand/foot version, or Push-ups hand/knee moderated version but not both.

THE DUKE OF EDINBURGH'S AWARD

SCORING FOR FEMALE CADETS
Points Scored

Events	1	2	3	4	5
Speed Test Time (secs)	32	28	27	26	25
Ball Speed Bounce. Catches in 30 secs	20	26	32	36	38
Trunk Curl Test. Number in 1 minute	10	20	28	32	36
Bailey Bridge Number in 30 secs	12	16	18	20	22
Push-Ups hand/foot version. No in 1 min	8	14	18	24	30
or Push-Up hand/knee moderated version. Number in 1 minute	14	24	28	40	45
Single Leg Squat Thrust. No in 30 secs	35	50	65	72	80
Run Time (minutes and seconds)	4.50	4.30	4.10	3.50	3.40

Note: Scores may be counted for either Push-ups hand/foot version or Push-Up hand knee moderated version, **but not both.**

Physical Achievement Programme

Points required for Star Awards.

The MINIMUM number of points for you to qualify at each level of this subject are set out in the chart below.

Training Level	Participation	Performance	Additional Pts	Pass Qual
Basic Training	6	3	3	12
One Star	10	4	4	18
Two Star	12	6	6	24
Three Star	12	6	12	30

Note: Points are awarded for *participation* on a basis of 1 point for each half-hour of training. No more than two participation points may be gained in any one week.

Additional points may be gained by either further participation or by improved performance

THE DUKE OF EDINBURGH'S AWARD

DESCRIPTION AND CONDITIONS OF TESTS

Speed Test: Cross **TEN** times between two lines marked on ground or floor NINE metres apart. Each line crossed or touched by one foot.

Stamina Run

Twenty laps of a regular circuit 12 metres by 8 metres, each corner marked by a small object. The score is determined by the time in which this exercise is completed.

Ball Speed Bounce

Using a Netball or a size 5 Football, stand behind a line 2 metres from a wall. Hold the ball with two hands against the chest. Ball must be thrown with two hands so as to rebound from the wall into the hands behind the restraining line.

Count each successfully caught ball in 30 seconds. It is recommended that a brick or similar solid surface is used for this event to ensure a satisfactory rebound.

Push-Ups

Hand/Foot version: Lie face down on the floor, hands under shoulders, palms flat on the floor.

Straighten arms without locking, to lift body, leaving only palms and toes on floor.

Bend elbows until nose only touches the floor or return to starting position.

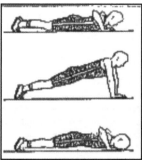

Repeat push-ups. Scoring ceases if body sags. The score is the number of push-ups completed in one minute.

THE DUKE OF EDINBURGH'S AWARD

or alternatively:-

Hand/knee moderated version:

Lie face down on the floor, hands under shoulders, palms flat on the floor with lower legs bent upwards from the knees.

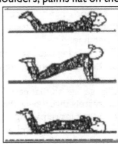

Straighten arms, without locking, to lift body, leaving only the palms and knees on floor, so that knees, hips and shoulders are in a straight line.

This straight line should be maintained and the hands should not be allowed to move back towards the knees. Bend elbows until nose touches the floor or return to starting position.

Repeat push-up. The score is the number of push-ups completed in one minute. Girls may find it easier to lie face down on the floor, hands under shoulders, palms flat on the floor with legs bent upwards from the knees on the floor.

Bailey Bridge

Start in the front support position (body in a straight line supported by hands and toes only) with shoulders near to and facing a chair, stool or box on which is placed a small object, bean bag, keys, a stone etc.,.

The seat of the chair should be 45cm from the floor.

Take the object from the chair seat with one hand, place it on the floor, pick up the object with the other hand and replace it on the chair seat.

Continue the cycle, using alternate hands. Count the number of times the object is successfully placed on the chair in 30 seconds

SINGLE LEG SQUAT THRUST
Starting Position:

Set up two lines 50cm apart. Crouch with both hands placed flat on the floor and with the toes touching the front line.

Take one leg back so that the foot is on the floor behind the rear line.

The test:

Change legs so that each foot is alternately thrust over the rear line, with the hips remaining high.

The score is the number of single leg squat thrusts, ie when each foot crosses the line, completed in the thirty seconds.

TRUNK CURL TEST

(To be performed on a towel, mat or suitable equivalent).

Lie on the back with legs bent. A 90 degree angle should be maintained between the upper and lower legs. Place hands on cheeks. Ankles should not be held. Sit, curling trunk and head until both elbows touch upper legs and then return to the starting position. Although the feet may leave the floor, the right angle between the upper and lower legs must be maintained. The score is the number of curls completed in one minute.

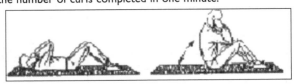

THE DUKE OF EDINBURGH'S AWARD

SELF TEST QUESTIONS

1. What four sections are common to all Awards.
2. What is the age you can enter the Bronze, Silver and Gold Awards?
3. At what Star level of your APC training are you most likely to qualify for the Bronze Award.
4. Give two examples of where a Senior Cadet Instructors Cadre might fit into an Award.
5. What is the upper age limit for gaining an Award.
6. How many kilometres are suggested for Bronze, Silver and Gold Expeditions on foot.
7. Before going on an Expedition what do you leave behind.
8. What is the minimum period of time you must undertake for a particular Skill at Silver level?
9. In the Physical Recreation section what is the minimum period of time you must take to qualify?
10. What is the important proviso which enables you to count Annual Camp as your Residential Project (apart from the time requirement)?
11. During Expeditions the minimum recommended calorie intake per day is 1000, 2000, 3000 or 4000?
12. Can Drill be taken as a Skill in the Award?
13. What do you have to buy to start your Award.
14. Do you all enter as a team in your unit for the Award?
15. Who is the Award Officer in your County?
16. Are you permitted to do an expedition other than on foot?
17. Can Skill at Arms be counted as a Skill towards the Award?
18. How many in the team doing a Qualifying Venture?
19. Who sets the targets to be achieved in Physical Recreation?
20. Who completes an account of the Expedition?
21. Name fourteen recognised 'skills'.
22. At what level of the Award do you do a Residential Project?
23. Name two alternative types of Expedition you can undertake over the age of 16?

Chapter 8
EXPEDITION TRAINING

Expedition training can be the most exciting and fun subject of your cadet training. It is also the most important, bringing other skills you have been taught in to practical use. The skills and knowledge you gain in expedition and adventurous training will benefit you throughout your life. Not forgetting that it is an important part of the Duke of Edinburgh's Award Scheme.

THE COUNTRY CODE
Expeditions may take you over Military Training Areas, privately owned property, or land where the public has rights of access. The Country Code applies wherever you are. You have a personal responsibility to ensure that you protect the natural beauty of the countryside and the wildlife living there. The message is, **abuse it and lose it.**

THE PRAYER OF THE TREE
You who pass by and would raise your hand against me, hearken ere you harm me.
I am the heat of your camp fire on a cold night, the friendly shade screening you from the summer sun.
My fruits are refreshing draughts quenching your thirst as you journey on.
I am the beam that holds your house, the board of your table, the bed on which you lie, the timber that builds your boat.
I am the handle of your hoe, the door of your homestead, the wood of your cradle, the shell of your last resting place.
I am the gift of God and the friend of man.
You who pass by, listen to my prayer, harm me not.
                                                        Anon

EXPEDITION TRAINING

The COUNTRY CODE is a series of ten reminders based on common sense – and common failings. Thoughtless disposal of litter is perhaps the most unsightly and costly problem our countryside faces. For instance, did you know that cows love shiny ring pulls from drink cans; they eat them along with the grass and they can perforate their stomachs. Next time you are in the country, have a look at the rubbish others leave behind – pretty isn't it?

"LEAVE NOTHING BUT YOUR FOOTPRINTS"

RESPECT THE PEOPLE AND LIFE OF THE COUNTRYSIDE

PROTECT ALL WILD LIFE

GO CAREFULLY ON COUNTRY ROADS

SECURELY FASTEN ALL GATES

EXPEDITION TRAINING

THE COUNTRY CODE

GUARD AGAINST RISK OF FIRE

USE GATES AND STILES

KEEP DOGS UNDER PROPER CONTROL

LEAVE NO LITTER

KEEP TO THE FOOTPATHS

SAFEGUARD WATER SUPPLIES

EXPEDITION TRAINING

DISCIPLINES OF PERSONAL HEALTH AND HYGIENE

HOW TO WALK – BOOTS AND FEET

You are issued with one pair of feet, with some of the most delicate bones in your body; so it makes sense to try and look after them! Some of you may already have problems with your feet through wearing badly fitting shoes.

BOOTS

It is most important to make sure that your boots are comfortable, giving your ankles the support and protection they require. They are expensive, and even if you can afford two pairs – one polished up for parades, the other kept for 'heavy work', unfortunately your feet will grow and trying to walk in boots at the age of 16 bought when you where 14, is a very painful experience and will do untold damage to your feet.

Good quality, well fitting boots or shoes are an investment, not only will they look after your feet, preventing problems later on, they SHOULD last longer.

FITTING BOOTS

1. When you go to buy new boots, take a thick pair of socks or two pairs of normal socks to wear when trying on your boots.
2. Make sure you can move your toes and that when standing still your toes do not touch the toe of the boot.
3. A method of testing the fitting is to be able to get a finger down between your heel and the back of the boot. If you can do this and your toes just touch the toe of the boot, they should fit you comfortably.
4. Fully lace up the boots to check that the uppers have enough room for your foot and that they are comfortable.

CARE OF BOOTS

1. Keep your boots 'well fed', leather will dry and crack if you do not put polish on them regularly.
2. If your boots get wet, do not dry them too close to heat, they will go hard and crack. Stuff them with newspaper; changing it often, this draws out the damp.
3. Always clean mud off your boots, it dries the polish out of the leather causing cracking and lack of water resistance.

EXPEDITION TRAINING

CARE OF YOUR FEET
SOCKS
To give you and your feet the best chance of comfort, it is important to have natural fibre socks. Make sure that you have at least two pairs of thick Wool, Cotton or a mix of the two is ideal. Natural fibre lets your feet 'breathe'. Keep your socks in good repair; 'holey' socks cause blisters. If you use the terry 'tube' socks, they are better worn inside out as there is less chance of friction.

FEET
When walking with a backpack, the extra weight you carry on your back is equivalent to more than three times the same weight on each foot. Your balance is more critcal and you will adjust to a different 'gait' When walking the weight of your body is transferred to the ball of your foot rather than the heel. Your normal "civilian pedestrian" feet will need some extra help to cope.

Make sure your boots are "broken in" before expedition work.

Wear thick 'boot socks'

Prepare your feet – if you have corns etc. see a chiropodist - if you don't wish to be a casualty

Keep your feet clean, dust them every morning (or more often if necessary) with a foot powder. Do not use too much powder, it will 'clump' and be uncomfortable.

Wash your feet regularly, rub them dry and check that your toe nails are not sharp.

Change your socks from one foot to the other, (stops the sock from forming too closely to your foot).

NEVER SOAK YOUR FEET WHEN ON THE MARCH, a quick dip, quick dry and then walk on is beneficial.

TREATMENT OF BLISTERS
Prevention is better than cure, if when you check your feet you find a reddened patch of skin, this is a blister waiting to happen. To prevent further pressure, apply a plaster or a strip of hypoallergenic tape to the affected area.

EXPEDITION TRAINING

If you already have a blister and wish to open it, either use a sterile lance or sterilize a needle by holding it in the flame of a match and letting it cool before use.

To lance the blister, prick the skin at the side then gently press the liquid out until the blister is flat. Apply a plaster or a sterile dressing secured by two strips of plaster applied like a cross. It is important to keep the area clean to guard against infection.

WET FEET

Should you get your feet wet, if at all possible dry them and your boots, putting on fresh socks. "Walking to dry them" will make your skin tender and you will end up a casualty.

CRAMP

If you have been walking for a long period, or perhaps your boots are laced up too tightly, you may get a sudden very painful spasm in your

are YOUR FEET always happy ?

leg muscles. Loosening off your boots and massaging the affected area is the best treatment. The cramp should go in a few minutes.

APART FROM YOUR FEET....

THIRST

After the first few hours of walking, particularly in hot weather, you may find that you develop a great thirst, not necessarily because your body has need of fluid, but by your mouth feeling dry. An alternative to drinking large quantities of water is to chew a blade of grass or suck a prune. A further alternative is to carry a piece of raw onion in your mouth; it also helps prevent your lips from cracking. (Petroleum jelly does the same job for your lips).

When on an organised Cadet or Duke of Edinburgh's Award expedition, care is always taken to ensure that there is an adequate supply of water available. Remember you should drink 3/4 litres of water each day. However, should you have been without water for a long period, sip slowly to prevent your stomach going into cramps. Never swallow snow or ice, let it melt first, preferably by boiling it. Do not assume that spring water is fit to drink, who knows what is in the water further upstream? Remember to sterilise your water bottle before you use it, by using a sterilising tablet.

ALCOHOL

As a Cadet you are not supposed to drink alcohol. Alcohol slows reaction, impairs thinking and in cold weather can make you more susceptible to hypothermia. Alcohol slows down the heart rate, and therefore slows the 'heating system' to the body.

PERSONAL MEDICATION

If you have a medical condition that requires you to take medication, **ENSURE THAT YOU HAVE ENOUGH WITH YOU, MAKE SURE YOU PACK IT WHERE YOU CAN FIND IT!**

PERSONAL HYGIENE

This might be seen as a low priority when you are on expedition or camping, yet the reverse is true. Sweat stays on the skin surface and if not removed can lose you friends and cause sores particularly between the legs, under the arms, around the waist and feet. It takes self-discipline to keep clean, particularly so if there is only cold water to wash in.

Clean your teeth regularly; a build up of old food and drink makes your mouth feel dry.

Weather and time permitting, wash out dirty socks and underwear, this will prevent them festering in your kit.

Wash Kit

Keep your soap in a soapbox; it prevents it from going soggy and becoming un-usable.

EXPEDITION TRAINING

Try and dry your towel out, it will stop it smelling - hang it out in the fresh air.

Keep all your wash kit in a plastic bag to keep it clean and dry.

CLOTHING AND EQUIPMENT

You are never certain what sort of weather you may be faced with in the UK, in less than an hour it can change from bright warm sun to cold, damp or rain. This makes it difficult to be dressed in the right gear. You need to remember that whatever you chose to wear needs to:

Keep water out – keep your body heat in"

JACKET/ANORAK

If your jacket lets water in, your clothing underneath will get damp or wet. Wet clothing will not insulate your body; in fact it will cool you quicker, increasing your chances of becoming a casualty through hypothermia.

Cheaper waterproofs are effective - they keep water out. The down side is that because the fabric cannot 'breathe' your body heat cannot escape and you may get very hot and damp from the inside.

Modern 'breathable' waterproofs are available. They are lightweight, keep you dry and are expensive! It is suggested that if you really enjoy walking or expeditions and plan to continue after you have completed your APC and/or Duke of Edinburgh's Award, then save up for one of these jackets.

A less expensive alternative is to have a decent warm jacket (non – waterproof), and buy a waterproof CAGOULE. Most have a ventilated yoke at the back and they pack neatly to sit on the top of your kit for easy access.

SHIRTS AND UNDERWEAR

Many experienced walkers wear woolen vests and tops because it has the best insulating and breathing properties. Some people find that wool next to the skin is most uncomfortable. Whatever you wear, apply the 'ONION SKIN PRINCIPLE'. This means wearing several thin layers of clothing (two minimum), to trap the warmth in. It is better to wear two thin layers rather than two thick – it holds more air in. Always keep an extra 'layer' in your kit, as you may well need it.

EXPEDITION TRAINING

HATS

If the sun is blazing down, wear a hat; it will protect you from uncomfortable sunburn and prevent possible sunstroke.

If the weather is cold and damp, wear a hat; it will prevent you losing valuable body heat. BALACLAVAS are a good choice as they can be pulled down over your ears and face if it is very cold or windy.

PERSONAL KIT LIST

Expeditions are either in uniform or civvies. Whatever the kit, wear your jacket. (Your County may well have cagoules to loan out for expedition work).

The following lists are an example of what you will need to carry with you.

To be carried on you:

Map, compass, Pathfinder Protractor/Romer, Whistle on lanyard. Matches in a waterproof container. Plasters, Pencil and notebook. Unless told otherwise a mobile phone in working order.

To be carried in your backpack:
Personal cleaning kit, towel, spare underclothes and socks, Mess tins with knife fork and spoon, pan scrub for cleaning your mess tins, reserve food such as Kendal mint cake, chocolate, raisins.

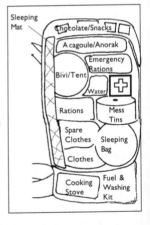

Remember – you carry what you take so think about weight.

Mug – metal preferred as you can heat it up, but plastic will do. A water bottle with a secure top. Groundsheet and a good length of strong string. A small torch, sleeping bag liner and a survival bag or blanket.

The following can be put into a kit bag to be delivered to camp site – if that is how the expedition is being organised, otherwise you will have to carry them yourself.

Sleeping bag, spare change of clothing, spare boots or shoes if available. Trainers, wool pullover. ***NOT TO FORGET YOUR BUNGEES***

EXPEDITION TRAINING

PACKING YOUR BACKPACK

The type and capacity of backpack you are able to use can make all the difference to the way it is packed. If it does not have a frame, you will need to be careful not to overload it as you may end up with hard and odd shaped items sticking into your back whilst carrying it.

The emphasis is packing INTO the backpack, not hanging boots or other items on the outside until you look like a Christmas tree on the move. Look carefully at the **LOAD CARRYING** and the **DISTRIBUTION** of the load as illustrated in the diagrams. Stove fuel should be packed in a well-sealed polythene bag stored well away from your rations. All clothing and your sleeping bag should also be kept in polythene bags. It is a good idea to use a strong polythene bag as a liner for your kit bag; it will keep the contents dry.

It is worthwhile taking some time to practice packing your backpack correctly and then wear/carry it to ensure that it is comfortable.

As a rough 'rule of thumb' you should not carry more than one quarter of your body weight.

LOAD CARRYING — The RIGHT and Wrong methods

RIGHT

LOAD
CARRIED
CORRECTLY

WEIGHT
APPLIED
VERTICALLY

WRONG

LOAD CARRIED
INCORRECTLY

HANGING
OUT FROM
SHOULDERS

LOOSE ITEMS
OF KIT
HANGING

Carry not more than a quarter of your body weight

EXPEDITION TRAINING

LAYOUT OF A CAMP SITE

Your Officer or Adult Instructor will have gained permission for you to camp on the land and for you to have the training time. If you are camping out with some friends for a few days, remember it is very important to gain permission from the landowners first.

The ideal campsite is one offering shelter from the prevailing wind, on well-drained fairly level area, facing East to hopefully catch the early morning sun. It should be as far away as possible from any houses, be close to a clean water supply and be in the open.

IS IT SAFE?

1. Is the site below the level of a river, lake, dam or reservoir, whose banks could burst or overflow in the event of a severe storm, or in a dried-up stream which 'comes to raging life' in a storm.
2. Is the site under overhanging rocks or cliffs, or any other form of danger, for example under a bridge or viaduct.
3. Ensure that the ground does not slope down from the bivi area to where the cooking area is set out, and that the tents are not close enough to be a fire risk.

CAMP LAYOUT

1. Can the tents/bivi's be correctly pitched in the area and sheltered from the wind and not under trees
2. If a platoon or section camp, a COOKING AREA sited where there is no risk of causing fire, properly set out for the purpose to be conveniently close to the bivis, but again, not too close in case of fire.

EXPEDITION TRAINING

3. Toilet/washing area defined, sited down wind and away from the
   tent site and cooking area. Latrines must be given some privacy.
4. Some access for a vehicle.

LATRINES

One of our normal everyday occurrences is the use of a toilet.
Normally you sit in solitary comfort, door shut and perhaps a magazine
to read. You will not find it quite so civilized in the field! There are a
few important things to remember.

Hygiene: In spite of being "in the field" you have to take more care
about using the toilet facilities and cleaning your hands. There is a
greater possibility of infection: to have digestive problems in the field is
no picnic.

CONSTRUCTION OF A FIELD LATRINE

On military land it is normal to see portable toilet units servicing
frequently used camp areas. Some
Counties have chemical toilets for field
use. However, should these items not
be available, knowing how to
construct a field latrine is a useful skill.
It will need a spade or shovel as digging
a hole in the ground is essential as any
exposed excrement attracts flies. Try
to lift any grass over the chosen site
carefully; it can be replaced before
leaving.

You will need to dig a hole not less
than 44cm (one foot six inches) deep and 22cm (nine inches) wide.
The earth taken from the hole should be piled up ready to be used by
each individual to cover excrement and finally to fill the hole before
leaving the site. If time permits, a 'seat' can be made for the latrine, see
diagram.

Before leaving, the ground used for the toilet must be clearly marked
with a sign stating that it is 'soiled ground'.

Privacy when using a latrine is an important factor, therefore some
sort of screen or concealment is desirable. Your Instructors will no
doubt introduce some sort of control.

One method is to provide a container for the toilet paper that is left in

EXPEDITION TRAINING

a prominent position. Each user must remember **to return it after use.** The message – when the toilet is "engaged" the container is **not there.** Simple, but effective.

Note: it is important to put the toilet roll in a plastic bag to keep it dry.

PREPARING FOOD IN THE FIELD

Your experience of cooking may be limited to zapping a pre-prepared meal in the microwave, cooking in the field is a little different.

Traditionally, one of the first tasks on reaching a campsite is to "brew-up" for the whole group.

During cold weather, particularly if you have been physically active or walking, it is important to have hot drinks regularly, and when you do have a meal, to ensure that it is hot, to sustain you.

COOKERS

You may use butane gas cookers, or 'hexi cookers' that use small blocks of solid fuel in a folding tin container. The most effective way of using a hexi cooker is to scrape a hole in the ground deep enough to shield your mess tins when they are on the cooker. This prevents any wind blowing your fuel out and keeps the food from chilling.

Important note: Make sure that you never use your hexi/butane/other cooker where it could cause a fire, for instance on dry leaf mould in wooded areas.

MESS TIN COOKING

Mess tin cooking is usually carried out with two of you "teaming up" as a cooker is efficient enough to produce hot food for two.

If you are issued with tinned rations, there are two important points for you to remember.

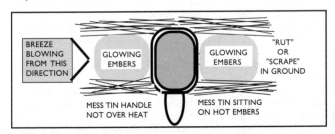

EXPEDITION TRAINING

1. Make sure there are two holes made in the top of the tin before you heat it, otherwise the tin could 'blow' and scald you badly.
2. If you have aluminum mess tins, do not use the water your tins have 'cooked in' to make a hot drink. It can be used for washing yourself or your tins.

Solid fuel cookers make a sticky black mess on the bottom of your mess tins, an easy way to remove most of it is to rub it hard along grass, then use a pan scrub to remove the rest. Remember to clean the inside, wipe out with grass, and then wash out.

FOOD RATIONS

A balanced diet becomes more important as the distance you travel or activity increases. If a journey is to take several days you will need to plan your menus carefully. The amount of food required each day depends on the country you are moving over. If it is mountainous then your body will use more energy and require more food. (Carbohydrates, sugar and starches).

Food has to be carried, too much is unnecessary weight, too little and you will go hungry. Dried potatoes weigh less than a bag of potatoes. Rice or pasta weighs little when uncooked. Dehydrated foods are excellent but expensive, plus the need to carry extra water. All in stews are a good standby; they only need one mess tin.

Whatever you decide to take, make sure that it is simple to cook and most important, you like it.

Ensure that you have sufficient to drink, avoid fizzy drinks; they do not quench your thirst.

FOOD HYGIENE

When on an expedition or exercise the very last thing you will think about will be food hygiene.

Food Poisoning - through using dirty mess tins or using fresh rations that have not ben properly cooked can really spoil your fun - and everyone elses!

1. While you are eating your hot food put a mess tin of water on to boil.
2. Ensure you clean your Mess Tins and KFS **properly** use very hot water.
3. Carefully wrap cooked food if you intend to eat it later.
4. NEVER EVER RE-HEAT RICE.
5. Take all your rubbish, tins, plastic with you -**leave nothing but your footprints**

EXPEDITION TRAINING

COMPOSITE RATIONS

As a Cadet you will have Service issue Composite Rations (**COMPO**) issued on field training. These rations have been developed over many years to give the soldier a high quality balanced diet.

CONTENT OF COMPO RATIONS

Compo is issued in a 24 hour Ration Pack ('rat pack'), which is produced in different menu selections. Compo rations are slowly being replaced by a pouched system. Pouched rations can be eaten hot or cold. If heating, follow the instructions on the pack ensure the food is hot. If a pouch is punctured and food is visible it should not be eaten.

BOIL IN THE BAG

Ensure that you carry extra water - or have access to extra water for these meals as they require more to cook correctly.
Cook your food in your mess tin to ensure it is thoroughly heated, thus preventing possible food poisoning

TO HEAT CANS

You can cook compo rations 'in the can' by piercing **TWO** holes in the lid of the can, stand the can in your mess tin and fill with water until the can is half submerged. Bring to the boil and boil for TEN minutes. Handle carefully when opening a hot can. This is a quick and easy method of cooking the food, but it does not taste quite as good as when heated out of the tin.

WATER PURIFICATION TABLETS

These are part of your ration pack and it is important that you know how to use them. Normally, drinking water is provided on Cadet organised training, but there may be an occasion where this does not happen. For Drinking Water, add one tablet to a litre of water, leave for TEN MINUTES before use. Leave for at least **THIRTY MINUTES** if using to make up your Lemon or Orange drinks. You must remember your **liquid intake** must be 3 to 4 litres per day. Once you are thirsty, it is too late.

WINDPROOF/WATERPROOF MATCHES

These matches MUST be kept for lighting your Hexamine blocks in bad weather conditions. Don't use them for any other reason or you will be in difficulty if rain or bad weather sets it and you have:

EXPEDITION TRAINING

NO WINDPROOF/WATERPROOF MATCHES ......
NO HOT FOOD – NO HOT DRINK – NO WARMTH

Don't forget you will be assessed on you outdoor cooking for your APC

USEFUL MEASURE TO NOTE

If you fill your small mess tin to the bottom rivet that holds the handle hinge, you will have HALF a PINT of water in the tin.

HILL WALKING SKILLS

Any walk over a reasonable period of time requires you to have a rhythm in the way you walk. This is especially so when HILL WALKING and carrying a loaded backpack. It is best to start out at a steady pace, one that you feel capable of keeping up for a few hours. If you are finding it difficult to talk or sing whilst walking, you are walking too fast – slow down. A slow plodding pace will get you to your next stop point as quickly as walking fast and having to take regular breaks. The other bonus is that you will not feel hot, sticky and overheated. Wise walkers conserve their energy and enjoy their walk.

WRONG | RIGHT

CLIMBING A HILL

Climbing directly up a hill puts strain on your calf muscles and Achilles tendons. Walking in a "zigzag" fashion across the slope your feet will be in full contact with the ground, with less chance of slipping. It may be slightly further to walk, but far less tiring.

EXPEDITION TRAINING

GOING DOWN HILL

Descending a slope safely carrying a full backpack requires some skill. Running or attempting to slide down is not recommended. Your balance plays a great part, the main thing is to bend both knees and lean forward. By adopting this stance your legs act as springs and absorb the shaking up your body would have had. Descend by traversing across the slope, keep your hand on the uphill side and near to the ground for support should you slip. Keep off any slopes with loose stones or scree. The golden rule is if a slope frightens you too much – find another way down.

KEEPING YOUR BALANCE

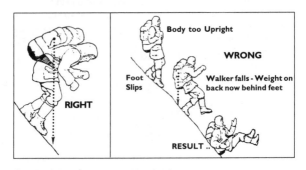

CROSSING RIVERS or STREAMS

In the first place never attempt to coss a river on your own.
Such hazards are best avoided unless there is no safer alternative. When crossing a stream or shallow river an Instructor must always be present. Never attempt to cross a river or stream in full flood. Water is a powerful element and it is easy to underestimate its force. There may also be hidden dangers such as stones, weed etc. that will cause you to fall. Remember, you will end up with wet boots and probably wet feet. The best plan is to find a good crossing point, a bridge or ford. Do not attempt to build a raft unless one of your qualified instructors are with you and checks it for safety before use.

EXPEDITION TRAINING

STOPPING FOR A REST

On any walk taking several hours you must stop and rest at regular intervals. The time between each stop will depend on the 'going' – difficult or easy. When resting lay down and raise your feet higher than your head. Don't halt for more than five minutes or your muscles will stiffen up.

CARE OF THE ENVIRONMENT

Trees are a valuable natural resource, which take many years to mature. Many of the wild animals, birds and insects rely on trees for their food and protection.

In Britain we cannot grow sufficient trees to meet our needs and import many million pounds worth of timber each year.

We must take care in preserving what we have, follow the Country Code. Do not break branches off trees, or carve in to the trunks. Remember the Prayer of the Tree at the beginning of this Chapter.

IMPROVISED SHELTER

There will be occasions when you do not have a tent to shelter in. The British soldier has the reputation of being able to improvise, "Any fool can rough it, but a good soldier will make himself comfortable under any conditions". As a Cadet, you should try and follow their lead. The following illustrations give a few ideas on how to put up improvised shelters.

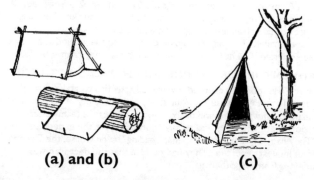

(a) and (b)   **(c)**

EXPEDITION TRAINING

(a). A shelter with two ponchos constructed on the same principle as a BIVI for two.

(b) A poncho shelter made against a fallen tree trunk for one person. The groundsheet must be on the side of the trunk away from the prevailing wind.

(c) Another example of a poncho type of shelter for one person. The rope must be strong enough and the open side of the poncho away from the prevailing wind.

GUY
ROPES
&
TENT
PEGS

IMPROVISED TENT

Using a string/rope between two supports, (perhaps suitable trees),tie poncho over the string, peggingthe bottom edges to the ground. This type of "tent" can also be put up against a fence or wall using one half of the tent as shown in the picture as the triangle A – B – C.

To make a Basha for two you need two ponchos string or bungees (at least 6), meat skewers or tent pegs are useful (8 or 12 are needed). A length of strong string is always useful to have in your kit. Tent pegs must not be driven into the ground with the head of an axe, use the proper mallet. The pegs should be driven in to the ground at an angle (see diagram) and not so far in the ground that they cannot be seen.

ADVENTUROUS TRAINING & PHYSICAL ACTIVITIES

Having a responsible attitude towards all activities you take part in goes a long way to ensuring your safety and the safety of others. This means careful planning and preparation. The Rescue teams often report that "The party was totally unprepared for the expedition", or "They had not been trained in map reading", even worse, the Coroner at an Inquest reported "They had no idea that the deceased was suffering from Hypothermia".

EXPEDITION TRAINING

Your Officers and Adult Instructors have the responsibility of ensuring that all adventurous training and physical activities are correctly planned; this includes suitably qualified persons to instruct or guide you through. Part of the planning is briefing you the Cadet in all aspects of the activity. This will include the kit you require, who will be in charge of the training/activity, who the designated First Aid Person is, where they will be sited.

You may also be given 'no go' areas, make sure you know where they are.

Your responsibility to yourself is to make sure you take the correct kit and follow instructions given.

Your responsibility to all the other Cadets is to be alert. Watch out for others, if you are working in hot weather, heat exhaustion can occur quickly. In cold or wet and windy weather, hypothermia can happen to the best of us. Your Instructors will be watching out, but it is almost impossible to see everything.

If you see another Cadet about to do something that will put him/herself or others at risk, don't be slow in trying to stop them. It is not 'sneaky' it is being responsible.

Perhaps most important of all, enjoy the experience – give it your best.

THE ACTIVITIES THAT ARE CONSIDERED AS ADVENTUROUS & PHYSICAL ARE AS FOLLOWS:

Mountaineering – including Hill Walking, Rock Climbing, Abseiling, Skiing, Caving, Canoeing, Off Shore Sailing, Rafting, Swimming, Gliding or Hang Gliding, Paracending, Sub – Aqua Diving and all activities involving the hazard of water.

OFFICIAL PERMISSION

On no account should you organise activities without the knowledge and assistance of your Officers or Instructors.

For your safety's sake,
REMEMBER – SHOULD THERE BE AN ACCIDENT YOU ARE ONLY COVERED BY INSURANCE IF THE ACTIVITY IS OFFICIALLY PLANNED AND ORGANISED.

EXPEDITION TRAINING

PREVENTION OF ACCIDENTS ON OUTDOOR ACTIVITIES - PLANNING

Your Instructors will expect you to work through and be involved withthe planning process as part of your training.

Plan your route beforehand, ensure all members of the group are fully briefed and all have copies of the Route Card, map refs and check points and RVs, campsites and your Estimated Time of Arrival all supported by **accurate map references.**

If you are walking in areas where there are rescue posts or mountain rescue posts, know their locations and procedures including the map references of telephone boxes. Decide on a **Lost Drill** e.g. "Go West till you strike the main road" or "Keep walking down – stream".

BEFORE YOU GO

1. As an individual, always carry a map, compass, protractor, pencil, whistle, small first aid kit and a torch in your jacket or in pockets
.2. Have emergency rations such as chocolate, glucose tablets, dried fruit etc. DON'T eat them unless in an emergency.
3. Always carry warm clothing, but reduce non – essentials like two sweaters when one will do.

BEFORE YOU SET OUT

1. Don't overdress, leave off the pullover – carry it on top of your pack until the harder part of the walk is over.
2. Report to the local Rescue Post giving them a copy of your Route Card and expected time back.
3. Check the weather conditions and the forecasts for the duration of your walk

OUT ON THE HILLS

1. Always stay together; unless there is an injured person, in which case half of the party should stay with the casualty, while the other half goes for help.
2. Walk at the pace of the slowest person.
3. If you go out as a group, never travel in groups of less than five.
4. Remember to observe the Country Code.
5. Carry at least one polythene survival sack or sleeping bag per two persons.

EXPEDITION TRAINING

6. Stick to the route agreed.
7. Make one decision among the group on the direction to take. If a
    compass bearing is used, have others check it, then trust your
    compass.
8. Do not assume that your mobile phone will work.
If the weather deteriorates – **DON'T PRESS ON; TURN BACK.**
9. If fog descends, **carefully** find a sheltered place, ensure you keep as
warm and dry as possible, have a hot drink. Use your whistle to make
the distress call if necessary.
10. Don't throw stones; these can dislodge bigger ones and could
cause an accident.

IF YOU DO GET LOST:

1.   **DO NOT SPLIT UP**

2.   **DO NOT PANIC**

3.   **DO NOT FORGET TO USE YOUR MAP,
        COMPASS AND COMMON SENSE**

4.   **REMEMBER THE INTERNATIONAL DISTRESS
        CALL – SIX BLASTS ON YOUR WHISTLE OR SIX
        TORCH FLASHES PER MINUTE.**

SAFETY ON THE HIGHWAYS

By day or night, when moving as an individual on foot you must:
1. Use a footpath; if there is not one, walk on the side of the road
    facing the nearest traffic (normally the right hand side), keep as
    close to the side as possible.
2. Cross motorways by bridges or underpasses, railways by bridges or
    level crossings.
3. When dark, keep an extra sharp lookout and wear a high visibility
    jacket/tabard or if not available, light coloured clothing which will
    show up in the lights of a vehicle.

Note: Walking on the highways at any time as a group should be
            organised and led by an Instructor.

EXPEDITION TRAINING

EMERGENCY PROCEDURES

Emergency Messages

The Police are responsible for calling out the rescue services. The information they will require is as follows:

A. The exact location of the injured person(s) with a six-figure grid reference and a description/landmarks of the area for a helicopter pilot to identify.

B. The number of injured persons and their names.

C. The nature of their injuries.

D. The time of the accident.

E. Mobile Phone number(s) held by members of the group.

Those going for help must remember the area and landscape with any particular reference point to help find the site on return with a rescue party. (Write the information down).

Waiting for help to arrive

1. Those looking after the injured should set up shelters and carry out emergency first aid with particular reference to the prevention of hypothermia/exposure.

2. It will be necessary to mark the site with light coloured clothing or bandages on sticks where they can easily attract attention.

3. There are International **Ground to Air Signals** that can be used to communicate with rescue aircraft; these are shown on the next page.

4. In addition to these signals, **A RED FLARE, A RED SQUARE OF CLOTH** or a **FIRE** are also recognised **International Alarm Signals.**

5. Setting out clothing or items of kit, or a person lying down taking up the shape of the letter can make the shape of each signal. Get help any way you can.

6. Be alert; watch out for the rescue party to guide them in by the quickest route.

7. Make yourselves as comfortable as possible; 'brew up', eat HOT food, keep together, keep warm, keep up the morale.

EXPEDITION TRAINING

GROUND TO AIR SIGNALS

letter	signal	
V		REQUEST ASSISTANCE
↑		WE ARE PROCEEDING IN THIS DIRECTION
X		MEDICAL ASSISTANCE REQUIRED
N		NO WE DO NOT NEED ANYTHING

EXPEDITION TRAINING

GO FLY - A SURVIVAL KITE

A Pocket Sized piece of kit to rescue those lost on an expedition or lost as darkness falls, may, if kitted out with a Survival Kite be brought to safety sooner.

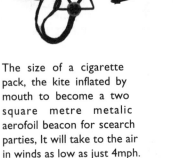

The size of a cigarette pack, the kite inflated by mouth to become a two square metre metalic aerofoil beacon for scearch parties, It will take to the air in winds as low as just 4mph. Its flight is so stable it remains airborne while survivors sleep.
Kite reflects radar signals and its visability can be further enhanced by adding a small "light stick", the brightly glowing chemical indicator.
Other uses, it can be worn as a vest under outer garments directing heat back to the body or wrapped around a broken limb and then inflated, used as a splint.

EXPEDITION TRAINING

WIND CHILL FACTOR

Insufficient attention is paid to the combined effect of air temperature and wind speed has on the human body. This combined effect is the **Wind Chill Factor.** The air temperature may be quite warm, but it only needs a wind blowing at 24 k.p.h. (15 m.p.h.) to cause body cooling, particularly to the head, face and hands.

Wind speeds above 24 k.p.h. cool the body slower, but can cause the body to burn up more energy; there is also the hazard of being blown over whilst walking. The following diagram is reproduced from the book Mountain craft and Leadership by Alec Langmuir and illustrates graphically how important it is to be aware of the Wind Chill Factor. As an example it shows:

The air temperature at +5 degrees C, at a wind speed of 50 k.p.h. (31 m.p.h.) it crosses the Wind Chill Line at "Very Cold".

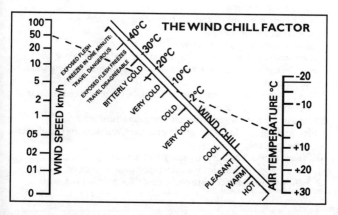

EXPEDITION TRAINING

PRECAUTIONS & ADVICE

Before setting out on a hill walk or expedition, you would be well advised to check out the wind speeds and ensure that you take adequate steps to prevent rapid chilling.

Try and keep warm and dry, wet clothing combined with Wind Chill can cause Hypothermia

Wear a hat and gloves

Eat the right food, keep energy levels high

Do not get too tired

Never underestimate or ignore the Wind Chill Factor.

Check First Aid Chapter for the treatment of Extremes of Temperature (heat and cold).

SUMMARY

Accidents don't just happen; they are CAUSED.

Most accidents occurring on outdoor adventurous activities no matter where they take place are due to one or more of the following reasons:

1. Not involving senior more experienced members of your unit and not gaining permission to carry out the activity.
2. Insufficient detailed preparation, planning and training. RECCE not done properly, no rehearsals. Menu not planned for the activity or area to be traveled.
3. Not having the right clothing, e.g. wearing jeans and unsuitable footwear for hill walking.
4. Carelessness or casual attitude by those taking part.
5. Overestimation of the strength and stamina of those taking part.
6. Not enough practical experience – especially in map reading and camp craft.
7. Not paying sufficient attention to detail, failing to notice the signs of deteriorating weather conditions.
8. Not turning back when common sense says 'turn back'.
9. Not 'looking out' for other group members, not noticing the effects of heat or cold
10. Failure to work as a team, getting into a panic.
11. Not accepting advice from experienced people while en-route.
12. Failing to provide accurate route cards, RV points, timings etc.

EXPEDITION TRAINING

KNOTS AND THEIR USES

A lot depends on knowing how to tie just the right knot or hitch for a particular job.

While learning to tie knots it is no use using a thin string or twine made up of loose strands. You need a piece of rope or cord not less than a quarter of an inch thick and several feet long.

An important point to remember is that it is not a good idea to ever cut a rope just to shorten it, as you will find that no sooner had you cut it, than you needed a longer rope for some other purpose.

As mentioned in the Expedition Training, it is always useful to have a length of string or rope with you, but there is not much point in having a rope if you don't know how to tie a useful knot in it.

Like most skills it is only through practice that you will become proficient, this is especially so with knots.

The occasion you need to use a knot will more than likely be in an emergency situation, you must realise that this will mean instant re-action with no time to think of what to do. This is when your ability to tie the — "right knot at the right time" — could prevent a disaster.

A ROPE

The main part of a rope is called the "standing part" - see illustration.

When the end is bent back toward the standing part, the loop formed is called a "bight", regardless of whether it crosses the rope or only lies parallel with it.

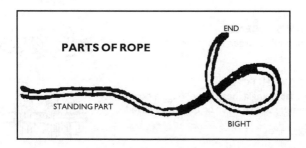

PARTS OF ROPE

END

STANDING PART

BIGHT

EXPEDITION TRAINING

KNOTS AND THEIR USES.

THUMB KNOT and FIGURE OF EIGHT KNOT
Both used to make a 'stop' on a rope: to prevent a rope from fraying at the end.

REEF KNOT.
For joining two dry ropes of the same size. The most generally useful knot. Always used in First Aid

SINGLE SHEET BEND.
For joining two ropes of different size.

DOUBLE SHEET BEND.
For joining two wet ropes of different size.

HAWSER BEND.
For joining larger ropes or cables.

DRAW HITCH.
For fastening a 'head rope' (e.g., a boat's painter) so that it can be quickly released.

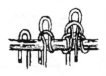

EXPEDITION TRAINING

CLOVE HITCH
This is the most useful knot that you will ever learn. It can be made under strain, will not slip on itself nor along a pole, and can easily be cast loose.

TIMBER HITCH
is useful for hauling, the more it is pulled the firmer it holds.

TWO HALF HITCHES.
Two turns of a rope, which, when drawn together, holds securely. It is the quickest and simplest way to make a rope fast to a post.

ROUND TURN and TWO HALF HITCHES.
The quickest way to make a rope fast under strain. One of the most useful and easily made knots .

FISHERMANS BEND.
For fastening ends of ropes to spars, poles, etc., or to other ropes.

BOWLINE ON THE BIGHT
To form a loop that will not slip. One loop is made larger than the other. This is the sling for lowering a person from a building.
It enables the person to be supported, with the longer loop under the knees and the short loop under the armpits.

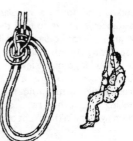

EXPEDITION TRAINING

THE SPANISH WINDLASS

This is not a knot, but is closely related to them. You may come across a situation where knowing how to use a Spanish Windlass could be helpful.

The windlass as you will see from the diagram, gives you great pulling power on a rope, by means of a lever using it to wind the rope round a post or stake, one end of which is in the ground.

The rope is wound round the post and a bar or piece of wood with the rope hitched over it.

The power given could be used to haul a boat out of the river or to move a vehicle, one end of the rope is fastened to the object to be moved, and the other is made fast on to a tree or some other suitable anchor. The stake or post must be strong and sound, likewise the material used for the lever as there is considerable pressure on both when in use.

Check your rope for any damage and be sure it is strong enough for the job.

Arrange your rope as in the diagram, pulling the lever round the stake.

The stake needs to be held firmly by driving it into the ground making the hole big enough for it to turn. It may be necessary to "overhaul" your windlass as too much rope may be wound round it, it will depend upon the size of the

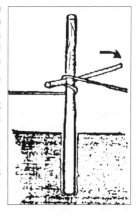

stake used for the windlass and the distance you have to haul the object.

Warning - it can be dangerous if you do not use strong enough material, or if it snaps or if you let go of the lever.

Check your rope and Windlass frequently, secure the load you are pulling with other rope to prevent it running away in the event of an accident.

EXPEDITION TRAINING

LASHINGS

Lashings are used for fastening poles or spars together they should be finished with a reef knot when both ends of the rope or yarn are available, or with a clove hitch if only one end is available.

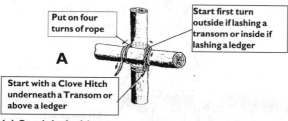

Put on four turns of rope

Start first turn outside if lashing a transom or inside if lashing a ledger

A

Start with a Clove Hitch underneath a Transom or above a ledger

(a) Straight lashing to spars.

For lengthening a spar or for repairing a broken spar. The lashing is made fast to the spar with a clove hitch, and is then passed round and round the spars; the end is made fast by another clove hitch or by passing the end under the last few turns and then tightening them up.

Two frapping turns shown as loose to make it clear. These to be pulled up tight and beaten in

B

Four complete turns of the lashing and an extra turn round this spar to bring the start of the frapping turns to the right place

b) Square lashing.

For lashing one spar to another at right angles. The lashing is started with a clove hitch, consists of at least four complete turns round the spars and two or more frapping turns, and is finished with two half-hitches round the most convenient spar.

Finish with two half hitches. Outside on a Transom inside - on a Ledger

SHEAR LEGS LASHING

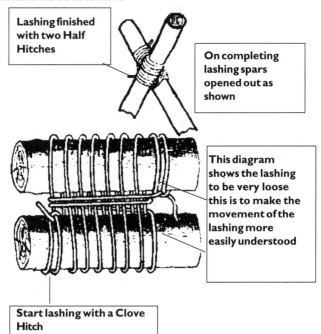

Lashing finished with two Half Hitches

On completing lashing spars opened out as shown

This diagram shows the lashing to be very loose this is to make the movement of the lashing more easily understood

Start lashing with a Clove Hitch

Shear legs lashing

For lashing spars at adjustable angles. The spars are placed side by side; a clove hitch is made round one spar and the rope is taken loosely six or eight times round both spars above the clove hitch without riding.

Two frapping turns are made round the lashing, and the end of the rope is made fast to the other spar by two half hitches just above the lashing.

EXPEDITION TRAINING

SPLICING

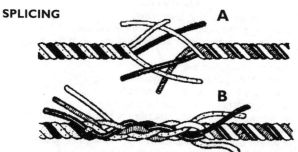

A

B

Diagram 'A' shows strands ready for splicing. Diagram 'B' shows the splice after each of the 6 strands have been passed through twice. From here, the strands are reduced in diameter by half and worked through once, then by half again, and through once to finish. Work from right to left, 'over and under'.

Splices are permanent and strong, and do not increase the thickness of the rope by much.

a. Short splice.   For joining two ropes.
b. Back splice.   For ending off a rope permanently.

WHIPPING

Whipping is used to prevent the end of a rope unravelling and is best done with sail twine; it is less permanent than the backsplice but does not greatly increase the thickness of the rope.

Rope 'Whipped' at end to prevent fraying

**KNOWING HOW TO TIE THE RIGHT KNOT, IS
A SKILL YOU WILL USE THROUGHOUT YOUR LIFE.
PRACTICE AND MORE PRACTICE MAKES PERFECT**

EXPEDITION TRAINING
QUESTIONS

1. What are the ten Country Code Rules.
2. What sort of socks should you wear on an expedition
3. The weight you carry on your back is equal to ....times the weight on your feet.
4. What do you dust your feet with.
5. How do you open a blister and what with.
6. If you are very thirsty, should you eat snow.
7. What do you carry on the outside of your ruck sack.
8. When looking for a camp site, what do you have to have from the owners.
9. What do you check out for safety when choosing a camp site
10. Is it a good idea to put up a tent under trees.
11. If you have to use water from a stream, what do you first do with it.
12. Where would you site the latrine and washing area, and why.
13. In a camp for several days you construct a latrine, how is it done and what are the important sizes.
14. When sighting a latrine what do you do about providing privacy, and how important is it.
15. How is privacy maintained for those using a Portaloo or field toilet.
16. What is the advantage of digging a small hole to put your cooker into.
17. What should you always leave behind at a camp site.
18. Why can't you go off on your own expedition as a Cadet,
19. Five of you are on an expedition, one is injured, how many would normally go for help.
20. When planning a route what must you produce and give someone a copy of .
21. The weather is getting bad on an expedition, do you go on or turn back.
22. What is the distress call/signal with: a. Whistle. b. Torch, and the Emergency Ground to Air Signals.
23. What do you understand by the Wind Chill Factor.
24. What added danger is there if you get wet on a cold and windy day.
25. You use ONE Water Purification Tablet to how much water.
26. Before heating tins in a mess tin of boiling water, what must you do.
27. Describe three types of improvised shelters.
28. How would you sterilize a water bottle.
29. How do you 'end-off' a rope.
30. What happens if you walk for some distance with boots full of water.

EXPEDITION TRAINING

31. How can you test a pair of boots are about the right size.
32. In cold weather without anything covering your head, how much body heat can you lose.
33. With pouched rations what is the best way to ensure you get a hot cooked meal.
34. What do you always take away from your camp site.

FINALLY -

When you draw a tent from the stores to use on exped, what state do you expect it to be in ?

Answer: dry, clean, good repair and complete with guy ropes, pegs and mallet all properly packed.

How do you ensure that your tent is as described above?

Answer: **POST EXPEDITION ADMINISTRATION** or in other words, ensure that all stores returned are clean, dry and complete as issued. Report defects/damage to the Quarter Master.

Your ability to carry out the Post Expedition Administration efficiently when you are tired and required to check that all is correct takes a great deal of self discipline - don't forget it is all a part of your test.

Chapter 9

FIRST AID, HEALTH & SAFETY

INTRODUCTION

At some point in your life you may face a situation where your knowledge of First Aid may save someone's life. First Aid is not "Just another subject" you need to pass: if you keep your knowledge up to date, it is a life-saving skill.

The First Aid At Work qualification, valid for three years, is recognised in the workplace. When you need to re-qualify there are many organisations providing courses including the British Red Cross and St John's Ambulance; should you no longer be a Cadet.

The following pages are not intended to take the place of good instruction and practice; they are to act as a 'trigger' to remind you of the priorities of looking after a casualty.

D.R.A.B.C.

Remember the meaning of the above initials and you should be able to manage accidents and emergency situations competently.

D - DANGER

The general rule in casualty and incident management is to treat the casualty where found, as moving them may cause further injury. However, a good First Aid person knows that if there is danger that cannot be removed, the casualty should be removed to a safer place in order to protect them and the person helping them. If there are other people nearby, ask them for their assistance.

R - RESPONSE

A fully conscious casualty is easily recognised; however there are various stages of consciousness and you need to assess this. The method is as follows:

FIRST AID, HEALTH & SAFETY

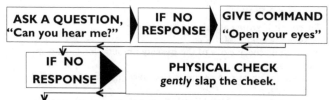

| ASK A QUESTION, "Can you hear me?" | → | IF NO RESPONSE | → | GIVE COMMAND "Open your eyes" |

| IF NO RESPONSE | → | PHYSICAL CHECK *gently* slap the cheek. |

If there is **NO RESPONSE** from the casualty, then it can be assumed that they are **UNCONSCIOUS**. *SHOUT FOR HELP*

A - AIRWAY

In an unconscious casualty, the greatest danger is that food, vomit, blood, water, other substance or the tongue may block the **AIRWAY** and prevent the casualty from breathing.

DO NOT DELAY, LOOSEN CLOTHING AT THE NECK AND WAIST, AND OPEN THE AIR-WAY.

LIFT THE CHIN FORWARDS WITH THE INDEX FINGER AND MIDDLE FINGERS OF ONE HAND, WHILST PRESSING THE FOREHEAD BACK WITH THE PALM OF THE OTHER HAND.

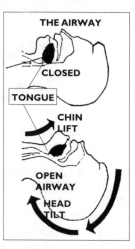

THE AIRWAY

CLOSED

TONGUE

CHIN LIFT

OPEN AIRWAY

HEAD TILT

QUICKLY CHECK THE MOUTH FOR OBVIOUS OBSTRUCTIONS – REMOVE IF FOUND.

FIRST AID, HEALTH & SAFETY

B - BREATHING

To check if your casualty is breathing:
- Note the colour of the skin
- Place your cheek close to the casualty's mouth, looking down towards their chest.
- Check for up to **ten seconds** to ensure that you can see/feel the breathing.
- If the casualty **IS BREATHING, check the circulation as described in C - CIRCULATION below, to be sure that the pulse feels normal.**
- Do an initial **Top to Toe Survey**, looking for obvious injuries; treat where found. **Keep checking the casualty's breathing.**
- **If the casualty's breathing becomes "laboured", place the casualty in the RECOVERY POSITION** continue treatment.

RECOVERY POSITION

REMEMBER – ANY CASUALTY WHO HAS BEEN UNCONSCIOUS EVEN FOR A SHORT PERIOD OF TIME, SHOULD GO TO HOSPITAL.
IF THERE IS NO SIGN OF BREATHING, GIVE THE CASUALTY TWO EFFECTIVE RESCUE BREATHS and check for:

C - CIRCULATION

To check for circulation:
- Look, listen and feel for signs of circulation. Do this for up to 10 seconds.
- If you are sure you have detected signs of circulation, continue Rescue Breathing.
- After every 10 breaths (about one minute) check for signs of circulation.

FIRST AID, HEALTH & SAFETY

- If the casualty starts breathing but remains unconscious, place in the **RECOVERY POSITION** and monitor vital signs.

If there are NO SIGNS OF CIRCULATION:
Commence CPR (Cardio Pulmonary Resuscitation)

- Kneel beside the casualty
- With the **Index and Middle fingers of your lower hand**, locate one of the **lowermost ribs** on the side nearest to you.
- Slide your fingertips along the rib to the point where the lowermost ribs meet the **Breastbone**.
- Place your **middle finger** at this point and your **index finger** beside in on the **lower breastbone**.
- Place the **heel** of your other hand on the **breastbone** and slide it down until it reaches your **index finger**.
- Place the **Heel** of your first hand on top of the other hand, and interlock your fingers.
- Leaning well over the casualty, arms straight, press down vertically on the **breastbone** and depress the chest by about **4 – 5cm (about 2 inches)**. Release the pressure **without removing your hands from the chest.**
- Compress the chest **15 times** at a rate of **100 compressions per   minute.**
- Tilt the head, lift the chin, and give two **Rescue Breaths**
- Continue this cycle until: emergency help arrives and takes over; the casualty makes movement of takes spontaneous breath; or you become so exhausted that you are unable to carry on.

> **Note: In the interests of your own health, if you have a disposable ventilation aid, use it. If not try to improvise.**

WHEN TO CALL FOR AN AMBULANCE

If you have a helper, send him/her to call for an ambulance as soon as you know that the casualty is not breathing.

If you are on your own, your course of action depends on the likely cause of the unconsciousness.

If you do not know what has happened, call for an ambulance immediately after noting that the breathing is absent. If the unconsciousness is due to injury, drowning or choking, and no help is

FIRST AID, HEALTH & SAFETY

available, give chest compressions and rescue breaths for **ONE MINUTE,** then call an ambulance.

TELEPHONING FOR HELP

Call 999 or 112

Police, Fire, Ambulance, Coastguards,
Mountain, Cave and Fell Rescue

You will be asked which service you require. Whenever casualties are involved, ask for the ambulance; the control officer will contact other services if necessary.

GIVE CLEAR DETAILS

- State your name **Clearly**
- The **telephone number** you are calling from
- The **exact location** of the incident; a road name, any junction or other landmarks. **DO NOT WORRY** if you do not know this, your call can be traced.
- The type and seriousness of the accident/incident
- The number, sex and approximate age(s) of the casualties and what you know of their condition
- Details of any hazards, such as power lines, gas, chemicals fog, ice or entrapment.
- DO NOT HANG UP UNTIL THE CONTROL OFFICER CLEARS THE LINE, THEY MAY REQUIRE FURTHER INFORMATION

BLEEDING

Remember: minor wounds the danger is infection: severe bleeding the danger is SHOCK, UNCONSCIOUSNESS and possible death.

Severe Bleeding

If possible, wear disposable gloves
- Where necessary, cut clothing to expose the wound
- Check wound to ensure that there is no foreign body present
- Apply **Direct Pressure** over the wound either with your fingers

or the palm of your hand, preferably over a sterile non-fluffy dressing. If the casualty is able, you can ask them to do this for themselves.

Where possible, raise and support the injured limb
- Help the casualty to lie down – on a blanket if you have one
- Secure the dressing tight enough to maintain pressure, but not too tight, restricting circulation.
- If bleeding continues, apply a second dressing on top of the first.
- If seepage occurs, apply a further dressing.
- Keep checking for signs that the bandage is too tight.
- Call for an ambulance

If there is a "Embedded object" in the wound:

- Press firmly on both sides of the embedded object to push the edges of the wound together.
- Assist casualty to lie down.
- Build up padding on either side of the object and carefully bandage over without pressing on the object.
- Support the injured part in a raised position to minimise swelling and control any bleeding.
- Call for an ambulance.

NEVER attempt to remove an embedded object

SHOCK

The circulatory system distributes blood around the body, passing oxygen and nutrients to organs and body tissues. When this system fails, circulatory shock develops. If this is not treated swiftly, vital organs such as the lungs and heart will fail, which can lead to death. The condition can be made worse by pain and fear.

Causes

Shock can develop if the heart fails to pump blood, shock may also occur if the blood supply to the body's vital organs is reduced through blood loss or loss of other body fluids through vomiting, severe diarrhoea or burns. The body initially responds by diverting the blood supply from the skin to vital organs.

FIRST AID, HEALTH & SAFETY

Recognition

As the brain's oxygen supply is weakened:
- *The casualty may become restless, even aggressive*
- *The casualty may yawn and gasp for air (air hunger)*
- *The casualty will become unconscious*
- *The heart may stop if positive action to reduce shock is not taken.*

PULSE Rapid, becoming 'thready'.

SKIN Pale, grey-blue around the lips, Earlobes and nose. Sweating, cold, clammy.

BREATHING Rapid and shallow

Treatment

1. Treat any external bleeding or burns you find.
2. Lay casualty down on a blanket to protect them from the cold, cover with a further blanket.
3. Loosen tight clothing.
4. If injuries allow, raise and support the legs to improve the blood supply to the head.
5. Check and record breathing, pulse and levels of response.
6. Reassure the casualty.
7. Be prepared to resuscitate if necessary
8. **DO NOT** let the casualty smoke, eat, drink or move un-necessarily. **DO NOT** attempt to warm the casualty with direct heat such as a hot water bottle.
9. If the casualty complains of thirst, moisten the lips with a little water.

BURNS AND SCALDS

Large area burns and scalds mean the loss of vital body fluids causing loss of oxygen to the vital organs.

Treatment

1. QUICKLY remove anything constrictive from the injured area, e.g. rings, or watch before swelling occurs.
2. Cool the area with cold water, preferably gently running water, for at least **10 minutes.**
3. When the affected area has been sufficiently cooled, cover loosely with non-fluffy material.

FIRST AID, HEALTH & SAFETY

4. Treat for shock.

5. DO NOT use creams or sprays, burst blisters or use plasters.

Note: Any burn or scald over 2.5 cm with more than superficial skin damage, or caused by electric current, must receive medical attention.

FRACTURES

Types of Fracture

A. Closed Fracture. Skin not broken.

B. Open Fracture. Bone has broken surface of skin. Dangerous; external loss of blood and serious risk of infection.

C. Complicated Fracture. When internal nerve or organ is also injured and when fracture is connected with a dislocated joint.

D. Symptoms and Signs. Casualty heard it break. Pain at site of injury. Swelling, bruising later. Deformity, bone grating and shock.

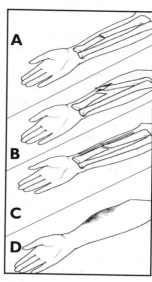

Recognition

Sometimes it is obvious that a bone is broken; however, if you are in any doubt, treat the injury as a fracture.

Signs and Symptoms

- Pain
- Swelling and bruising
- Deformity
- Immobility
- Visible sign of bone either under the skin or protruding through.
- Sound of bone grating against bone

FIRST AID, HEALTH & SAFETY

Treatment – Lower limbs

If an ambulance is available within **15 minutes** it is preferable to immobilise the injured limb using blankets, coats, bags etc. The First Aid person can also support the injured area using one hand above and one below the site of the fracture. (The first aid person must be comfortably positioned before attempting this, as any involuntary movement on their behalf may cause more pain to the casualty).

If the casualty has to be moved for their safety, or medical assistance will not be available for some time, the following should be done:

1. Advise casualty not to move
2. Dress any wound.
3. Gently bring the 'good' leg towards the injured leg.
4. Place broad bandages at the thigh, knee, above and below the site of the fracture and round the ankles.
5. Place padding in between the legs particularly at the knee and ankle
6. Tie off bandages on the **uninjured side.**
7. Treat for shock

Treatment – Upper limbs

1. Dress any wound.
2. If possible, secure the injured arm in a sling
3. Tie to the chest to immobilise
4. Treat for shock
5. Seek medical help

HEAD INJURY

Blows to the head should always be taken seriously, if you are in any doubt about the severity, call for an ambulance. Severe injury does not always show straight away, it may take up to 24 hours or more to develop.

The following are signs that probable severe injury has occurred; urgent medical attention is required should any one of them be present.

1. **Unconsciousness – however brief.**
2. **Clear, slightly yellow discharge, possibly with blood flecks, coming from the inner ear or nose.**

FIRST AID, HEALTH & SAFETY

3. Bleeding from the inner ear.
4. Whites of eyes suffused with blood, probable 'black eyes'.
5. Unevenly dilated pupils.
6. Vomiting
7. Loss of vision
8. Severe headache and dizziness.

EXTREMES OF TEMPERATURE

HYPOTHERMIA or EXPOSURE

Hypothermia can kill. It is caused by exposure to conditions where the body heat is reduced to a point where the deep body temperature (vital organs) begins to fall. It is not easy to recognise a mild case of hypothermia, but 'looking out' for other members of the group could be vital.

Signs and Symptoms

1. Unexpected behaviour; wandering away from the main group, irritability.
2. Physical fatigue, failure to understand questions/instructions.
3. Complaints of being cold and tired.
4. Failure of vision, stumbling, slurring of speech.
5. Outbursts of unexpected energy, violent language, physical resistance to help.
6. Violent shivering fits, muscle cramps.
7. Dizziness, fainting

If a member of your group gets to the violent shivering fits before you stop and give assistance, take note, you have the beginnings of a medical emergency to deal with.

Treatment

1. Move the casualty and the rest of the group to a place of shelter. If you are carrying a tent, use it. If not, get other members of the group to build a shelter.
2. Detail someone to 'brew up'.
3. If the casualty's clothes are wet, replace with dry clothes.

4. If the casualty is conscious, persuade them to eat something with high sugar content. Give them a **warm** not hot drink, put sugar in the drink if they refuse to eat.

5. Increase the casualty's body temperature by ensuring their head is covered and placing them in a sleeping bag or thermal blanket, if possible get other group members to lie either side of the casualty to give extra warmth.

6. Arrange for medical assistance to be brought out to the casualty, particularly if they have been unconscious. **Do not let them walk on.**

7. Be aware that breathing may cease in cases of severe hypothermia, be ready to resuscitate if necessary.

COLD + WIND + WETNESS + FATIGUE = HYPOTHERMIA

FROSTNIP AND FROSTBITE

These conditions occur when the weather conditions are very cold. Circulation to the extremities of the body, ears, nose, fingers and toes is reduced causing rapid cooling. If adequate care is not taken to cover and warm through the affected areas, Frostnip will occur, turning these areas white. A sure sign of Frostnip is the hands and feet feeling warm then cold.

Failure to treat Frostnip can lead to Frostbite.

Treatment – Frostnip

1. Warm hands by placing them under the armpits
2. Ears and nose – use the body heat of your buddy
3. Feet – use the body heat of your buddy

Frostbite

Superficial frostbite is where the skin tissues are white/gray, frozen solid to the touch. Left untreated, severe frostbite can develop causing possible loss of fingers, toes, or in very severe cases, the whole hand or foot. **Immediate treatment** can lead to full recovery.

FIRST AID, HEALTH & SAFETY

Treatment – FROSTBITE

1. DO NOT rub the affected areas – it will damage tissues
2. Remove the casualty to shelter
3. Introduce warmth to the affected areas, keeping the weight of blankets etc. off the area.
4. Immediate evacuation from the area should be arranged.
5. If there is to be delay, treat for exposure, give continuous warmth and shelter.

EFFECTS OF HEAT

The body's defence against excessive heat are:
1. Increased blood flow.
2. Increased sweating.
3. Increased respiration

These responses cause increased evaporation of body fluid resulting in a cooling effect. If action is not taken promptly to prevent body fluid loss, the following conditions may occur:

HEAT EXHAUSTION

This is caused by loss of fluid and salt in the body. It primarily affects those who are not used to hot environments and may be accompanied by diarrhoea and vomiting.

Heat exhaustion can occur in violent exercise such as running or long distance walks even in this country, especially if you do not feel well, or your clothing prevents free circulation of air near your skin.

Signs and Symptoms

1. Casualty feels faint.
2. Dizziness, nausea.
3. Moist, clammy skin.
4. Pulse – rapid and weak.
5. Temperature not much above normal.

Treatment

1. Lay casualty down in a cool place.
2. Give sips of water to which salt has been added (half a teaspoon to half a litre of water).
3. Do not allow the casualty to 'over chill'.

FIRST AID, HEALTH & SAFETY

HEAT STROKE

This condition is caused by a failure of the body's 'thermostat' in the brain. The body becomes dangerously overheated due to high fever or prolonged exposure to heat. In some cases, it can follow Heat Exhaustion. Heat Stroke can occur suddenly, causing unconsciousness within minutes.

Signs and Symptoms

1. Sudden loss of consciousness
2. Casualty feels hot, restless and complains of headache.
3. Skin is flushed, warm and dry
4. Pulse is strong and rapid.
5. Body is 'burning up' (fever).

Treatment

1. Lay casualty down in a cool place.
2. Wet casualty all over with cold (NOT ICED) water. The cooling process is helped if a sheet is wrapped around the casualty and kept wet to decrease the heat loss.
3. Get urgent medical assistance.
4. If unconscious, place in the Recovery Position.
5. Be prepared to resuscitate.

**Bearer Company of the
1st. Cadet Battalion King's Royal Rifle Corps.**

The lessons of the South African War led to wholesale changes in the way in which the regular army was trained. This was reflected in the new training manuals prepared for cadets and resulting programmes were both lively and varied. Ironically, the tactics of manoeuvre on which training was based in no way prepared for the trench war that was to come.

Standards were high, matching up to a system in which units were inspected annually and the efficiency of each cadet tested. In the larger units, specialist sections or companies were the order of the day. They included bands, signallers, pioneers, ambulance sections and cyclist sections. This was indeed a golden age and few modern cadet units could match either the variety of activities or the high standards set.

FIRST AID, HEALTH & SAFETY

We illustrate members of the Bearer Company of the 1st. Cadet Battalion King's Royal Rifle Corps. These were fully trained cadets who had gone on to qualify in ambulance work.

As with shooting, there was active competition in this field. In 1906 this particular unit won the Challenge Shield of the Volunteer Medical Association.

The cadets wear the rifle green uniform of the K.R.R.C. with the interesting addition of matching slouch hats with green plumes.

For a number of years following the South African War slouch hats remained in fashion for field training

Bearer Company. 1st. Cadet.Bn. King's Royal Rifle Corps. 1907.

MAKING UP YOUR OWN TRAINING AIDS ADDS A GREAT DEAL OF SATISFACTION TO LEARNING THE SUBJECT. 'WOUNDS' ARE EASILY MADE, SOME CAN BE VERY REALISTIC - IF YOU DON'T KNOW THEY ARE 'MOCK-UPS'.
VERY LITTLE MATERIAL IS REQUIRED, JUST SOME IMAGINATION AND A WORD WITH YOUR FIRST AID TRAINERS OR THE LOCAL ST JOHNS FOR SOME ADVICE.

FIRST AID, HEALTH & SAFETY

DON'T PUT *YOUR* HEAD IN THE SAND!

The development of the contraceptive pill in the 1960's led to females taking responsibility for ensuring they did not become pregnant. Antibiotics meant that Sexually Transmitted Diseases (STDs) and Venereal Disease (VD) could be easily cured. The result was a revolution of sexual habits and social conduct across the world.

The Present is not quite so clear cut; several new sexually transmitted diseases have emerged that cannot be easily cured, such as Herpes, Chlamydia and Pelvic Inflammatory Disease, Hepatitis B and C, not forgetting the discovery of HIV and AIDS. The message is that unprotected sex can cause real discomfort, infertility or a fatal and incurable disease. Find out about these diseases, you need to know!

As a result, young people having or contemplating having sex should make sure they use a condom; "being on the pill' will not protect you.

You need to learn about condoms. Learn how to use one and how to put one on the right way. Used properly they can be an enjoyable part of sex and they could even save your life.

If you cannot afford to buy them, they give them out free at the local Family Planning Clinic or Brook Advisory Centre. These places are totally confidential, you can drop in and pick some up anonymously, or stay and talk through any problems you may have in total confidence. The Brook Advisory Centre will tell you where your nearest local centre is: Tel: 0800 0185 023

Don't be like

one of these

The above information was provided by Lifeline Publications, Manchester M4 1NA **www. lifeline.org.uk**

FIRST AID, HEALTH & SAFETY

SUBSTANCE MISUSE

In First Aid, you learn that a poison is any substance that taken in sufficient quantity can cause temporary or permanent damage to your health. Believe it or not, it is quite possible to poison yourself with water.

The pharmaceutical industry has invested countless billions of pounds to 'invent' drugs to assist our Doctors and Specialists in the prevention and control of medical and psychological conditions. Many of these 'drugs' have side affects; at some time you have probably taken medication that has made you feel sleepy, dizzy or worse! Taken in controlled conditions these side affects can be monitored and the dosage or drug altered. When these 'drugs' are misused, there is a real danger of 'Poisoning' your body.

Who says you get what you pay for?

If you buy a CD from a shop, you know exactly what you are getting. If the CD is faulty, you return it to the shop and either have it replaced or your money refunded.

If you become a 'miss user' of substances then there is a good probability that the substances you buy are not what they seem. They may have been 'bulked up' with things like sugar, laxatives or a cheaper, more lethal cocktail of substances. What you see is not necessarily what you get; you cannot get a refund – even if you are well enough to ask for one.

Mixing Substances. Loading any drug on top of another is very risky. It requires a much lower dose of each drug to provide a 'killer cocktail' – again you do not know exactly what quantities of each substance are – or what they will do to you.

The first paragraph mentions 'any substance'; this section will cover the majority of substances that people 'misuse', what it is, how to take it and the probable side affects.

TOBACCO

Tobacco is one of the most widely used addictive substances in this country. *If you get through 20 cigarettes a day over one year, that is 365 packets costing you well over* **ONE THOUSAND POUNDS!**

FIRST AID, HEALTH & SAFETY

What is does to you: when smoking, you take tar, nicotine and carbon monoxide into your body. (Those around you also inhale these substances). Smokers claim that cigarettes help them concentrate or relax. Some smokers believe that it helps keep their weight down.

The more you smoke the more likely you are to suffer from heart disease, blood clots, cancer, strokes, bronchitis, poor circulation and lung disease. Pregnant women who smoke tend to have smaller babies and run a greater risk of losing the child before or shortly after birth. Tobacco causes over 1000,000 early deaths each year.

ALCOHOL

Alcohol is produced by the fermentation of fruits, vegetables or grain. Beer contains about one part of alcohol to twenty parts of water. Spirits, like whisky or vodka, are almost half alcohol.

What it does to you: The effects of alcohol begin quickly and can last for several hours or more, depending on what you drink and how much. Usually, after a couple of drinks most people feel relaxed and confident. Tolerance to alcohol is an individual thing; some can drink large quantities and show little affect; others, two pints and they have slurred speech, become 'silly' or worse, become aggressive. For many people, drinking moderately is an enjoyable and sociable experience. To avoid probable damage to your health it is a good idea to stick to sensible limits – less than 21 units per week for men and 14 units for women. (One unit is the equivalent of half a pint of ordinary strength beer, lager or cider, a small glass of wine or a single pub measure of spirits). Heavy drinkers face the possibility of liver damage (cirrhosis), heart problems, brain damage, ulcers, etc. in the long term. In the short term, there is always the possibility of alcohol poisoning, (which can be fatal), or being involved in an accident; over 600 people are killed each year in alcohol related accidents such as traffic incidents, falling, choking to death, death in fire – the list goes on.

AMPHETAMINES

Street names: SPEED, UPPERS, SULPHATE, SULPH, WHIZ
Amphetamines were widely prescribed for depression and to suppress appetite. They come in pill or powder form (to be sniffed). It can also be injected.

FIRST AID, HEALTH & SAFETY

What they do to you: Amphetamines arouse the body, giving a sense of energy and confidence, followed by anxiety and irritability. High doses are liable to give you panic attacks, which can last for up to two days. With this substance there is no such thing as enough. To maintain the effect, regular users have to take increasing doses. Each time they stop, depression and hunger force the user back on to the drug. Resistance to disease is lowered; this can be particularly dangerous if the drug is taken by injection.

COCAINE

Street names: SNOW, ROCK, CRACK, BASE

Cocaine is a powerful stimulant with properties similar to those of Amphetamines. It's a white power made from the leaves of the Andean Coca shrub. It is sometimes injected, (often mixed with heroin), but is more likely to be sniffed through a tube into the nose where it is quickly absorbed into the blood through the thin skin which lines the nose. Persistent 'snorters' will damage the structure of the nose, which will require plastic surgery repair.

'Crack ' is cheaper than Cocaine, but far more dangerous. It is cocaine that has been treated with chemicals to enable it to be smoked. The initial 'high' is followed by unpleasant after effects that not only encourage compulsive use, but also encourage dependence.

What is does to you: Cocaine produces feelings of mental exhilaration, well being, indifference to pain and illusions of physical and mental strength. Sometimes these feelings are followed by anxiety, even panic. The effects tend to peak quickly and lessen rapidly. The drug then has to be taken more often to maintain the 'high' and this may lead to dependence.

Over the long term, happiness is replaced by sickness, lack of sleep, and weight loss.

ECSTASY

Mainly known as E or MDMA, comes in tablets or different coloured capsules, liquid or powder form. You could also be offered it under different names, such as Dennis the Menace, Rhubarb and Custard, New Yorkers, Love Doves, Disco Burgers or Phase 4 to name but a few. If it is taken in a hot atmosphere, at a Rave for example, it may cause Heatstroke. There have been several deaths attributable to Ecstasy.

What it does to you: Ecstasy can make people friendly towards each other, or give the feeling of extra energy. Once the effect wears off, it can leave you feeling pretty miserable. Taken in larger amounts, it can cause feelings of anxiety, confusion and paranoia. It can affect the body co-ordination, making it dangerous to do things like driving. Studies also show that it may cause brain damage; long-term use could cause liver damage and insomnia. Some girls find that it makes their periods heavier. It is particularly dangerous those who have a heart condition or Epilepsy.

LSD

Also known as ACID, is a man made substance; minute quantities are impregnated into small squares of blotting paper, which are then allowed to dissolve on the tongue. The squares often have colourful designs on them.
Note: sometimes squares sold as LSD contain none at all.
What it does to you: A trip begins about one hour after taking, and fades gradually in about twelve hours, depending on the dose. Effects depend on the user's mood, where they are, whom they are with and the strength of the dose. Trips often include distortion of vision and hearing, or a feeling of being outside the body. Bad trips can lead to depression, dizziness, even panic. Bad trips are more likely is the user is anxious or in unfamiliar surroundings. Anyone driving whilst under the influence of LSD will endanger themselves and others.

MAGIC MUSHROOMS

There are several types of wild mushroom that can produce dreams or visions. Of these the best known is the Liberty Cap, which contains hallucinogenic chemicals. It is not illegal to pick magic mushrooms and eat them raw; once you dry them or turn them into any kind of preparation you could be outside the law.
What they do to you: A magic mushroom trip is rather like an LSD trip. The difference is that it takes affect quicker and does not last as long. Magic mushrooms can also cause nausea and severe stomach cramps. In this country there are many poisonous fungi, for instance, distinguishing between the Liberty Cap and the highly poisonous Amanita is not easy.

FIRST AID, HEALTH & SAFETY

CANNABIS

Street names: DOPE, BLOW, WACKY BACKY, SHIT, GRASS

Cannabis comes from a plant know as Cannabis Sativa. **Hash** is the commonest form in this country, is resin blocks made from the sap of the plant. Herbal cannabis or marijuana is generally mixed with tobacco, rolled into a cigarette and smoked.

What it does to you: Cannabis makes people feel more relaxed and talkative. It can also reduce the ability to carry out complicated tasks; which would make it dangerous to operate machinery or drive whilst under the effects of the substance. Inexperienced people using high doses, or taking it when depressed, may sometimes experience panic attacks. *Cannabis takes effect very quickly. It can be mixed with food or drink and it is difficult to assess how much has been taken. This can be distressing for the user, particularly if un –knowingly taken, or alcohol is taken at the same time.* Cannabis is not addictive, but users come to rely on it as a method of relaxing.

SOLVENTS

Solvents are found in products like glue, lighter fuel, paint, aerosols and petrol. When the vapours from these substances are inhaled, they produce a similar affect to alcohol. Some users increase the effect by inhaling inside a plastic bag placed over the head.

What is does to you: The effects are similar to being drunk (including the hangover). Vapours are absorbed through the lungs and quickly reach the brain. Repeated inhaling can cause loss of control.

A NASTY WAY TO DIE! *A number of users have died as a result of the miss use because they have squirted aerosol gases directly into their mouths, thus freezing their air passages.* Sniffers can be accidentally injured when they are 'high' because they are in an unsafe place – on a roof or by a railway line; perceptions of danger are non – existent. Sniffers can suffocate I they inhale the solvents by putting plastic bags over their heads. The mouth and nose areas of users are often reddened and blistered. There is a real danger of Sniffers becoming unconscious and choking on their own vomit. Heavy solvent abuse can result in lasting damage to the brain, kidneys and liver.

FIRST AID, HEALTH & SAFETY

BARBITURATES

Street names: BARBS, BLUES, REDS, SEKKIES

Barbiturates - DOWNERS, are used medically to calm people down (as sedatives) and as sleeping pills (hypnotics). Most come in powdered form and are sold in coloured capsules. Users will swallow them, occasionally with alcohol, or inject. *Injecting Barbiturates is one of the most dangerous forms of drug misuse.*

What they do to you: Users of this drug tend to develop a tolerance to them and then a physical as well as mental dependence. Sudden withdrawal can even kill. The effects can include irritability, nervousness, faintness, sleeplessness, sickness, twitching, delirium and convulsions.

TRANQUILLISERS

Street names: TRANX, BENZOS, EGGS, JELLIES

Doctors prescribe tranquillisers to control anxiety and tension, or to help people sleep. Although they are supposed to be taken in pill form, users sometimes inject them in to the body.

What they do to you: they lessen alertness and affect skills where concentration is required. They can also release aggression by lowering inhibitions. Mixed with alcohol they can even cause death. Dependence is fairly common among long-term users. Once people stop taking the drug, they can feel confused, irritable, anxious and unable to carry on with their normal routines.

HEROIN

Street names: SMACK, JUNK, 'H', SKAG

Heroin along with other opiates is made from the opium poppy. In its purest form, it is a white powder. Heroin is sometimes sniffed like cocaine, sometimes smoked, sometimes injected.

What it does to you: Heroin depresses brain activity, widens the blood vessels (giving a feeling of warmth) and causes severe constipation. Opiates create a feeling of total relaxation and detachment from pain or anxiety. They make people warm, drowsy, content, and it appears to relieve stress and discomfort. But this is where the bad news starts. Once physical dependence has established itself simply the relief of getting hold of the drug replaces this pleasure. Users find that they need more and more of the drug to get the same feeling of well being.

FIRST AID, HEALTH & SAFETY

As the intake increases, as it inevitably must, the user feels the effects, even between doses. These include aches, tremors, sweating, chills, and sneezing, yawning and muscular spasms.

Overdosing or using a bad fix results in unconsciousness and coma: often if the user is not discovered in time, death from breathing failure. The chances of dying are even greater if other drugs such as alcohol are used at the same time. First time users often feel sick and vomit, especially if they have injected. Damage to the body is common with users. It is usually caused by repeated injections with dirty needles and by the substances mixed with the heroin by the suppliers to make more money from the batch they are selling. By this time, the user lives for the next 'fix', spending their time trying to raise the money by whatever means they can. An existence

General Note: Users who share needles place themselves at risk of at the least, infection, at the worst, Hepatitis or contracting HIV the virus that can lead to AIDS. Most large towns and cities have chemists who have the facility of providing users with clean hypodermics and needles.

DRUG AND OTHER ABUSE POISONING

You will be well aware of the use of drugs, which is the "broad heading" given to Painkillers, Tranquillisers, Stimulants, amphetamines and LSD, Cocaine, Narcotics, Solvents and in addition Alcohol Poisoning.

In the majority of cases the casualty will have been responsible for their own state or condition, although some casualties may have accidentally taken an overdose. It will be necessary for you to keep strictly to the ABC of First Aid when dealing with them.

We set out on the following pages a chart showing the "cause" and "effect" of drug poisoning which vary depending on the drug taken and the method by which it has been taken.

Although not strictly a drug we have included Alcohol Poisioning as it is a very common situation that the first aider has to deal with and often not taken seriously enough.

FIRST AID, HEALTH & SAFETY

DRUG	EFFECT
Painkillers Aspirin (commonly swallowed)	Upper abdominal pain, nausea, and vomiting (possibly blood stained) Ringing in the ears. "Sighing" breathing. Confusion or delirium.
Paracetamol (commonly swallowed)	Little effect at first. Later, features of liver damage, upper abdominal pain and tenderness, nausea, and vomiting.
Nervous system depressants barbiturates and tranquillisers (commonly swallowed)	Lethargy and sleepiness, leading to unconsciousness. "Shallow" breathing. A weak irregular, or abnormally slow or fast pulse.
Stimulants and hallucinogens - amphetamines and LSD. (commonly swallowed) cocaine (commonly inhaled)	Excitable, hyperactive behaviour, wildness and frenzy. Sweating. Tremor of the hands. Hallucinations, casualty may be "hearing" voices, and/or "seeing" things.

FIRST AID, HEALTH & SAFETY

DRUG	EFFECT
Narcotics - morphine, heroin (commonly injected)	Constricted pupils. Sluggishness and confusion, possibly leading to unconsciousness. Slow, shallow breathing, which may cease. Needle marks may be infected, or infection may be introduced by <u>dirty</u> needles.
Solvents (commonly inhaled) - glue, lighter fuel	Nausea, vomiting and headaches. Hallucinations. Possibly unconsciousness. Rarely, cardiac arrest

TREATMENT
YOUR AIMS ARE: To maintain AIRWAY, BREATHING & CIRCULATION.   To arrange urgent removal to hospital.
CARRY OUT THE ABC of FIRST AID.
   DO NOT ATTEMPT TO INDUCE VOMITING.

ALCOHOL POISONING

Early Stage
Smell, flushed face, deep noisy breathing, full bounding pulse.
Later
Swollen face, shallow breathing, weak, rapid pulse.
DANGER The unconscious casualty may well choke on their vomit.
Hypothermia may develop *if* casualty is not kept warm.

BE AWARE - Alcohol may conceal other serious injury.

TREATMENT Carry out the ABC of First Aid. *if* casualty is unconscious - place in Recovery Position.
   URGENT REMOVAL TO HOSPITAL.

SELF TEST QUESTIONS

1. Name the three types of fracture.
2. Name two signs of a possible fracture
3. When do you carry out a Top to Toe survey?
4. What causes Shock?
5. What is the treatment for Shock?
6. What must a casualty not do if suffering from Shock?
7. How do you tell if a casualty is breathing?
8. In what position do you place an Unconscious, Breathing casualty
9. What is the treatment for a burn or scald?
10. What size burn or scald requires medical attention?
11. In Casualty Management, which casualty must have priority?
12. Name the three key points in the treatment of severe bleeding.
13. What is the treatment for Heat Exhaustion?
14. What is the cause of Heat Stroke?
15. What is your action when you are on your own, and have a
    casualty who is not breathing and shows NO sign of physical
    injury or drowning?
16. How long should you check to see if a casualty is breathing?
17. Where do you find the Carotid pulse?
18. When doing Cardio Pulmonary Resuscitation, when do you stop
    and check that there is no heart beat?
19. What is the ratio of ventilation to compression for C.P.R?
20. What three things do you do to check the level of
    consciousness?
21. Treating a casualty for shock, what are the four things you do
    NOT do.
22. Treating Heat Stroke,what keeps temperature down.
23. Free circulation of air near skin, prevents what.
24. What may cause a patient to have dilated pupils.
25. Give the four effects it has on a brain when its oxygen supply is
    weakened.
26. Who are the principal First Aid Authorities in the UK
27. Explain what the initials D.R.A.B.C mean and how they are
    applied.
28. When do you especially SHOUT HELP.

FIRST AID, HEALTH & SAFETY

.29. What are the AIMS of First Aid.

30. What factors are considered when Assessing the Emergency.

31. Diagnosis, three "key words", what are they and explain the meaning of each one.

32. You can save a life by maintaining a casualties vital needs, what are they.

33. What could cause "noisy, bubbling, gasping breathing".

34. How can you tell if the casualty is breathing.

35. Ventilation: how soon should you give the first ventilations.

36. Where is the Carotid artery.

37. How do you carry out Chest Compression and when is it done.

38. When is the recovery position used.

39. If the casualty has severe bleeding their vital organs are deprived of what.

40. How do you control severe bleeding.

41. A casualty with severe burns or scalds will lose what, and as a result what condition will occur.

42 What do you understand by anything constrictive in the injured area.

43. What MUST NOT be used on a burn or scald.

44. Name three types of fracture.

45. How do you immobilise an injured arm.

46. How do you immobilise an injured leg.

47. What are the symptoms of a casualty with SHOCK

48. What must you NEVER DO with an unconscious casualty.

49. Explain what DILATED PUPILS look like.

50. What affects the "CORE" temperature in the body.

51. What is HEAT EXHAUSTION, its cause and treatment.

52. What is HEATSTROKE, its cause and treatment.

53. If you are gong to make up aa set of training aids for First Aid training who could you get advice from.

54. In health terms what does the abreviation 'STD' refer too.

55. Describe what should be the content of your Detachment First Aid Box.

56. When did you last have a Detachment Fire Drill.

Chapter 10

SIGNALS TRAINING.

INTRODUCTION

Signals equipment issued for your use costs the Ministry of Defence a considerable amount of money to buy and maintain. Therefore it is important that it is cared for and used correctly, at the same time you must learn how to operate efficiently, using procedures the same as the Army and TA. If you don't, then you will be a menace if taking part in exercises or visiting units.

Communications for a modern army are as important as ammunition and petrol, as without good communications things can very quickly go wrong, supplies will not get through, casualties not evacuated etc. The following notes are intended to help you with some basic background information which you need to know. The important thing is to become disciplined in the procedures and practices to such an extent that it becomes second nature when YOU GO "ON THE AIR".

SECURITY

You must realise that if you transmit a message on a radio then it will be heard by both friendly and opposing forces.

It follows that you must become security minded "on the air". In addition the opposition may have a Direction Finding capability, which means if you send long messages they will find out where you are, with the obvious consequences, so, you will discipline yourself to automatically obey the following rules.

- Keep your message as short as possible.

- Speak clearly without over emphasis

- If possible make a note or rehearse what you are going to say, don't think 'on net'.

- If it is a long message split it into parts.

- Encode those parts of the message which might give valuable information such as grid references and timings.

- If you cannot get through to other stations, move, and try a different position for your antenna before increasing power.

SIGNALS TRAINING

CODES

The usual method of ensuring that the opposition does not find out what you are up to is through the use of codes.

The most secure of these is what is known as a one time code, that is, a code which is used only once and then discarded.

The British army now uses a code of this type called BATCO, short for Battle Code. It is easy to use for simple Grid References or long messages. You may be able to learn more of this should you go on exercises with your own TA Unit or have a signals troop/section in your ACF area.

APPOINTMENT TITLES

Appointment titles used to be used for all key personnel, they have now been replaced by call signs except for the appointment title SUNRAY who is any Commander. e.g. Bde, Regt, Bn, Coy, Pl, Tp or Section.

In addition the second in command is known as SUNRAY-MINOR. This is useful since you and the person you are talking to will know who you are talking about, but others will not.

CALL SIGNS

All radio stations on a military net have a call sign. This identifies the user to other users without the need to give away unit names. Always find out which call sign you are before you use a radio The call sign should be *preceded* by a letter of the alphabet which usually changes daily. This letter is known as the *callsign indicator*

SIMPLE VOICE PROCEDURE (VP)
THE REASON WHY VP

1. Because every word spoken on a transmission can be listened to by everyone.
2. Because no matter how smart your equipment is, communications can suffer from interference and your message may not be understood.
3. Because if everyone spoke at the same time it would be chaos.

SIGNALS TRAINING

ABBREVIATIONS and AIDS for ACCURACY

To assist in accurate reception of messages, figures, orders etc. and in addition to the use of the PHONETIC ALPHABET, specially selected words are used in transmissions.

These words are called **'PRO WORDS'**. Each word has a special meaning used within your transmission information.

This enables signallers to keep 'chat' on the radio to a minimum since all messages take the same form this is done with the use of PRO WORDS

PHONETIC ALPHABET

Because letters and figures form the greater part of most transmissions, it is important that all users have a standard method of pronunciation, this is especially important if communications are difficult.

For this reason the PHONETIC ALPHABET has been adopted. You may need to spell out a message, in this case you would use the phonetic alphabet, you will often find that it is useful on a telephone to be certain that detail being given is correctly received.

Always precede the spelling with the words " I SPELL " to give the signaller at the other end warning that he will need to be prepared to write down the letters.

The Phonetic Alphabet

A Alpha	B Bravo	C Charlie
D Delta	E Echo	F Foxtrot
G Golf	H Hotel	I India
J Juliett	K Kilo	L Lima
M Mike	N November	O Oscar
P Papa	Q Quebec	R Romeo
S Sierra	T Tango	U Uniform
V Victor	W Whiskey	X X-Ray
Y Yankee	Z Zulu	

SIGNALS TRAINING

e.g. The town name "York" would be sent as
        " I spell Yankee Oscar Romeo Kilo.
Numbers/Figures can also be sent digit by digit in bad conditions.
e.g.. "Twenty three fifty nine hours " would be sent as
        "FIGURES two three five nine hours"

PRO WORDS

Those PRO WORDS in common use are set out below.

"I SPELL" - I'm going to spell out a word, letter by letter. e.g. YORK
- "I spell Yankee Oscar Romeo Kilo"

"FIGURES" - I'm going to send a number, figure by figure.
        e.g. FIGURES - "Three Six Eight Five Eight Two" (368582)

You can combine PRO WORDS if it is required:
        e.g.. "FIGURES One Nine. I SPELL Alpha Golf.
        FIGURES Six Six" (19AG66)

"HELLO" - Is used to introduce an initial call.

"MESSAGE" - Indicates a message you must write down. **"SEND"** -
go ahead with your transmission.

"OVER" - This is the end of my transmission, I want a reply, go ahead
and send it.

"OUT" - This is the END of my transmission. No reply is expected.

"WAIT OUT" - Your transmission has been received, further
transmission on the same matter will follow later.

"ROGER - SO FAR - OVER" - Have received/sent message more to
follow on this transmission.

"ROGER" - Message received OK, or I have received your last
transmission OK.

"WRONG" - What has been sent is wrong, the correct version is ....

EXAMPLES USING PRO WORDS:-

1. ALL messages start in the following manner.

"HELLO" - followed by the CALL SIGN of the station you wish to talk
to. e.g.. "HELLO A23 THIS IS A11"

2. If the message is short it would immediately follow this.

e.g.. "HELLO A23 THIS IS A11 send rations now"

3. If you do not require an answer end the message with "OUT".

> e.g.. *"HELLO A23 THIS IS A I I send rations now OUT"*

4. If the message is long send it in parts, each part ending with
> *' ROGER SO FAR OVER'.*

This indicates that there is more to follow.

The other station will answer with
> *'ROGER SO FAR OVER'*

to confirm he has received it and is ready for the next part. After you have sent the last part say 'OUT' to end message.

5. Remember - **"OVER"** - means I have finished and am ready/waiting for your reply.

"OUT" - means I have finished and need no reply.

This means that you should **NEVER SAY**, as they do in the Movie's :-- **"OVER and OUT"**.

6. You must also learn **NEVER** to ever say **"REPEAT"** on the radio if you cannot hear or have missed a part of the message, always use **"SAY AGAIN"**.

The word "REPEAT" is used by mortars and artillery **only** to mean FIRE at the same target again, not that you as a cadet will be in such a situation, but it could become a habit if using it.

This might be very upsetting for someone if used wrongly and at the wrong time.

7. If you are looking after a radio, and receive a message asking for information which you do not have readily available or for someone who is not present, use the PRO WORD - **"WAIT OUT"**, make a note of the CALL SIGN, then get the information or fetch the person concerned.

CONTROL OF YOUR VOICE WHEN TRANSMITTING

The manner in which your voice is transmitted can make all the difference to the quality of the signal received at the other end. Practice and remember the following :--

RHYTHM - keep a natural rhythm by dividing the message into suitable phrases.

SPEED - slightly slower than normal conversation - it has to be written down.

SIGNALS TRAINING

VOLUME - as normal volume, there is no need to shout.
PITCH - a higher pitch transmits clearer, but not to feel 'uncomfortable'.

USE OF ABBREVIATIONS

When used abbreviations can save time in talking and writing down a message. Many are used in our daily conversation, so it is quite natural to use some of them 'on the air'. e.g., NCO, ACF, CO, MT.

IF WORKING IN GOOD CONDITIONS

Common abbreviations are spoken as in normal conversation:-
NCO as NCO instead of November Charlie Oscar.
ACF as ACF instead of Alpha Charlie Foxtrot.
CO as CO instead of Charlie Oscar
ETA as ETA. ETD as ETD etc.,

IF WORKING IN BAD CONDITIONS

Abbreviations should only be used if they are going to save valuable time, it would be better to use correct full words.
Headquarters - is shorter than
         "*I SPELL Hotel Quebec*"
Reconnaissance - is shorter than
         "*I SPELL Romeo Echo Charlie Charlie Echo*".

DISCIPLINE

The Operator at the **CONTROL** no matter what his rank, is in charge of the NET and is responsible for it's efficient operation.
  As already said chaos will reign if more than one station speaks at a time so to prevent confusion there are strict rules to follow as below:-

1. LISTEN OUT to make sure the frequency is clear before speaking.
 Don't try to cut-in to other transmissions.

2. Make a SHORT PAUSE at the end of a phrase or part of your message, remember the person receiving will be writing it down.

3. ANSWER all calls immediately and in the correct order.

SIGNALS TRAINING

ORGANISATION - A RADIO NET

The term NET is the abbreviation of NETWORK, meaning where several transmitting stations are grouped together for the purpose of talking to each other.

There are TWO types of STATION:

1. The CONTROL. 2. The SUB-STATION.

A10 In the diagram below the CONTROL STATION has a CALL SIGN - 0

The SUB-STATION "CALL SIGNS" are A10, B10, B20, and B30.

The CALL SIGNS are a combination of LETTERS and FIGURES, which enables them to be identified as a communications station, an organisation or an individual on the radio net.

SEQUENCE OF ANSWERING CALLS.

An important discipline in answering calls is that they must be answered in ALPHABETICAL ORDER FIRST, then in their NUMBER ORDER throughout the NET.

CONTROL ALWAYS ANSWERS FIRST - if it is included in the call.

TYPES OF CALL Types of CALLS can be grouped under FOUR headings as follows:-

1. **SINGLE CALL** - from one Station to another:
    e.g., *"HELLO B10 this is B20"* or *"HELLO A10 this is 0"*

2. **A MULTIPLE CALL** - from one STATION to TWO or MORE STATIONS, BUT NOT the whole NET:
    e.g., *"HELLO 0, B10 and A10 this is B20"* or
    "HELLO 0, A10 and B10 this is B20"

3. An **ALL STATIONS CALL** - from ONE STATION to ALL STATIONS:
    "HELLO all STATIONS this is 0 " or
    "HELLO ALL STATIONS this is B10"

4. **COLLECTIVE CALL** - a CALL to TWO or more STATIONS on the NET who have a pre-arranged call designated to them:
e.g.,

SIGNALS TRAINING

"HELLO CHARLIE, CHARLIE I this is 0"

AN OFFER

An **OFFER** - this is like a 'warning order', a SHORT
transmission to warn STATION(S) that a message follows.

I. An OFFER is made when the SENDER has reason to believe that the

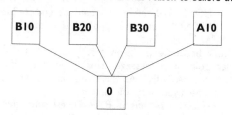

RECEIVER may be involved for some reason that they might NOT
receive the message at all.

In this example the STATION CALL sign B10 has a message for CALL sign
B20 which does not have to be written down, but is not sure that they
are in a position to receive it - in fact they are able to:

"HELLO B20 this is B10 over"."B20 send over"

"B10 move when ready, over/out".

"B20 ROGER out"

2. When the RECEIVER has to take notes it will depend upon the length
and content of the message, but the SENDER must use his common
sense as to when the OFFER should be made. e.g.,

"HELLO 0 and B20 this is B10 message over"

"0 send over" "B20 send over" "B10 no MT at grid 6STWTDAZ
or grid AGSVRT or grid HJKBTR DR now returned - over"

"0 roger out" "B20 roger   out"

SIGNALS TRAINING

CORRECTING MISTAKES AND REPETITION OF MESSAGES

When SENDING you may make a mistake during the TRANSMISSION and will have to correct it.

This is done by using the PRO WORD "WRONG" and going back to the last correct word transmitted as in the example below:

> *"HELLO A10 this is 0 rations at grid 342467*
> *WRONG" "rations at grid 342476 over"*
> *"A10 roger out""*

There may be some occasion that you have to emphasize a particular point in a message. This is done by using the PRO WORD "I SAY AGAIN". As this takes up valuable time it should not be used very often. e.g.,

> *"HELLO A10 this is 0 no cheese with the rations"*
> *"I SAY AGAIN no cheese with the rations*
> *"0   roger out"*

If you wanted to emphasize the whole message, you would say "I SAY AGAIN" at the end of the message and send the whole message again

When receiving a message, you may for many reasons miss a part of it. It would be a waste of time to have all the message sent again and there is a method used in this instance.

You obtain the parts that are missing by referring to a part already received, these parts are known as 'catch words' or 'catch phrases' and you will indicate what you need repeating by using the following PRO WORDS:-

SAY AGAIN,   WORD BEFORE,   WORD AFTER,
ALL BEFORE,   ALL AFTER,   FROM ..... TO ...

If you needed the whole of the message you would use "SAY AGAIN". e.g.,

> *"HELLO B20 this is A10 send transport before*
> *1800 hrs over" "B20 say again" "A10 send*
> *transport   before   1800 hrs over"   "B20 roger out"*

SIGNALS TRAINING

NOTES.

Stations are dealt with individually, using the correct sequence of answering, until "ROGER" is obtained.

The SENDING STATION does not use "I SAY AGAIN" in reply to a request for a REPETITION.

CATCH WORDS or CATCH PHRASES must be easy to identify, it is wrong to use a word that appears in the message more than once as it causes confusion.

The PRO WORD "OUT" should be used whenever possible in GOOD working conditions.

On SINGLE CALLS, the CALL SIGN may be dropped after the initial exchange.

The expression **'OK'** is used only when reporting signal strengths e.g. 'OK, difficult', 'Unworkable', 'Nothing Heard'

It is **NOT** to be used in any other context on the air. The PROWORD **'ROGER'** would usually be correctly used.

LIMITED RESPONSE

When it is established that all CALLED STATIONS are in communication, you should make use of LIMITED RESPONSE in order to improve security since the CALL SIGN responding to CHARLIE CHARLIE (Collective Call) and ALL STATIONS calls are of value to anyone listening in.

The procedure is to nominate one or two STATIONS ONLY to acknowledge as shown in the following examples:

1.   "HELLO ALL STATIONS this is 0, text, A10
        ACKNOWLEDGE over" "A10 roger out"

2.   "HELLO CHARLIE CHARLIE 3 this is 0, text, A10
        and B30 ACKNOWLEDGE over" "A10 roger out"
        "B30 roger out"

IN YOUR OWN INTEREST

The impression that signals training is rather technical may have been overcome now that you have read this section.

Apart from being a very interesting cadet activity, your ability to operate a radio transmitter correctly is not only a valuable skill, but also very desirable one, take every opportunity offered to you for signals training.

SIGNALS TRAINING

Once you have become a proficient signaller there will be many opportunities for you to use that skill.

On attachments to the Army or on exercises with the TA you will become more involved and appreciate how useful it is to be a skilled operator.

The disciplines and procedures are used today by a great many organisations in industry, commerce, and the emergency services.

You never know when in an emergency, you might be called upon to use these skills, don't be found wanting if the situation presented itself.

You can practice by using the procedures and applying the disciplines and principles every day in many situation.

SIGNALLING A 4 STAR OPTION

Signalling will be an option at 4 Star level. Once you are tested and certificated your cadet signalling qualifications can count towards your Duke of Edinburgh's Award.

Qualifications. Signalling courses at the Royal School of Signals, Blandford, Dorset.

On qualifying as a 'crossed flags' Cadet Signaller you will be eligible to attend the Post-classification' and 'Advanced' courses held during the Easter and Summer holidays at the Royal School of Signals, Blandford, Dorset.

Your Detachment receives the programme and full details on an annual basis, book your place early to avoid disappointment!

SIGNALS TRAINING

SELF TEST QUESTIONS

1. What are the six rules for "Security on the air".
2. Why use codes.
3. Who is a SUNRAY and a SUNRAY MINOR.
4. What identifies the user to another user.
5. Give the three reasons for having Voice Procedure.
6. Say the Phonetic Alphabet.
7. What is a Pro Word used for and why.
8. If you are to spell out a word, how do you start.
9. If sending numbers, how do you send them.
10. How do you introduce an initial call.
11. How do you know if you must write down a message.
12. How do you know when to send a transmission.
13. What do you say at the end of a transmission.
14. What do you say at the end of your message if you want a reply.
15. Having sent part of a message with more to send, how do you tell the receiver there is more coming.
16. What does ROGER mean.
17. How do you tell a receiver when you have sent incorrect information in your transmission.
18. Why should you NEVER say "Over and Out"
19. Who uses the message "REPEAT"
20. If you cannot hear or miss a word, how do you ask for it to be repeated.
21. In the middle of a message you need to stop, how do you tell the sender.
22. What do RHYTHM, SPEED, VOLUME and PITCH refer to, explain what each of them mean.
23. When are Common Abbreviations used.

SIGNALS TRAINING

24. How do you give Common Abbreviations when working in bad conditions.

25. Which operator is in charge of the NET.

26. What is the sequence of answering calls.

27. Name the different types of call and explain the difference between them.

28. What do you understand by an "OFFER".

29. What is a "Catch Word" or a "Catch Phrase".

30. Why use a LIMITED RESPONSE call.

THERE IS GREAT PERSONAL VALUE IN ATTAINING THE DUKE OF EDINBURGH'S GOLD AWARD.
PEOPLE WILL RECOGNISE YOUR ABILITY AND SELF DISCIPLINE TO HAVE ACHIEVED THIS COVETED AWARD.

Signal Section. Imperial Cadet Yeomanry 1912
Proficiency Arm Badge Signaller.

Signal Section. Imperial Cadet Yeomanry 1912

In 1910 the War Office set up the Territorial Cadet Force, an organisation which was to include all cadet units giving military training, other than those school corps which in 1908 had elected to become part of the Officers Training Corps. Powers to recognise and administer cadet units were delegated to the Territorial Force Association of each county. Behind the new move was a feeling that cadet units had an important part to play in providing recruits for the Territorial Force.

Most cadet units were now affiliated to a Territorial Force unit. Here we see members of a signal section receiving instruction. They form part of the Yorkshire Squadron, Imperial Cadet Yeomanry, affiliated to the Yorkshire Hussars. Another squadron of the Imperial Cadet Yeomanry was based in City of London. It should be pointed out that no mounted instruction was undertaken, all cadet units had to follow a programme of infantry training.

Increasing numbers of cadet units now wore khaki service dress, though more colourful uniforms still persisted. The speed of change was governed by cost, uniforms were still paid for either by the individual cadet or locally raised funds.

Chapter 11
BANDS IN THE ARMY CADET FORCE

INTRODUCTION

If you joined a Cadet Band in the past, not only did you have band practice, you had to keep up with ALL the APC training as well.

BAND UNITS/DETACHMENTS

Many Counties have Detachments or Units where all the Cadets are members of the Band. This does not mean that it is to the exclusion of other training, you will have to pass your One Star training alongside your Band training. The syllabus then changes from Two Star onwards, and is directly related to improving standards and ability with the instrument(s) you have chosen to play. Many 'Band Cadets' chose to continue with their APC training, often to assist them in completing their Duke of Edinburgh's Award work. It is worth noting that a Band Cadet who chooses to continue with their APC and Band training has far more to learn than a non – band Cadet. The Cadet who has some distance to travel to his/her Band Unit rather than attend the local Cadet Detachment also shows considerable commitment.

This is before all the extra nights down at the Detachment practicing for a special parade, the cleaning and maintenance of instruments, special uniforms and equipment – that's DEDICATION!

DRUM AND BUGLE BANDS

Many Cadet Detachments have their own bands, the majority of which are Drum and Bugle. Although there may only be a few in a Detachment who play, they normally join together with other Detachment Bands for practices and parades, especially at Annual Camp.

OTHER SKILLS REQUIRED

As a Bands person you not only have to play your instrument well, you have to be proficient at foot drill and do both together, not as easy as it may appear. It is also expected that your Turnout must be immaculate at all times.

BANDS IN THE ACF

The reason for this is twofold, firstly, you. Why spoil all your hard work by not looking and sounding the best? Secondly, the public frequently sees your Band; you are representing your County and the ACF each time you are on parade. Feel good about it!

QUALIFICATIONS AND EQUIPMENT

Qualifications: this is dependent on whether you are either able to take lessons through your school or the level of musical instruction your Instructors in the Band can take you to. However, if you are keen enough to continue, being able to play a musical instrument well is a much envied and rewarding talent. Parents are usually very supportive (and proud!) when they see you doing something so worthwhile.

If you have the opportunity to play in a Full Military Band and be trained in Woodwind, Brass or Percussion, you will be tested on the Full Military Band Syllabus for your instrument(s). Either the Associated Board of Music or the Grade Examinations for Trinity College of Music, London, sets the standards for the tests. To attain this grade of proficiency may well be useful if you wish to follow music as a career either in the Army or a professional band/orchestra. The grades achieved for passes in your APC levels are as follows:

NOTE - See details for BTEC First Diploma in Music on page 13-23

BAND – APC QUALIFICATIONS

2 STAR
Pass Grade 3 in Associated Board or Trinity College practical exam

3 STAR
Pass Grade 4 in Associated Board or Trinity College practical exam

4 STAR
Pass Grade 5 in Associated Board or Trinity College practical exam

DRUM AND PIPE BANDS

As with the Full Military Band testing, appropriate levels of attainment are set out for the Bagpipes the Band Instructors will advise you. Instruments: some Bands have a pool of instruments for Cadets to

BANDS IN THE ACF

use, but the majority expects Cadets to buy their own instrument. These can be costly, especially if bought new. Second hand instruments are often advertised in the press, specialist music magazines or on the Internet; shop around you may find a bargain. Another resource could be family or friends; they may have just what you are looking for tucked away in the loft.

FINANCE AND SUPPORT

Bands in the Cadet Force are NOT supported financially by the Ministry of Defence or issued with instruments, uniforms or other equipment. Travel to engagements is often difficult; many parents, Band Officers and Instructors will use their own transport to ensure Cadets get to the engagement. However, Cadet Bands do get encouragement and support from their County and Band helpers to raise funds. They also receive donations or a fee when they attend a function.

BEARDMORE CADET CORPS 1918

The 1914-18 war saw a massive expansion of the Cadet Force, once initial losses of adults to the regular forces had been overcome. Existing units increased in size and many new ones were formed. In spite of a small War Office capitation grant, the movement had to remain largely self-sufficient and uniforms had to be purchased. Few weapons remained available and most units trained with dummy rifles or obsolete carbines. Our illustration shows a bugler of the Beardmore Cadet Corps, Glasgow. This was a unit recruited from employees of the Beardmore Engineering Company and was affiliated to the 7th. Battalion Highland Light Infantry. By now, khaki was in general use for cadet units, but Scottish units could present a more colourful picture.

A rifle green glengarry is being worn, carrying the regimental badge. The khaki tunic is of the pattern peculiar to Scottish regiments, the bottom edge being rounded and cut away at the front.

BANDS IN THE ACF

On the shoulder straps a bugle is worn over the word BEARDMORE. Though affiliated to a lowland regiment, a kilt is worn in the Mackenzie tartan. Trews are confined to officers of the unit.

The sporran has a black top which carries a regimental badge, the hair is in black with three tassels in white. Red and white hose tops together with white spats complete the uniform.

Unlike many units, the Beardmore Cadets continued to operate during the post-war years and by 1929 could still muster 120 cadets. With the temporary withdrawal of official recognition in

1930, the unit became 'Beardmore Company of Scottish Cadets' and the cap badge of the Corps of Scottish Cadets was worn. Though the Beardmore works is no more, the unit continues in existence. Today it is affiliated to the Royal Highland Fusiliers, the regiment formed by the amalgamation of the Highland Light Infantry and the Royal Scots Fusiliers. The background of the picture depicts the Toll Booth Glasgow.

Chapter 12

METHODS OF INSTRUCTION

The 'Golden Rule' of successful instruction:

THE SIX P'S

PRIOR PREPARATION AND PRACTICE PREVENTS POOR PERFORMANCE

INTRODUCTION

Methods of Instruction, (MOI) follows the system used by the Army. Providing you apply the well tried and practiced framework called a **Lesson Plan** you will find that instructing becomes simplified and there is less chance of you 'losing your way' in a class.

As a Senior Cadet, the skills you acquire following this system will improve your confidence; it is a skill that you may be able to put to good use in your career.

QUALITIES REQUIRED

The main qualities you need as an instructor are:

1. Enthusiasm – boredom is infectious
2. Self confidence – through following the 6 P's
3. Good knowledge of your subject. Your class soon picks up on 'Surface knowledge'.
4. Look the part – be smart
5. Good manner and bearing - look up whilst you speak, your voice will travel further.
6. Vary the pitch/strength of your voice to stress a particular point and keep the class alert.
7. Be firm but fair - encourage your class to join in – to a point!

METHOD OF INSTRUCTION

8. Never be satisfied with your standard of instruction, always look for ways to improve your presentation skills
9. The ability to instruct **clearly, completely, patiently, giving information at a suitable pace, one stage at a time.**

AVOID

The following are the **"DO NOT's"**

1. Use sarcasm to get a laugh
2. Make a fool of one of the cadets in front of the class
3. Use remarks that have a double meaning or that may offend one of the class
4. Pick on one cadet to answer questions too often
5. Do not 'cut corners' by omitting important information or assuming knowledge
6. Overload your lesson with too many aids, e.g. a projector, flip chart, overhead projector video recorder, camera and computer for one lesson will detract from subject matter. Keep it simple but effective.
7. Watch yourself for distracting mannerisms such as saying 'OK' or 'RIGHT' after each statement, scratching your nose etc. You know how it is when you are the student and your teacher/ instructor's mannerisms become more interesting than the lesson.

PREPARE AND PLAN

1. What is the objective?
2. Which is the best method – lecture, lesson, discussion, exercise or demonstration.
3. Where is the instruction to take place – a small room may rule out some of the activities you may wish to use.
4. What is the size of the class?
5. What time is available?
6. What equipment and training aids are available?
7. Are the aids suitable, simple enough, large enough or even necessary?
8. What handout notes should be produced?
9. What is the present standard of the class's knowledge?
10. Prepare your list of questions and answers for this lesson and have your questions and answers ready from the previous lesson if appropriate.

METHOD OF INSTRUCTION

SKILLS LESSONS – (Drill, Skill at Arms, etc.)

Remember and use the sequence: (EDIP)

EXPLANATION – DEMONSTRATION
– IMITATION - PRACTICE

STAGE	KEY POINT
BREAK DOWN THE LESSON TO AS MANY STAGES AS YOU LIKE	IMPORTANT POINTS NOT TO BE MISSED
1	STRESS SAFETY, ANYTHING THAT CAN CAUSE DAMAGE
2	"MEMORY TICKLER" FOR SIZES, MEASUREMENTS REFERENCES, COLOURS ETC

A SIMPLE LESSON PLAN

Rule up sheets of paper using the sample as a guide, setting out the **STAGES** or **BLOCKS** of information as headings on the subject, and the **KEY POINTS** which are the important points to be made, such as safety, figures, codes, references and the correct training aid to use at this particular point, use this section as a prompt, drawing as many lines as you require. Don't forget to write large enough and clearly as you may be using your plan when standing up - **NOT** held in your hand, reading from it!

The plan is divided in to three stages:

STAGE ONE – BEGINNING

Subject: Class/Squad: Time: Location:

Dress: Stores required and Training Aids:

Time allowed:

METHOD OF INSTRUCTION

'Prelims': Roll Call: Safety Precautions: Class Formation: Seating Plan: Comfort of the Class: Lighting Levels: Standard of Visual Aids. Training aids make sure they all work and you have sufficient for the class; spare bulbs for OHP

Introduction: Make sure the class know your name.

Objective: must be clearly stated and understood, attainable in the time allowed.

Reason Why: give a realistic reason, incentive to achieve

Results: Benefits to be gained from the lesson.

Revision: Check the classes' knowledge/skills in the subject previously taught. Cadets soon forget.

STAGE TWO – THE MIDDLE

The main instruction to be taught. Time allowed – divide the subject in to several **STAGES**, select from each stage the **KEY POINTS** that you must bring out in your instruction, for example, SAFETY to ensure a complete understanding of the lesson.

CONFIRMATION

At the end of each **STAGE** of the instruction, confirm that the key points have been understood. It is important to ensure that all the class are 'kept on their toes' you must therefore **pose the question to the whole squad,** wait for a few moments for them **ALL** to think of the answer, then **select or nominate one of them to answer.**

Note: if a cadet is unable to answer the question, give a little time, then re-nominate. Correct any errors as they occur. Do not keep nominating the same cadet – even if they give the correct answers!

ASK - PAUSE – NOMINATE

METHOD OF INSTRUCTION

STAGE THREE – THE END

Invite questions from the class; if you are asked a question and do not know the answer, do not try and bluff your way out, ADMIT IT, but find out and let them know – **MAKE SURE THAT Y OU DO!**

Use your prepared questions to confirm that the class has achieved the objective of the lesson. In the case of skills based instruction you will confirm by practical assessment.

Summary: – bring out and stress the achievement of the objective. Once you have taken the time to plan and produce a Lesson Plan - stick to it - it is so much easier than getting lost for words!

Look forward: state when the next lesson will be/what the next lesson will be.

KEEP ALL YOUR LESSON PLANS – CAREFULLY FILE THEM FOR EASY REFERENCE. THE NEXT TIME YOU TAKE THAT LESSON – HALF YOUR WORK WILL ALREADY BE DONE.

TRAINING AIDS

There are various methods of presentation available today such as OHP, Power Point, Videos, etc all of which have their advantages and disadvantages.

Whatever medium you decide to use always be prpared for a 'system failure' or lack or equiment. Have a 'back up' and be prepared to improvise.

You will have to allow plenty of time to set up equipment and ensure it is all working. Likewise check that any handouts are available and set out in the order they are required. Rehearse any demonstration and check that those who may be assisting do know what and when to perform.

IMPROVISED TRAINING AIDS

Many Detachments will have a box in their stores of 'training aids' which amongst other item will have an old blanket used as a 'cloth model' for tactical training or perhaps a lump of plasticene for teaching contours and relief for map reading. What appears to be a blood stained trophy is in fact an improvised wound for a compound fracture. If your Detachment does not have improvised Training Aids

METHOD OF INSTRUCTION

SELF TEST QUESTIONS

1. What is the "Framework" used for good instruction.
2. When preparing a lesson what do you have to take to do it correctly.
3. What are the qualities required of a good instructor.
4. What should you do about habits.
5. Look up when you speak, — why.
6. What do you understand by "looking the part".
7. Complete the following sentence; "Instruct, Clearly, completely one _ _ _ _ at a _ _ _ _
8. As an instructor how can you check your own performance.
9. What are the six "Basic Points of Instruction.
10 Name six of the ten things to do before you Prepare and Plan a lesson.
11. How do you use the "Questioning Technique".
12. If instructing a SKILL, what is the "Sequence of Instruction".
13. What do you understand by a. "A STAGE. b. "A KEY POINT".
14. A COMPLETE lesson is broken into how many parts or stages, what is the name of each one.
15. What are you doing if you are carrying out the "PRELIMS".
16. What do you do about Training Aids before a lesson.
17. If asked a valid question and you don't know the answer, what do you do about it.
18. Name three methods to confirm that all your class members have learned the lesson given.
19. Why and how should you keep the lesson plan that you have just used.
20. What is the last thing you tell a class before finishing.
21. If the lesson is on any Skill at Arms subject, (including Shooting), what is the FIRST and most important action to carry out and who takes part in it.

Chapter 13
THE CADET N.C.O. & OPPORTUNITIES AFTER TWO STAR

County ACFs have different methods of NCO selection and training. The following are intended as general comments.

Every Cadet has the opportunity to earn promotion. The skills and abilities you require can only be developed by training and practice. To a great extent your opportunity for promotion is entirely in your hands. From your first Parade night your attitude towards your mates, how you respond to being given instructions and how well you carry them out. Some of the essential qualities are:

Loyalty and pride in the Regiment or Corps to which you are badged, your County and Detachment and the Army Cadet Force.

Enthusiasm in all that you do, encouraging other Cadets to imitate you.

Sense of humour: especially when things go wrong. Do not laugh AT others; laugh with them.

Initiative to anticipate what will be required of you.

Knowledge of your subjects – giving others confidence in your ability

Instructional ability, watch and learn from good instructors

Self discipline in the way you behave

Reliability is important, if you say that you will do something, DO IT

Good manners are never forgotten

PROMOTION IS NEVER AUTOMATIC

Promotion is related to your qualifications as well as your ability. You will need to achieve the standards set out below and be recommended for consideration as a candidate for promotion by your Officers and Instructors.

Lance Corporal	Not before passing **One Star**
Corporal	Not before passing **Two Star**
Sergeant	Not before passing **Three Star**
Master Cadet	having attained your Four Star, completed the Master Cadet Course at Frimley Park, and subsequently been recommended by your County Cadet Commandant.

THE CADET N.C.O. & OPPORTUNITIES AFTER 2 STAR

Under Officer having passed your Four Star and also been recommended by your County Cadet Commandant.
Changes to these rules will only be permissible in exceptional circumstances and with the approval of your County Cadet Commandant.

PROMOTION CADRES

Most County Cadet Forces take the promoting of their Cadets very seriously. They have a system of promotion courses similar to the Army system; these courses are called NCO's Cadres.
The Cadres are usually organised over a weekend or perhaps at Annual Camp, when potential NCOs are brought together and given the opportunity of showing how the have developed, not only in their APC skills, but to see how they behave when with their fellow candidates. The Cadre usually follows the form of planning and taking lessons, command exercises, lecturettes, initiative tests, games and other activities.
Cadets who have taken part usually say that it is great fun and a good method of finding out their strengths and weaknesses, to see how you behave under different circumstances and conditions. All the Officers and Instructors make an assessment before final recommendations are made concerning your suitability as an NCO.

CADET NCOs

Duties and Responsibilities
Junior N.C.O.

You will learn how to instruct the basic APC subjects and also how to take command of a squad.
With the other NCOs in the Detachment, you are responsible to your Detachment Commander to assist with the organisation and smooth running of your Detachment at the level of your rank.
When you earn your first stripe, it is easy to start "throwing your weight around". The first to know about it are the mates who were happy to have a laugh with you before, but now avoid you. It could be that they respect your promotion, now you have to prove to them and yourself that you are worthy of it. This is a good time to consider some of the actions and failings of bad **Cadet NCOs.**

FAILINGS

1. Intimidate individuals by shouting at them, particularly when standing close up to them.
2. Making personal contact (touch) when addressing them.
3. Use foul language, make offensive personal remarks about an individuals background, height etc, or make threats of what might become of them.
4. Make an example of an individual by punishing without due reason, or belittling them in front of others.
5. Keep picking on an individual in front of others. If they are persistent offenders, not reporting individual for OC to deal with.
6. Borrowing money or asking favours of Cadets.
7. Not sharing duties or "chores" fairly, not having a duty roster displayed.
8. Being late with orders/information, not allowing time for all to respond.
9. Asking Cadets to clean, press etc. your personal kit or equipment.
10. Not reading Orders, being un-informed of duties, events.
11. Fail to check untidy Cadets and/or their rooms.
12. Always late for parades and duties.
13. Puts off dealing with complaints and problems reported to them.
14. Does not praise or give encouragement for good work.
15. Passes on responsibilities to others, lacks personal discipline; does not bother to prepare lesson plans.
16. Using first names when "On Parade" – difficult, but surnames should be used.
17. Failing to report serious breaches in discipline, theft, illegal substance taking, Cadets out of bounds.
18. Sets a bad example by being untidy in uniform and civilian clothes.
19. Annoying mannerisms such as saying "OK" or "Right" after every sentence etc.
20. Throwing their weight about, always going to the front of the queue in the Naafi or Dining Hall.
21. Behaviour either as an individual or a member of a group that may harm the reputation of the ACF and the Detachment.

No doubt you can think of many more, make sure you are not guilty of them!

Don't forget that:
WITH AUTHORITY GOES _RESPONSIBILITY_

THE CADET N.C.O. & OPPORTUNITIES AFTER 2 STAR

Senior N.C.O.

As a Senior Cadet NCO in your Detachment, you have responsibilities at all times; on or off Parade. In any activity where Cadets are involved or it is known that you are a member of the Army Cadet Force.
You will be directly responsible to your Detachment Commander for the Cadets in your Detachment.

Delegation of Responsibility

The Detachment Commander and Instructors in your Detachment 'share' some of their authority in running the Detachment with you. This means that they must be seen to give you the backing or authority to carry out tasks within the Detachment leaving you to probably make mistakes. This is all part of the learning curve; providing you do learn from your mistakes.
In return your Detachment Commander and Instructors will expect you to measure up to the trust they have in you.

DEVELOPING YOUR ABILITY AS AN NCO

RESPECT AND DISCIPLINE

"Respect is not a right, it has to be earned"

Respect and discipline are together; one cannot exist without the other. How can you gain respect? There are two ways firstly through fear, by proving you are bigger, stronger, can hit harder and swear better. To put it briefly, by being a bully.
Secondly, by gaining the Cadets trust and through that their respect and wish to do as you ask.
In America in 1940, they needed one million managers to run their war effort. They were aware of the need for good relations in the work place, resulting in the introduction of the **"Foundation For Good Relations"**. They have been converted into "Cadet speak" as follows:

1. Let your Cadets know in advance of things that affect them; what's on, date, time, place and the reason why it is being done.
2. If someone does well – give him or her the credit for it when it is due – at the time, NOT afterwards.
3. NEVER criticize or check other NCO's or Cadets in front of assembled Cadets.
4. Always take the individual "out of earshot" of others if you are to reprimand them.

5. Recognise the ability of other Cadets and NCO's, give them every opportunity to show and use their talents.

If Cadets know that you will ensure they are kept informed, trust, respect and good teamwork will follow. Listen to those who supervise you both now and throughout your career. You will know immediately those who value Good Relations and the importance they place upon it.

Following the **Foundation For Good Relations"** requires the same control as remembering not to swear, shout and dish out punishments for every minor offence; self-discipline. You will get far more out of your squad wheresoever you are, **"Speaking softly, but carrying a big stick"**. In other words, use the trust and respect you have earned to control your Cadets; not shouting or using discipline unnessarily.

WORKING WITH SUBORDINATES

Unlike your counterparts in the Regular or Territorial Army, you have no power to order any form of punishment. Physical punishment such as 'push ups' or making the Cadet look small in front of other Cadets is not allowed. NEVER touch, i.e. *personal contact*, strike, push trip up or in any other way deliberately touch a subordinate Cadet, it could result in legal action being taken, and it is a form of bullying.

When a Cadet's uniform needs adjusting, let them do it themselves, that way they learn by their mistakes.

DISCIPLINING A CADET

When disciplining a Cadet, ensure that the reprimand is not made in the hearing or presence of others and that it is done at the time or immediately after the incident. Where possible, use constructive criticism, for example, a Cadet is fooling about in a lesson, when you speak to him/her you could say; "You have been doing so well at (whatever subject they are good at), I am disappointed that you are not making the same effort in (whatever subject the lesson is), I expected better of you". It takes practice to get constructive criticism right, but it really does work well if your Cadets have respect for you as an NCO.

BULLYING

Bullying comes in many forms, and most of us have been victims, perhaps without realising it.

Earlier on in this Chapter there is a list of some of the actions of a bad NCO, many of these are recognised as bullying. As an NCO you must guard against appearing to "pick" on a particular Cadet, it gives them bad feelings about the Cadet Force and it **IS** bullying. Issuing threats and promises is another common form of bullying and an easy trap to fall in to. As a senior Cadet NCO, watch newly appointed junior NCOs to ensure they get it right from the start and follow the **Foundation For Good Relations.**

Bullying destroys a person's self esteem; it makes them withdraw from the 'team', lose interest in activities, and stops them attending Detachment Parades. If you recognise the signs in a Cadet, watch, listen and when you have **proof**, report it.

As an NCO you will perhaps find a junior Cadet "Disclosing". This is the term used for a child or young person admitting to physical or mental abuse against them. If this occurs, you must tell the Cadet concerned that you have to inform your Officer in Charge. DO NOT try to deal with the problem yourself, or talk to anyone other than the people in charge, it is a serious matter and requires official action.

WHEN YOU MAKE MISTAKES

The more inexperienced you are, the more likely you are to be reprimanded by your superiors. At times you may feel a rebuke was not warranted and unfair. It is not so much what you may have done, but the way you take being 'torn off a strip'. Never sulk, or feel someone has a 'down on you', accept that the rebuke was carried out in good faith. However, if the matter is serious and you genuinely were not at fault, do not complain to everyone within earshot, it does not help your image. Accept the rebuke, then gather your facts together, ask for an interview with the Officer or Instructor concerned **- in private** and present your facts.

ATTITUDE TO ORDERS

There are times when you will be required to carry out an order given by a superior which you know will be unpopular with the Cadets. This order should be given as 'your order', never apologise for it, just carry it out to the letter. If it is an order or instruction that you disagree with, carry it out, gather your facts and evidence in logical sequence and present them to the Officer or Instructor concerned. Use the procedure described in 'when you make mistakes'.

Should you be given an order or instruction which through the individual's lack of specific knowledge or experience is illegal, dangerous or in contravention of safety rules, then in spite of the individual being of superior rank, it would be important to point out the facts to them. Try and do this away from other people if possible, but safety is paramount, you cannot be ordered to break safety rules.

COURTESY TO SUPERIORS

At times you may find it difficult to give the respect due to certain Officers and Instructors in your County. It helps to remember that you are giving respect to their rank not the individual. Question yourself about why you feel the way you do, what is it about the individual's behaviour/attitude; ensure that you do not make the same mistakes and continue to give the rank the respect it requires.

THE PARADE GROUND

In some Regular Army units you may find that the square is the 'personal property' of the RSM and is only used for drill parades and should NEVER be walked across in a casual way. It perhaps would be as well to assume this when visiting a Regular Army base and ensure that all Cadets are encouraged to follow your example.

OFFICER'S, WARRANT OFFICERS & SERGEANT'S MESS

Many Counties arrange for the more senior Cadets (3 and 4 Star) to visit the Mess on the afternoon prior to their formal Mess Dinner, and as a Cadet Under Officer you will attend these functions. The following may help you. Your guide is usually a senior member of the Mess, who will explain the history of the Mess silver, procedures and etiquette that is expected from Mess Members when attending a Mess Dinner. These dinners are usually formal, and follow the Regular Army in format.

Some of the more senior Cadets will be invited to 'wait on table' for Mess Dinners, and may receive some training in what should be done.

THE CADET N.C.O. & OPPORTUNITIES AFTER 2 STAR

1. The Mess Steward will allocate your duties, you may be given a section of table to care for, or you may be given specific items to serve.

2. You will be taken in to the Dining Room to familiarise yourself with the layout, where items are to be found and how your duties will be carried out.

3. You may well assist in the placing of the cutlery and glasses, a sample layout of a "Dinner cover" or "Place setting" is shown further on in this section along with an explanation of how to 'navigate' the setting should you ever be invited to a formal dinner.

4. **The evening commences:** it is common practice for the diners to congregate at the Mess approximately 30 minutes before the Dinner is to commence. You will perhaps be asked to serve sherry to Mess Members and their guests. You will notice that no one is late for this 'gathering', it is seen as an insult to the Mess.

5. The Mess Steward will gain the attention of the Mess Members, (usually by a gong, and shouting out "Ladies and Gentlemen, Dinner is served"). The Senior Officers and Guests are allowed to enter the Dining Room first, followed by others in order of rank. The reason for this is clear when you study the Seating Plan, the more senior ranking Officers are nearest the 'top table' it is therefore common sense as well as courtesy that they should enter the room first.

6. All remain standing until Grace is said, then when the top table is seated, all others take their seat. A note here, if there are female Mess Members or Guests, it is still seen as 'good manners' to pull her chair back and assist her to the seat. In some Messes, it is a 'Waiter' who performs this task, in others it is expected of a male diner seated next to her.

7. **The Meal:** The Mess Steward will 'give the nod' for you to begin serving food. You will be shown how to serve food; it is not as easy as it looks! No plates are cleared from any table until all the diners have completed the course.

8. Keep a sharp eye out for signals from diners, they may have dropped a knife or fork, spilt some wine etc. it is part of your duties to provide clean cutlery or a cloth for mopping should it be required.

9. **Wine:** If you experience problems with a Mess Member concerning the amount of wine he/she is demanding, be polite and quickly advise the Mess Steward who will take the appropriate action.

Some Cadets take the opportunity to 'refresh' themselves with the nearly empty bottles of wine. **TAKE CARE!** You have probably been training in the morning, working in the Mess in the afternoon and will not get to bed until after midnight. Wine will cloud your judgment of distance, and make you sleepy. Keep alert, save the wine until the work is finished.

10. **The Loyal Toast: Port** is served to the Mess Members, watch for those who do not wish to have Port, they will require water in their glass in order to drink to the toasts called.

11. **Leaving the Table:** When the Senior Officers present and their guests stand to leave their tables, one of two things may occur, firstly, all other diners remain seated, or secondly, all other diners stand until the parties have left the Dining Room and moved to the Ante-room.

Hors d'Oeuvre: is a dish served as a relish at the beginning of a meal. If you are offered a selection, choose three or four; don't aim to sample them all! They are eaten with both a fish knife and fork or with a tea spoon depending on the item, for melon, a dessert spoon and knife or fruit fork and knife are used.

Soup: taken with a round-bowled soup spoon. Drink your soup from the **side** of the spoon

• Tip the soup bowl **away** from you to finish the last of the soup
• The bread bun should be **broken not cut**
• Do not put the bread in your soup or use it to clean the soup bowl
• If you wish to use butter, butter a small bite sized piece of bread at a time.

Fish: use a fish knife and fork, if you have used your fish knife and fork for the Hors d'Oeuvre, and you have not been provided with 'new', ask the waiter for them.

• If the fish is on the bone, do not turn it over; you will never get the bones out!
• If you are unlucky enough to get a fishbone in your mouth, it is the **only time** you can remove it from your mouth with your fingers (unobtrusively behind your napkin).

Entrée: this is a dish served between the fish course and the main course, eaten with a knife and fork.

Main Course: self-explanatory, usually meat or poultry. If you find gristle or bone in your mouth, remove with your fork and place on the side of your plate.

THE CADET N.C.O. & OPPORTUNITIES AFTER 2 STAR

Pudding: usually eaten with a spoon and fork. The fork may be used alone, but not the spoon unless a special spoon is provided for ice cream or fruit salad.

Dessert: are items such as petit fours (marzipan sweetmeats).

Fruit: eaten with a dessert knife and fork, normally cut up (or peeled), before eating. Use the finger bowl if provided, to clean sticky fingers, just dip them in the water and dry on your napkin.

Cheese board: usually with a selection of cheeses and biscuits. Take small quantities of three or four cheeses.

General Notes:

1. **Salt, Pepper and Mustard:** salt should be placed on the side of your plate, not scattered over the meal, as pepper is. Mustard should also be placed on the side of the plate, do not tap the spoon on the plate to dislodge the mustard.

2. **Mess Silver:** when dining in an Officer's or Warrant Officer's Mess, do not touch the Mess Silver. In some messes this can mean a fine.

3. **Other diners:** always be mindful of their needs, ask if they require the salt, etc.

4. **Ask:** do not reach far across the table for an item; ask for it to be passed to you, or request the waiter/steward to get it for you.

5. **Dropped cutlery:** do not dive under the table, ask the waiter to provide clean.

6. **Talk to your neighbours:** at either side and directly across the table, do not attempt to talk to a person where it means either shouting, or leaning in front of someone. This does **NOT** include catapulting peas or pieces of paper at them; it will earn you a severe telling off from the PMC. (President, Mess Committee).

7. **Napkins:** at the end of the meal, rough folded it and left on the table.

8. **General Behaviour:** in some Messes, it is the custom that once the senior mess members and guests have departed, the junior mess members 'Let off steam'. This often includes finishing the port, playing forfeits etc.

Dancing on the table and playing football with the mess silver is not a recommended course of action - let others make that mistake! Excuse yourself and disappear.

THE CADET N.C.O. & OPPORTUNITIES AFTER 2 STAR

The diagram below shows a typical "Cover" or "Place setting" for a four-course meal. The following section is for those of you who wish to know how to 'navigate' the array of knives and forks, and check that they have the basic good table manners they will perhaps need for the future, when dining with the Managing Director of their company, or indeed if they decide to enter the Armed Forces (particularly as an Officer).

A Dinner usually consists of at least four courses; the cutlery is laid out in accordance with the menu and is used from the outside towards the centre. The napkin should **not** be tucked into your shirt neck!

DINNER COVER LAY-UP

The diagram above of a *cover lay-up* or a *place setting* is related to the Menu. On studying any menu you can relate the items of knives, forks and spoons to be used with each course on the menu.

Start by using each pair of *KFS* from the extreme left and right of the place setting.

The knife on the side plate is for spreading butter on pieces of a Roll or toast, NOT for cutting either.

You always break a roll on your side plate using both hands, and if you wish to butter the Roll use 'bite-size' pieces and butter each piece as you eat them.

THE CADET N.C.O. & OPPORTUNITIES AFTER 2 STAR

OPPORTUNITIES AFTER 2 STAR

INTRODUCTION

A Cadet with APC 2 Star has "One foot on the lower rung of the ladder" giving access to a whole variety of exciting and challenging opportunities. APC training can at times be difficult and demanding, but it is also rewarding especially now it is linked to the Duke of Edinburgh's Award Scheme, although not part of the APC Syllabus or testing. This offers you better opportunities than many other national youth organisations, read about it in the chapter about the Award Scheme.

Outside the APC Syllabus there are courses organised by the Ministry of Defence for 3 Star training Cadets and above. They are a bonus for you as a Cadet, introducing you to the practical and technical skills and trades within the Army. These courses are normally run during the Easter and summer holiday period and depend entirely on the availability of Army personnel and facilities. It should be appreciated that these courses are subject to change and the information given is purely a guide to encourage you to talk to your Detachment Commander about what is available. Course places are limited; 'bids' need to be made in good time for you to stand a chance of gaining a place.

The Army puts time and resources into the planning and organising of these **Special To Arm** courses. The best way to show your appreciation is to make sure that all the places are taken up – if you are lucky enough to be selected, you **should make sure you attend.** If for some reason it is impossible, make sure that you let your Detachment Commander know as soon as possible so that another Cadet can take your place and to save the good name of your County.

When attending one of these courses, you may well be required to pay a Daily Ration Fee, similar to your weekend camp ration money. Remember to ensure that this is paid either through your Detachment Commander or by taking the money with you; either way, get a receipt.

THE CADET N.C.O. & OPPORTUNITIES AFTER 2 STAR

Special To Arm courses all take place at Army establishments. Be smart, behave, be keen, be ready to learn all you can and ENJOY yourself. That is all the Army will require of you.

The following are examples of the variety of courses, where they are held, the duration and objectives of the course and what qualifications you require to attend. Another reminder that these courses are subject to change, new courses established, others withdrawn, please check with your Officers and Adult Instructors.

THE ROYAL ARTILLERY
Courses are held at the Royal School of Artillery, for a five-day period.
Qualifications: for Cadets badged to the Royal Artillery
Object of the course: To introduce you to field gunnery.

ROYAL SIGNALS
CLASSIFIED SIGNALLERS COURSE
Courses are held at the Royal School of Signals for a five-day period.
Qualifications: You must have a thorough knowledge of Voice and Operating Procedures and must have passed your Cadet Signals Classification Test.
Object of the course: As a classified signaler to give you an insight into Army Signaling. To demonstrate and give practice in handling signaling equipment used within an Infantry Battalion.

ADVANCED SIGNALLERS COURSE
Courses are held at the Royal School of Signals for a five-day period.
Qualifications: Passed GCSE Math's and Physics Grade A, B or C, if not passed, should actually be studying these subjects at this level in the year you are nominated for the course. You must have a thorough knowledge of Voice and Operating Procedures and passed your Cadet Signal Classification Test.
The aim of the course: The Advanced Signaling Course is one form of post classification training for the senior Cadet.
Object of the course: Is to train selected Cadets in more advanced signaling and to widen your technical interest in the Royal Signals.

THE CADET N.C.O. & OPPORTUNITIES AFTER 2 STAR

ROYAL ELECTRICAL & MECHANICAL ENGINEERS
MECHANICAL AND AUTOMOTIVE ENGINEERING COURSE

Courses are held at the School of Electrical and Mechanical Engineering for a period of twelve days.

Qualifications: Required to have APC 3 Star or above, be 16 years of age or over and should if possible be serving a recognised apprenticeship at a trade associated with Automotive Engineering.

Object of the course: To give you an elementary knowledge of general engineering, including bench fitting, welding and automotive engineering which will assist you either in the Services or Industry.

ELECTRONICS APPRECIATION COURSE

Held at the REME School of Electronic Engineering for four days.

Qualifications: Required to have APC 3 Star or above, be 16 years of age or over, have GCSE Math's/Physics or if not actually passed, should be studying these subjects at this level in the year of nomination.

Object of the course: To introduce you to Electronics and electronic equipment currently in use in the Army.

ARMY CATERING CORPS
INTRODUCTION TO BASIC COOKERY COURSE

Held at the Army Catering Corps Training Centre for five days.

Qualifications: You are required to have your APC 2 Star or above, have a particular interest in cookery/catering.

Object of the course: To introduce you to methods of catering used in the Army, the efficient use of rations and the planning and preparation of menus.

ARMY PHYSICAL TRAINING CORPS
PHYSICAL TRAINING CADET PT LEADERS COURSE

Held at the Army School of Physical Training or at the UKLF School of Physical Training for five days.

Qualifications: You are required to have your APC 2 Star or above and be physically fit, with an interest in physical Training.

Object of the course: To teach you the basic principles of Physical and Recreational Training.

PHYSICAL TRAINING CADET PT INSTRUCTORS COURSE

Courses are held at the UKLF School of Physical and Recreational Training for five days.

Qualifications: You are required to have your APC 2 Star or above and be 16 years of age or over.

Object of the course: Is to teach you the principles and organisation of Physical and Recreational Training as required by the APC Syllabus.

OUTWARD BOUND COURSE

Courses are held at the Joint Services Mountain Training Centre for a period of fourteen days.

Qualifications: You must be between the age of sixteen and a half and nineteen years old, be physically fit and able to carry a 40lb pack on a 3 day mountain expedition. It is essential to have had practical experience and a good knowledge of Map and Compass (3 Star level).

Object of the course: To offer you the opportunity to develop our leadership skills through taking part in mountain expeditions, rock climbing, canoeing etc.

UK LAND CADET LEADERSHIP COURSE

Courses held at various venues, duration eight to nine days.

Qualifications: You must be over sixteen and under seventeen and a half on the 1st April. You are required to have passed your APC 3 Star, or be considered sufficiently knowledgeable to manage the instruction given. Be a Cadet NCO, physically fit, capable of marching twelve miles in boots. Able to take part in obstacle and confidence courses. Rations: you will be expected to pay Ration costs similar to Annual Camp Messing fees.

You must have applied to your Cadet Commandant, who in turn will have to recommend you to take part in the course.

Object of the course: To develop the more senior Cadet's ability as a leader.

Special Note: Full instructions and kit list will be provided prior to the course. Your Parent/Guardian will be asked to sign a form permitting you to fly in service aircraft, whether you can swim, and consent for you to undergo surgery in an emergency.

THE CADET N.C.O. & OPPORTUNITIES AFTER 2 STAR

CADET TRAINING CENTRE LEADERSHIP COURSE

Courses are held at the Cadet Training Centre, Frimley Park, the course lasts one week.

Qualifications: It is open to Cadets of the CCF (all three service sections), The Air Training Corps, The Sea Cadets and Army Cadets. Those nominated to attend should be Cadet NCOs who have obtained APC (CCF) Advanced, or APC (ACF) 3 Star or hold an equivalent qualification in the Sea Cadets and Air Cadets. You are expected to have at least one year or more to serve in the cadet force. You must be fit, over sixteen and not over 18 at the time of attending the course. Ensure that you are physically fit to 'stay the course'.

Object of the course: To develop your initiative and self-reliance. You will carry out exercises involving problems of practical leadership.

CANADIAN ARMY CADET LEADERSHIP AND CHALLENGE COURSE

Courses are held at Banff, Western Canada and last for six weeks

Qualifications: Open to those who are already 4 Star Cadets and over sixteen years of age. You need to be fit as strict fitness requirements are laid down:

Run 1.5 miles	(male) 11.15 min	(female)	13.45 in min.
Sit Ups	(male) 42 in min.	(female)	36 in min.
Push Ups	(male) 29 in min.	(female)	25 in min.
Chin Ups	(male) 5	(female)	3

You must be able to hike a distance of 20km. You must be able to hike a distance of 15km carrying a load of 15kg within 240 minutes. Note: There is a cost for this course; some Cadets fund raise to pay their way.

BAOR VISITS

Courses are held at various locations in Germany. The duration is one week.

Qualifications: You must have your APC 1 Star or above at the time of your visit and must be fifteen years of age or have had a minimum of eighteen months service in the ACF. If you have shown a keen interest in the Army and are strongly recommended by your OC, it will help you get a place on a visit.

THE CADET N.C.O. & OPPORTUNITIES AFTER 2 STAR

Object of the visit: To give you the opportunity to be attached to a Field Force unit of the Army serving in BAOR to gain some experience of the Regular Army at work; to gain from the social experience of visiting a foreign country.

Note: Each year there is an allocation of funding towards BAOR visits awarded to each County. This award is towards traveling to Germany and rations during your stay. Cadets will be asked to contribute towards additional costs.

THE LORD LIEUTENANT'S CADET

Background: There is a Lord Lieutenant appointed by Her Majesty the Queen for every County in Britain. It is an honorary appointment; the role is that of a personal representative of Her Majesty. In recognition of the appointment, the Lord Lieutenant is treated with due respect and courtesy. The Lord Lieutenant performs duties on behalf of the Queen, from attending events such as the annual Remembrance Parade, Military parades, functions, and open days, formally opening public buildings, hospitals etc. and supporting large scale public celebrations.

INTEREST IN THE CADET FORCES

As a mark of the Lord Lieutenant's interest in the Cadet movements, many County Cadet Forces (Sea, Army and Air) are required to annually appoint a Lord Lieutenant's Cadet. In the majority of counties, the Lord Lieutenants keep their Cadets very busy, accompanying them on many of their official engagements, acting as escort and carrying out minor duties on their behalf.

TOP JOB

This is a job for the 'Top Cadet' in the County. To be seen in public at the side of the Queens Representative requires an individual with special qualities; being a good Cadet can attain these. It is a particular honour to be selected as the **Lord Lieutenant's Cadet** and carries with it the responsibility of representing all the members of the ACF in the County.

THE CADET N.C.O. & OPPORTUNITIES AFTER 2 STAR

SELECTION

Most Counties have a nomination system followed by a selection board often held at Annual Camp. Cadets who wish to be nominated will probably have passed their APC 3 Star, be 16 years old, of particularly smart appearance, keen and at ease when talking to their seniors. They will require an out-going personality and will probably have attained the rank of Cadet Sergeant. They may well be taking part in the Duke of Edinburgh's Award Scheme.

Some Counties have different requirements, but if you ask your Officers/Instructors they will give you information as the Cadet Commandant usually publishes the 'rules'.

Working towards being nominated for Lord Lieutenant's Cadet is not a short-term project. You will need to ensure you are known for entering into your Cadet life with:

- Determination
- Enthusiasm that encourages other Cadets
- Firm but fair with your juniors
- Enjoyment
- Being a good listener
- Confident enough to speak up when necessary
- Look the part; be smart, well pressed and clean even in your civvies.
- Remember your good manners

The above are not in any particular order, but as mentioned before, being a good Cadet goes a long way towards attaining a nomination for Lord Lieutenant's Cadet. If you are successful, it will remain the most unforgettable 'milestone' in your Cadet career.

CONDITIONS CHART

The chart on the next page shows the different 'routes' you might take on your 'cadet career'. You will notice that some of the boxes on the chart have messages in them. The **'notes'** referred to are set out on following page 13-20.

THE CADET N.C.O. & OPPORTUNITIES AFTER 2 STAR

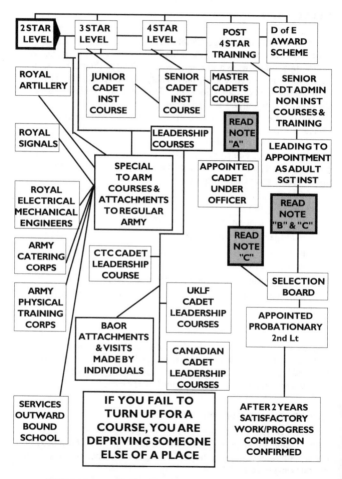

SEE PAGE 13-20 REFERENCE CHART NOTES "A", "B" & "C"

THE CADET N.C.O. & OPPORTUNITIES AFTER 2 STAR

CONDITIONS CHART NOTE "A"

It is a requirement to have successfully completed the 4 STAR to become eligible for consideration and subsequent appointment as an Under Officer.

This is **NOT AUTOMATIC;** you will have to prove over a period of time that by performance and aptitude as a responsible senior cadet you have the qualities that are considered essential for further progress.

A good report on the **MASTER CADETS COURSE** will help. Your dedication to the Cadets in your unit, your manners and behavior on and off parade, your reputation within the County and the recommendation of your Officers will all be taken into consideration before you are recommended as a potential Under Officer. You will have to attend selection interviews within your County Cadet Force.

CONDITIONS CHART NOTE "B"

Having been recommended by your Officers and instructors to be appointed as an Adult Sergeant Instructor, and approved by the County Cadet Commandant, you will become a member of the Warrant Officers and Sergeants Mess.

Your Regimental Sergeant Major will without doubt, take a special interest in you as a member of the Mess. He will expect you to observe the rules of the Mess, be a supportive Member of all Mess activities and become a member of the County team of senior ranks. Your progress will be watched, you will be expected to attain a high standard in all you do. Further opportunities will be made available to you as your service and experience progresses.

CONDITIONS CHART NOTE "C"

If it becomes apparent that your interest in the ACF and your performance as an adult member of the County is outstanding in every respect, then you may well be considered as a potential officer.

As a potential officer you will be involved in the selection process, which will be fully explained to you. If you are appointed to a commission it will be for a probationary period of two years, during which time you will be expected to fulfil certain training obligations.

THE CADET N.C.O. & OPPORTUNITIES AFTER 2 STAR

They are as follows:

1. During your first year you will complete your Initial Training Course, which is usually within your own County.
2. During your second year you will be expected to attend the Cadet Training Centre, Frimley Park to do your Instructors Course. It will also be expected of you to attend at least one Annual Camp during the two years.

On completion of this period, and having carried out the obligations required, earned a satisfactory report on your performance and suitability as an officer, your commission may be confirmed – subject to your Cadet Commandant's recommendation.

Promotion is not automatic in the Army Cadet Force;
All officers attend the Cadet Training Centre for courses to qualify for promotion to Captain, Major and Lt Colonel/Colonel. Each County Cadet Force has what is known as an 'establishment' of officers and instructors. This controls the number of officers or instructors in each rank that may be appointed; therefore promotion is often subject to a vacancy being available in a particular rank.

YOUR OPPORTUNITY TO STEP FORWARD AND STAND OUT

Cadet Vocational Qualification Office (CVQO)

Based at the Cadet Training Centre in Camberley, Surrey, CVQO is a registered Charity responsible for managing vocational qualifications for members of the Combined Cadet Forces, Sea Cadet Corps, Army Cadet Force and Air Training Corps.

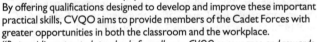

The qualifications on offer have been carefully selected to show employers and educators the wide range of skills that young people and adults learn in the Cadet Forces. These skills include leadership, teambuilding, problem-solving, communication, health and physical fitness.

By offering qualifications designed to develop and improve these important practical skills, CVQO aims to provide members of the Cadet Forces with greater opportunities in both the classroom and the workplace.

"By providing a trusted standard of excellence, CVQO encourages and rewards achievement in both vocational and academic education."
Lieutenant Colonel Edward Woods, Director, CVQO

CVQO is accredited by Edexcel, City & Guilds and the Institute of Leadership and Management (ILM) to deliver a wide range of qualifications including the BTEC First Diploma in Public Services and the BTEC First Diploma in Music for Cadets, and up to level 5 Graduateship Awards for Adult Instructors.

BTEC First Diploma in Public Service

This internationally respected qualification is equivalent to 4 GCSEs at A*-C level (4 Standard Grades at levels 1-3 in Scotland). The course mixes theory and practical elements with an emphasis on leadership, teamwork, communications, problem solving and fitness.

The syllabus has been designed to improve valuable life skills including CV preparation, interviewing techniques, communication, first aid, adventure training, health and nutrition.

THE CADET N.C.O. & OPPORTUNITIES AFTER 2 STAR

Cadets must be at least 16 years old to enrol.
In addition to existing Cadet activities, Cadets are required to complete the course syllabus which includes supervised adventure training activities and occasional weekend training.
The BTEC Award is accredited by Edexcel.
The BTEC Programme is FREE for Cadets.
To enrol, contact your local Cadet headquarters.

"When I applied to university, the admission's tutors were very interested in the fact that I had earned a qualification completely in my own time outside of school and I feel it helped set me apart from the other applicants." Joanna Woods, former Cadet RSM from Sussex ACF

BTEC First Diploma in Music

"The qualifications offered by CVQO focus on communication, leadership and teamwork; all important skills that Universities look for in potential students." Dr. Alan Pearson, Principal of St Hild and St Bede, Durham University

Since September 2005, Cadets over 16 with an interest in music are able to earn a vocational qualification equivalent to 4 GCSEs at A*-C level (4 standard grades at levels 1-3 in Scotland).

The BTEC First Diploma in Music curriculum has been designed to develop a basic understanding of the music industry and combines technical skills with theory and practical elements. The BTEC Award is accredited by Edexcel.

Upon successful completion, Cadets will have demonstrated an understanding of all aspects of the music business including music selection, composition, performance, marketing, legal issues and budget forecasting. Cadets are expected to be able to play a musical instrument prior to enrolling on the course.

The BTEC Programme is FREE for Army Cadets.
To enrol, ask to your Detachment Commander or contact your local Cadet Headquarters or log onto
www.vqaward.org

'Gaining recognised CVQ qualifications is a valueable career investment'

Duke of Westminster Award

The Duke of Westminster Award is an annual prize which has been created by CVQO to recognise outstanding Cadet.

To be considered for the Duke of Westminster Award, Cadets must possess a wide range of skills and have demonstrated these attributes through a consistently high level of commitment and ac throughout his/her Cadet career.

Cadets are nominated by their unit headquarters and must be enrolled in CVQO's BTEC Program to be considered for the award.

Once nominated, Cadets must write a letter to CVQO explaining why they should be considerec From these letters, a short list is produced and the finalists are interviewed by members of CVQO management team.

Nominees are judged on academic achievement, contribution to society, communication skills, and contribution to Cadets.

The winning Cadet is presented with a certificate along with a cash prize to be used towards further training.

Adult Qualifications

For those of you who stay on in the ACF as adults there is the added advantage of continuing your vocational training. Whether you are teaching nutrition in the classroom or survival skills in the forest, Adult Instructors are inspiring today's youth to become tomorrow's leaders. It is the aim of CVQO to reward the efforts of those individuals, by providing them with the opportunity to earn a respected vocational qualification that recognises their achievements within the Cadet Forces and will also be beneficial in their civilian career

With a wide range of awards on offer, CVQO has the ideal qualifications to help Adult Instructors get ahead both personally and professionally.

THE CADET N.C.O. & OPPORTUNITIES AFTER 2 STAR

Qualifications on Offer

Qualifications	NVQ	Awarding Body
Learning and Development		
L10 & L11 - Enables Teaching Through Instruction,	Part Level 3	Edexcel
Presentation and Demonstration		
A1 - Assessment Using a Range of Methods	Level 3	Edexcel
A2 - Assessmentl through Observation	Level 3	Edexcel
V1 - Verification Award. Demonstrates Ability to	Level 4	Edexcel
Conduct Quality Assurance of Assessment Process		
First Line Management		
Introductory Certificate in First Line Management	Level 3	ILM
Licentiateship		
Licentiateship in Youth Leadership & Training	Level 4	City & Guilds
Graduateship		
Graduateship in Youth Management & Training	Level 5	City & Guilds

No funding is available at this time for Adult Qualifications and participating adults are responsible for all costs. For more information on each qualification please visit **www.vgaward.org**

> "What I find particularly appealing about this innovative scheme is that young people, the future of this country, are being encouraged to achieve.
> Furthermore, it is entirely complementary to the education system"
>
> **Major General, Duke of Westminster, Assistant Chief of the Defence Staff (Reserves and Cadets).**

THE CADET N.C.O. & OPPORTUNITIES AFTER 2 STAR

INTRODUCTION

This introduction to Welbeck - The Defence Sixth Form College should be useful in gaining an insight into the unique role Welbeck plays in providing a first-class education for young men and women making a head start to careers in the Armed Services and the Ministry of Defence Civil Service.

Currently based on the Welbeck Estate in Nottinghamshire, Welbeck has provided the Army with many of its future Technical Officers for over fifty years.

The College has become one of the UK's top sixth form colleges and has an outstanding academic reputation. In 2004 the College became a quad-Service institution, admitting students with a career ambition to join The Royal Navy, The Army, The Royal Air Force or to become Ministry of Defence Civil Service engineers.

Welbeck's continued success has enabled the Ministry of Defence to invest in a brand new purpose-built site for the College at Woodhouse near Loughborough in Leicestershire.

From 2005 students entering Welbeck will join a state-of-the-art college with the highest quality residential and teaching facilities, benefiting from the latest educational and technological advances.

The College offers a unique programme of personal, physical and intellectual development which will provide students with a rounded education specifically designed to meet the needs of today's modern technical Armed Services. The programme does not end after a two-year A-level programme: the four Services continue to monitor and support students through university and on to professional training with their respective Armed Service or within the Ministry of Defence Civil Service.

THE CADET N.C.O. & OPPORTUNITIES AFTER 2 STAR

When you join as a student, you gain the experience of a lifetime.
At Welbeck you will face a variety of intellectual and physical challenges that will test your abilities and stretch your mind.

You will pursue sports, travel overseas and experience adventurous activities that build your self-confidence and develop your leadership potential.

The College team of trained and experienced staff - both civilian and military - is always available to assist, encourage and support you, providing every chance to make the best of the wonderful opportunities Welbeck offers.

The Welbeck Experience

Each year the College welcomes one hundred and seventy-five high-calibre young men and women from a variety of backgrounds, all looking for something that exceeds the average sixth form experience. Alongside academic study, you will learn how to develop loyalty and teamwork, as well as how to communicate as a leader.

The programme of extra-curricular activities includes a heavy emphasis on sport and fitness including outward-bound 'activities such as rock climbing, dinghy sailing and navigation. In addition, all Welbeck students join the Combined Cadet Force and take part in regular military training activities, including a range of adventurous training pursuits. Study at Welbeck and you will leave the College a more confident and responsible individual, fully equipped to read for a degree that will in turn be the gateway to a truly rewarding career:

2 years' sixth form study at Welbeck
Lower sixth: 4 AS-levels
- Upper sixth: 3 A-levels

3- or 4-year degree at a leading UK University
- Usually Newcastle, Southampton, Aston, Northumbria, Loughborough, or exceptionally Cambridge or Oxford

Initial Officer/Professional Development Training

- At Britannia Royal Naval College Dartmouth, the Royal Military Academy Sandhurst or RAF College Cranwell - Ministry of Defence Civil Service candidates will undertake up to 2 years' Initial Professional Development
Gain a commission in one of the Armed Services leading to a career as an Officer, or join the Ministry of Defence Civil Service as a graduate engineer.

THE CADET N.C.O. & OPPORTUNITIES AFTER 2 STAR

Eligibility and application procedure

To apply to Welbeck and subsequently the Armed Sevices you should be a medically fit UK, Commonwealth or Irish citizen aged between 15 years and 17 years 6 monts on 1st September in the year of entry to te College.

However, certain sigle-Service conditions will be explained at the time of application.

To join Welbeck as a Ministry of Defence Civil Service candidate you must be a British citizen or hold dual nationality, one of which must be British. The Ministry of Defence Civil Service welcomes applicants from disabled candidates.

Minimum entry requirements are 5 GCSEs (or equivalent) at grades A-C, including B in Mathematics and Physics (or a science subject that includes Physics). Your school or college must supply a reference showing that you are expected to achieve at least grade C in your likely main A-level subjects.

WELBECK - THE DEFENCE SIXTH FORM COLLEGE
www. welbeck.ac.uk

A LIFE LESS ORDINARY ..... THE REGULAR ARMY

Army life and professional, practical qualifications are an unbeatable combination. The Army will help you get into shape physically and mentally. You will be having so much fun you won't even notice that you are developing your natural abilities in a practical way.

The Army lets you share your world with people your own age, working together under pressure, facing physical and mental problems and finding the solutions.

If you choose to make the Army your career, there are several routes of entry. If you are under 18, there are four junior entry schemes you may like to consider.

The Army has four colleges. **The Army Foundation College (Harrogate)** offers a 42 week course for school leavers who want to become combat soldiers. **The Army Technical Foundation College (Aborfield)** is for those who want to learn a trade – an intensive 28 week course combining basic military training with technical education leading to Key Skills and NVQs.

THE CADET N.C.O. & OPPORTUNITIES AFTER 2 STAR

The Army Training Regiment (Bassingbourn) trains soldiers for all branches of the Army (except the Paras, Royal Artillery and Royal Armoured Corps) and offers two courses for sixteen year olds. Finally, there's **Welbeck College**, the Army's own sixth form college for those who want to be officers.

Attending one of the colleges means that you commit to the Army for a certain period of time, but if things don't work out there is an opportunity to leave the scheme. All four colleges offer potential students the opportunity to visit, along with their families, to help you decide which one is for you.

All four schemes offer the chance to train as a soldier plus the opportunity to gain practical skills and qualifications which are recognised and welcomed both in the Army and Industry.

Apart from those who attend Welbeck College, you will be paid from the start and there will be lots of action, sport and adventure.

The Army Foundation College, Harrogate

Offers a 42 week course for school leavers who want to train to become combat soldiers in the following:

To join you need to be between 16 and 17 years and one month when the course starts and you'll need to pass the Army entrance tests. The courses include 23 weeks on Military Training, 5 on Leadership and Initiative Training and 24 on Vocational Education. It is tough, but there are breaks at the end of each of three terms and at half terms.

Equal Opportunities (Regular Army)

We aim to treat everyone fairly and will not tolerate unlawful discrimination, including harassment and bullying. We recognise that everyone is unique and will give them the opportunity to develop their abilities fully. We expect all of our soldiers to operate as members of a close-knit community, where trust, cohesion and teamwork are decisive factors in our success on operations. We rely upon leadership at all levels, and the effective contribution of every individual, to achieve.

THE CADET N.C.O. & OPPORTUNITIES AFTER 2 STAR

The Army Foundation Courses gives you better military knowledge. You know the system better, you have a better understanding of Army life than other recruits"

You can concentrate on training to be a soldier for the following Corps and Regiments. Each have their own areas of expertise and opportunities...

INFANTRY

If you want to be at the heart of all soldiering, join the Infantry, part of Combat Arms. You'll be trained to fight and survive on the front line and seize enemy territory, whether you get there on foot, by vehicle or air.

HOUSEHOLD CAVALRY OR ROYAL ARMOURED CORPS

If you'd like to be on horseback as a part of the Queen's personal bodyguard, in a Challenger tank learning manoeuvre warfare or in a light tank on reconnaissance missions, try the Household Cavalry or Royal Armoured Corps.

ROYAL ARTILLERY

To get trained to use some of the most powerful and sophisticated weapons around, including missile systems for heavy bombardment, become a gunner in the Royal Artillery.

ARMY AIR CORPS

Supporting, manning and piloting the Army's aircraft, you'll be working with cutting-edge technology whether you pursue a career on the ground or in the air.

The Army Technical Foundation College, Arborfield

Royal Signals – Using every kind of technology from hand held radios to satellite to ensure accurate and secure transmission of information

Royal Logistic Corps – Sustaining the Army anywhere in the world, from front line to storehouse.

Royal Electrical and Mechanical Engineers – Vehicle Mechanic, Vehicle Electrician, Armourer, Metal smith, or Recovery Mechanic ensuring all equipment is ready at a moment's notice

Royal Engineers – As a Combat Engineer building bridges, navigating rivers or crossing minefields; not an office job!

Conditions of Entry

To gain a place at the Army Technical Foundation College, you need to be aged between 16 and 17 years and one month at the start of the course and have passed the Army Entrance tests. You will also need to have (or be expected to pass) GCSEs or the Scottish equivalents in Maths and English, and possibly certain other subjects depending on the job you wish to go into.

This is the specialist college for school leavers who want a career in one of the Army's technical corps. The course is of 28 weeks, combining basic military training with technical education. Soon after completing the course you could be a Systems Engineer Technician, a Marine Engineer, a Vehicle Mechanic or one of the many other technical specialists.

THE CADET N.C.O. & OPPORTUNITIES AFTER 2 STAR

The training leads to Key Skills and National Vocational Qualifications (NVQs), and can set you on track towards a Modern Apprenticeship, showing you have up – to – date skills that you can build on and take with you into civilian life.

The Army Training Regiment, Bassingbourn

To gain a place at the ATR you need to be aged between 16 and 17 years and one month when the course starts. Formal qualifications are needed to gain a place at the ATR for some trades.

The course lasts 20 weeks, including a week of leave half way through.

 INFANTRY – Learn how to operate in the toughest environments, use armoured cars or train in air assault techniques

 MILITARY CLERK – ADJUTANT GENERAL'S CORPS – Three career paths, Human Resources/Personnel Support, Business Administration or Payroll Management, finance and accounting.

 COMBAT MEDICAL TECHNICIAN – Where the Army goes you will be there to provide medical support from first aid to long term health care

 REME TRADES – Vehicle Mechanic, Vehicle Electrician, Armourer, Metalsmith, Recovery Mechanic, Electronics, Avionics or Aircraft Technician.

 ARMY AIR CORPS – Supporting, staffing and piloting the Army's aircraft

Army Training Regiment Bassingbourne (continued)

 ROYAL LOGISTIC CORPS – Many trades from every stage of the supply chain from sourcing equipment through to storage and distribution to the troops

 ROYAL SIGNALS – Provide vital IT and communications links

 ROYAL ENGINEERS – Trained to keep the Army moving with your combat construction and demolition skills

 ROYAL ARMOURED CORPS – Tank Crewmen trained in the ability to find, fix on and strike the enemy's weak point.

 ROYAL ARTILLERY – Gunner using some of the most powerful sophisticated weapons including missile systems.

THE CADET N.C.O. & OPPORTUNITIES AFTER 2 STAR

ARMY EDUCATION GRANTS & 'GOLDEN HELLOS'

These offer financial support to those who:

• wish to study a vocational subject, prior to enlisting as a soldier
• have studied a specified vocational subject to a set level
• or wish to enter one of the technically demanding trades at the
   basic level.

Who can apply for an Army Grant?

The scheme is open to any British applicant at school or college in the UK, Channel Isles, the Isle of Man or at an Army school overseas Candidates should be in year 11 or S4 and considering going on to Sixth Form College or further education in year 13 or S5 – 6 and considering going on to higher education.

In principle, the Army is looking for A levels or National Qualifications (Scotland) or vocational awards equivalent to A level. This would include the advanced level (AVCE) or BTEC at National Diploma Level in the following broad range of vocations:

Construction and Built Environment
Engineering
Health and Social Care
Hospitality and Catering
Information and Communication Technology
Science

You will be aware that a single AVCE is equivalent to 1 A Level

Your commitment to the Army is a standard minimum engagement of 4 years from date of entry.

Where would you be employed in the Army?

Royal Engineers -
Clerk of Works.ME (Military Engineer) Fitter (all)

Royal Logistic Corps:
Ammunition Technician. Chef. Movement Controller Petroleum Operator.

Royal Electrical and Mechanical Engineers :
Vehicle Mechanic

Intelligence Corps:
Operator Military Intelligence (Language)

Army Medical Services
Student Nurse. Biomedical Scientist. Pharmacy Technician.

THE CADET N.C.O. & OPPORTUNITIES AFTER 2 STAR

The 'Golden Hello' may be paid to those who are already qualified – providing they are eligible.

There are no retrospective payments on this scheme, however, if you have a full Academic year to complete, you may be considered for a bursary, or advised to apply for a 'Golden Hello".

THE ARMY SCHOLARSHIP SCHEME

If you are considered one of the top students in your school or college, and show academic, sporting and leadership potential, you can apply for an Army 6th Form Scholarship.

This provides you with financial support during your 'A' Level/Higher studies. It also guarantees you Officer training and gives you the chance to go on to university with an undergraduate financial award. You benefit by receiving Army support, as well as guaranteed acceptance into Sandhurst. This gives you an assured future that allows you to get the most out of your studies.

What age do I need to be?

You need to be between 16 years and 16 years, 6 months old. The awards are granted irrespective of background or method of schooling.

There are two Army Scholarship Competitions each year. Candidates should normally be aged between 16 years and 16 years, 6 months on 1 January for the Spring competition, and 1 July for the Autumn competition.

THE UNDERGRADUATE BURSARY

If you are thinking about completing a degree and pursuing a future in the Army, you should consider applying for an Army Undergraduate Award. The Army recognizes that may young people prefer to study for a degree before beginning a career. The Undergraduate Awards offer financial support and the chance to broaden your mind, intelligence and experiences.

You remain a civilian throughout your university course, receive financial support, and gain the opportunity to take advantage of paid training whilst at university.

On graduation, your immediate future is assured. You will begin training at Sandhurst with a further monetary grant.

Your minimum commitment thereafter is for three years commissioned service, with the opportunity of progressing to a full career.

Chapter 14

LIFE AFTER CADETS

The world of work becomes more competitive each year; there is also a growing industry in new technology presenting challenges and many opportunities.

As a member of the Cadet Force you will have learned some useful skills, knowledge and experience. Now is the time to think of taking it a stage further by joining in the CVQ scheme leading to BTEC Diplomas and later in your Career as an adult.

Information on CVQ can be found at the end of this Chapter.

FURTHER EDUCATION

You may have left school without many qualifications or, need further qualifications to follow your chosen career. Colleges of Further Education offer career studies and leisure courses in formats to fit in with most people's lives. Many thousands of people of all ages study through the Open University, an excellent way to take your own time in gaining qualifications, perhaps even a degree.

THE FACTS OF LIFE

Contributing a percentage of your wages to pay for housekeeping should not include all washing, ironing, cleaning and cooking. Take the opportunity to learn how to do these things - you may need them when you set up on your own.

LEAVING HOME

During your Cadet career, you were away from home on weekends and Annual Camps, although this may give you an advantage over those who have never been away without their parents, it is still a very emotional time. You may be only too pleased to leave 'home' and feel a sense of relief at finally escaping, but If you have been fortunate in having a caring home environment, where despite disagreements you share common interests and count your parent(s) or those who have guided you through childhood as friends, it is more difficult to leave without real heartache and bouts of homesickness.

Write, phone, text, email, visit - let your family and friends know your safe, share in your successes and support you when things are not so good.

LIFE AFTER CADETS

HOBBIES AND INTERESTS

Perhaps you already have a hobby that gives you hours of pleasure, it may even be the foundation of your future career, for example you may make your own clothes and go on to become a designer or perhaps you were introduced to woodworking by a member of your family, enjoyed it so much you decide to become a carpenter/joiner. Many people do not have a formal hobby; they use their time within the community, working with people with disabilities, fund raising for the local Hospice, teaching people with literacy problems to read, or helping one of the many charities, the list is endless. For those of you that have not yet found a hobby keep looking.

DECISION MAKING

JOIN THE S.W.O.T. TEAM

S.W.O.T. means Strengths, Weaknesses, Opportunities, Threats. Doing a SWOT list is an excellent aid to decision-making, particularly career choices. It is simple to create the form but more difficult to complete, as you must be honest with yourself.

Take a sheet of paper and draw four columns. Place the headings along the top of the page along with the subject of your SWOT list. You may well find that one of the difficulties in completing the form is that your Threats can also be seen as Opportunities; your Weaknesses, Threats or Opportunities. That is the idea of this list, to make you think where you need to improve and to highlight your Strengths. When you have completed your lists, number each point in order of importance and make your decisions using all the information you have on your form.

THE WORLD OF WORK

When you have made your choice, whether it is further education or the workplace, you will still need to complete application forms and write letters to prospective employers.

From the moment you apply for the application form your aim is to convince the employer that you are the person for the job. The following list is provided as a prompt.

1. Photocopy your application form, or use sheets of paper to draft out what you want to say.

2. When you have completed your application form - take a photocopy to remind you of what you have written, very useful if

LIFE AFTER CADETS

    you are fortunate enough to gain an interview. It may also be
    useful for completing other application forms.

3. Some advertisements ask for applications "in your own writing". This
    may be because the vacancy requires some written work.

4. Put a covering letter with your application saying what job you are
    applying for.

5. Where an advertisement states "Letter of application and CV" use
    the Specimen Letter provided in this section as a guide.

7. Make sure that the completed letter is neat, well set out and with no
    spelling mistakes. Use good quality paper, and where appropriate,
    matching envelope.

8. You can, if you would like a job at a particular firm/business, write
    and enquire about possible vacancies. Address your letter to
    the appropriate person and ensure you have their correct name,
    job title and address.

9. CURRICULUM VITAE means the course of your life' is normally
    abbreviated to CV. when writing be honest about experience and
    qualifications. Remember to update it regularly your Careers
    Advisor will have given/can give you useful formats for this
    document.

10. Keep your CV short, factual and a maximum of two A4 pages, if
    possible.

11. Personal References and Testimonials: Chose someone who knows
    you well, your AC Company Commander, any adult outside the
    family circle. You will be asked for the name of your previous
    employer if applicable. Do not forget to ask these people before
    you give their names.

YOU HAVE AN INTERVIEW

Congratulations! All your hard work has had the desired result. Now,
prepare properly for the final stage - your interview.

THE AIM OF AN INTERVIEW

The prospective employer has sifted through all the application forms
and short-listed several suitable candidates. Obviously, they will need
to meet you, ask questions, and expand on the information you have
given them.

LIFE AFTER CADETS

WHAT YOU NEED TO KNOW ABOUT THE EMPLOYER

1. What sort of training will they give you, is it formal and part of your contract of Employment?
2. Do they allow time off for block release or Further Education as part of your training, and encourage staff to attend?
3. How easy or difficult is it going to be to get to and from work, how long does it take, how much will it cost.
4. If you are a member of the Territorial Army, or Cadet Force, will they grant you leave for Annual Camp or courses.
5. Are there any outside activities, sports etc. that the company encourages?
6. How do they promote people - is it internal or internal and external applications
7. Make clear notes of what questions you want answered at the interview; remember to take the notes with you.

YOUR IMAGE

If you want the job, you have got to make the right impression on the person(s) interviewing you.

• Ensure your appearance is smart but comfortable.
• Be on time, five minutes before due time if possible.
• Take your Record of Achievements, Certificates etc. and put them in a folder.
• On entering the interview room, make eye contact, shake hands with the Interviewers and make a greeting (good morning/afternoon etc.).
• Sit comfortably, and do not slouch.
• Think through your answer, and then speak. Always try and answer as fully as possible, don't 'woffle'.
• Make eye contact with your interviewer(s) when answering their questions
• If you do not understand the question, say so.
• If you are asked if you have any questions, those that have arisen from the interview should come first, then produce your question list, and ask!

Questions that might be asked at an Interview

1. Tell me/us about yourself
2. Why do you want to work for this company
3. What makes you think you would be suitable for this job
4. What personal qualities do you have to offer us

LIFE AFTER CADETS

5. Where do you see yourself in 5 years from now
6. What subject did you enjoy most and why (taken from your CV)
7. Have you had any experience of work
8. Why did you leave your last employment
9. Would you be interested in attending training courses.
10. Would you be prepared to go to day release
11. Would working overtime be any problem for you.
12. Would you be prepared/like to move between departments
13. Are you prepared to move from the area if necessary
14. Can you work on your own
15. Do you play any sports if so who for.
16. What other hobbies and interests do you have
17. Do you use a computer at home
18. Would you like to ask any questions

AFTER INTERVIEW

If you were successful, congratulations, if not, wait a few days then, phone the company and ask for feedback. They may give you some constructive criticism to help you with your next interview - if it is for the same company, you will be remembered positively.

YOUR JOB

Being a member of the Cadet Force will help you fit in with the disciplines of working life. Apply the principles of being a good Cadet to being a good employee, and remember, all experience is useful even if it does not appear so at the time.

LIFE AFTER CADETS

SPECIMEN LETTER

Mr J.M.Jones (Initials & name of the person)   Your home
The Job Title. Director. Manager. Partner etc.   address
The Name of the Firm.   here on the right
Number & Name of Street,   Telephone/ Email
 Name of Town/City.   to contact you
County & Post Code.   Day/Date/Month/Year

Dear Sir/Madam or the persons surname Mr/Mrs if you already know them.

The first sentence saying what job it is you are applying for.

Details of your age, school attended, say what subjects you have studied and to what standard.

Any part-time jobs you have had, training schemes taken part in.

A paragraph about yourself, school duties, clubs or organisations you belong to and any responsibilities you have had.

Your hobbies or interests, sports activities.or involvement in the ACF, Duke of Edinburgh Award or any other achievements that would be of interest to a potential employer.

Tell them that you would like to work for them and that you would like to be considered for an interview.

A sentence at the end saying when you would be available to attend for an interview if you were chosen as a potential employee.

You finish it off

Yours faithfully,

Sign your name - then under it

PRINT YOUR NAME - NEATLY - IN BLOCK CAPITAL LETTERS.

ABBREVIATIONS

ACF	Army Cadet Force	DOP	Dropping Off Point
ACFA	Army Cadet Force Assoc	DS	Directing Staff
AI	Adult Instructor	DP	Drill Purposes
APC	Army Proficiency Certificate	DTG	Date Time Group
ACIO	Army Careers Information Office	DZ	Dropping Zone
		ECC	External Chest Compression
Adj	Adjutant		
AM	Ante Meridian	E S	Extreme Spread
ATO	Ammunition Technical Officer	ESA	Expected Scoring Area
		ETA	Estimated Time of Arrival
AWOL	Absent Without Leave	ETD	Estimated Time of Departure
BAOR	British Army of the Rhine		
BC	Battery Commander	En	Enemy
Bn	Battalion	Engr	Engineer
Brig	Brigadier	Eqpt	Equipment
BRCS	British Red Cross Society	Fmn	Formation
CAA	Cadet Administrative Assistant	FEBA	Forward Edge of Battle Area
Capt	Captain	Fup	Forming Up Place
cam	camouflage	FPF	Final Protective Fire
CCRS	Council for Cadet Rifle Shooting	FFI	Free From Infection
		freq	Frequency
CP	Command Post	F&M	Fire and Movement
CPOA	Corrected Point Of Aim	FRV	First Rendezvous
CTC	Cadet Training Centre	Gen	General
CCF	Combined Cadet Force	GN	Grid North
CTT	Cadet Training Team	GMA	Grid Magnetic Angle
Cdt	Cadet	G P	General Purpose
CEO	Cadet Executive Officer	GPMG	General Purpose Machine Gun
CO	Commanding Officer		
C of E	Church of England	GRID	Grid Reference
Col	Colonel	HE	High Explosive
Coy	Company	HQ	Headquarters
Cpl	Corporal	HQ Land	Headquarters Land Command
CSM	Company Sergeant Major		
CQMS	Company Quarter Master Sergeant	IA	Immediate Action
		i/c	In Command
CWS	Common Weapon Sight	ICE	Individual Compass Error
CZP	Correct Zeroing Position	II	Image Intensification
D of E	Duke of Edinburgh's Award	ISCRM	Inter Services Cadet Rifle Meeting
Dets	Detachments	JCIC	Junior Cadet Instructors Course
DF	Defensive Fire		
Dvr	Driver	Km	Kilometre

ABBREVIATIONS

Km/h	Kilometres Per Hour	RF & CA	Res Forces & Cadet Assn
L/Cpl	Lance Corporal	RV	Rendezvous
LAW	Light Anti-Tank Weapon	SAA	Small Arms Ammunition
LMG	Light Machine Gun	SCIC	Senior Cadet Instructors Course
Lts	Lights		
Lt/Lieut	Lieutenant	Sgt	Sergeant
Lt Col	Lieutenant Colonel	SI	Sergeant Instructor
Maj	Major	S/Sgt	Staff Sergeant
Mt	Motor Transport	Sig	Signaler
MTO	Motor Transport Officer	SITREP	Situation Report
MO	Medical Officer	SLO	Schools Liaison Officer
MP	Military Police	SOP	Standing Operating Procedure
MPI	Mean Point of Impact		
MN	Magnetic North	SSI	School Staff Instructor
MOD	Ministry Of Defence	SUSAT	Sight Unit Small Arms Trilux
MR	Map Reference		
MTM	Mouth To Mouth	Tech	Technical
NBC	Nuclear Biological Chemical	TI	Thermal Imaging
		Tk	Tank
NSP	Normal Safety Precautions	TO	Training Officer
NCO	Non Commissioned Officer	TEWC	Tactical Exercise Without Cadets
NRA	National Rifle Association	TMH	Trigger Mechanism Housing
Ni	Night		
OC	Officer Commanding	Trilux	Lamp in SUSAT Sight
OIC	Officer In Charge (pl.tp,patrol etc)	Wdr	Withdraw
		WOI	Warrant Officer 1st Class
offr	Officer	WOII	Warrant Officer 2nd Class
'O' Gp	Orders Group	Wpns	Weapons
OP	Observation Post	U/S	Unserviceable
Ops	Operations	USOP	Unit Standing Operating Procedure
OS	Ordnance Survey		
Pl	Platoon	VCP	Vehicle Check Point
Psn	Position	veh	Vehicle
PM	Post Meridian	Wng O	Warning Order
POA	Point Of Aim	wpn	Weapon
Ptls	Patrols		
PUP	Pick Up Point		
PV	Permissible Variation		
QM	Quartermaster		
RO	Retired Officer		
RSM	Regimental Sergeant Major		
RC	Roman Catholic		